Antique Trad

Perfume Bottles

PRICE GUIDE

3-28-11

Editor

Kyle Husfloen

Contributing Editor

Penny Dolnick

©2008 by Krause Publications

Published by

A subsidiary of F+W Media, Inc.

700 East State Street • Iola, WI 54990-0001
715-445-2214 • 888-457-2873
www.krausebooks.com

Our toll-free number to place an order or obtain
a free catalog is (800) 258-0929.

Library of Congress Control Number: 2008929066

ISBN-13: 978-0-89689-671-0
ISBN-10: 0-89689-671-4

Designed by Wendy Wendt
Edited by Kyle Husfloen

Printed in China

TABLE OF CONTENTS

INTRODUCTION

Although the human sense of smell isn't nearly as acute as that of many other mammals, we have long been affected by the odors in the world around us. Pleasant fragrances make us feel good; bad smells usually signal danger or something repulsive. This new *Antique Trader Perfume Bottles Price Guide* will concentrate only on the "good" aromas.

No one knows for certain when humans first rubbed themselves with some plant or herb to improve their appeal to other humans, usually of the opposite sex. However, it is clear that the use of unguents and scented materials was widely practiced as far back as Ancient Egypt. Some of the first objects made of glass, in fact, were small cast vials used for storing such mixtures. By the age of the Roman Empire, scented waters and other mixtures were even more important and were widely available in small glass flasks or bottles. Since that time glass has been the material of choice for storing scented concoctions, and during the past 200 years some of the most exquisite glass objects produced were designed for that purpose.

As you will learn as you read through this book, it wasn't until around the middle of the 19th century that specialized bottles and vials were produced to hold commercially manufactured scents. Some such aromatic mixtures were worn on special occasions, while many others were splashed on to help mask body odor. For centuries it had been common practice for "sophisticated" people to carry on their person a scented pouch or similar accoutrement, since daily bathing was unheard of and laundering methods were pretty primitive.

I have learned a great deal about the world of perfume and perfume bottles while editing this volume. It's fascinating to realize that commercially produced and brand name perfumes and colognes have really only been common since the late 19th and early 20th centuries. The French started the ball rolling during the first half of the 19th century when D'Orsay and Guerlain began producing special scents. The first American entrepreneur to step into this field was Richard Hudnut, whose firm was established in 1880. During the second half of the 19th century most scents carried simple labels and sold in simple, fairly generic glass bottles. Only in the early 20th century did parfumeurs introduce specially designed labels and bottles to hold their most popular perfumes. Coty, founded in 1904, was one of the first to do this, and they turned to Rene Lalique for a special bottle design around 1908. Other French firms, such as Bourjois (1903), Caron (1903) and D'Orsay (1904) were soon following this trend.

Our contributing editor, Penny Dolnick, has done a masterful job of bringing the vast history of perfume and perfume bottles together in this guide. In addition to her historical study, she also was responsible for obtaining a large majority of our nearly 1,200 price listings highlighted by over 950 color photographs. The full range of perfume and "scent" containers is covered here, including a few ancient examples as well as the fine "art glass" containers of the late 19th and early 20th century right through to more modern dime store bottles. There are hundreds and hundreds of collectors of perfume bottles all over the world, and our *Antique Trader Perfume Bottles Price Guide* provides something of interest to all of them. Even those who are not serious collectors will enjoy reading about how the world of perfumes has grown and changed over the years. We may even stir pleasant memories of a scent worn by someone's mother or grandmother. Science has shown that scents or smells can directly affect our mood or behavior. Reading through the following pages will certainly help everyone understand how this "secret science" has evolved over the millennia to become the big business that it is today.

Here's hoping the *Antique Trader Perfume Bottles Price Guide* will stimulate ALL your senses.

Kyle Husfloen, Editor

Please note: Although our descriptions, prices and illustrations have been double-checked to ensure accuracy, neither the editors, publisher nor contributors can assume responsibility for any losses that might be incurred as a result of consulting this guide, or of typographical or other errors.

On The Cover: Far back, left to right: A Czechoslovakian atomizer in orange and swirled red, white and orange, replacement cord and bulb, ca. 1920s-30s, 7 Ω" h., **$200-250**; German porcelain figural perfume bottle and powder box, a lady in 18th century dress, ca. 1930s, 7 π" h., **$525**. **Middle row, left to right**: Czechoslovakian clear cut glass pyramidal perfume bottle w/a tall flat blue glass stopper with the intaglio figure of a troubadour, ca. 1920s-30s, 5 ∫ h., **$240-275**; Czechoslovakian cut black glass stepped perfume bottle with a tall pointed cut lilac stopper, original "Irice – Made in Czechoslovakia" paper label, ca. 1920s-30s, **$300-350**; Lalique clear glass flattened bottle with a diamond point design and glass stopper, designed for "Capricci" by Nina Ricci, **$100**; **Front row, left to right:** Baccarat limited edition clear turtle-shaped bottle designed for "Champs Elysees" by Guerlain, ca. 1904, 4 ∫" h., **$800-1,250**; clear cut glass cornucopia-shaped perfume with facet-cut stopper, attributed to Czechoslovakia, ca. 1910, 4 π" l., **$200**.

PERFUME BOTTLE COLLECTING

By Penny Dolnick

People collect two kinds of perfume bottles—decorative and commercial. Decorative bottles include any bottles sold empty and meant to be filled with your choice of scent. Until about a hundred years ago, it was usual for a woman to bring her bottle to her favorite apothecary to be filled with her chosen fragrance. Commercial bottles are any that were sold filled with scent and usually have the label of a perfume company. Since there are so many thousands of different perfume bottles, most collectors specialize in some subcategory. Specialize is my number one piece of advice!

Popular specialties among decorative perfume bottle collectors include ancient Roman or Egyptian bottles, cut glass bottles with or without gold or sterling silver trim or overlay, bottles by famous glassmakers such as Moser, Steuben, Webb, Lalique, Galle, Daum, Baccarat, Saint Louis, figural porcelain bottles from the 18th and 19th century or from Germany in the 1920s and 30s, perfume lamps (with wells to fill with scent), perfume burners, laydown and double-ended scent bottles, chatelaines, atomizer bottles, pressed or molded Early American glass bottles, matched dresser sets of bottles, or hand-cut Czechoslovakian bottles from the early 20th century.

Among collectors of commercial perfumes, some favorite specialty collections are those including a special color of glass bottle, bottles by a single parfumeur, such as Guerlain or Caron or Prince Matchabelli, bottles by famous fashion designers such as Worth, Paul Poiret, Chanel, Dior, Schiaparelli or Jean Patou, bottles by a particular glassmaker or designer, such as Lalique, Baccarat, Viard or Depinoix, giant factice bottles (store display bottles not filled with genuine fragrance), little compacts holding solid (cream) perfume, which are often figural, tester bottles (small bottles with long glass daubers), figural and novelty bottles and miniature perfumes (usually replicas of regular bottles given as free samples at perfume counters).

Many people include perfume bottles in crossover collections as well—figural dog perfume bottles for the collector of dog figures or heart-shaped bottles for the collector of hearts, for example. There are also many related collections that may or may not include actual perfume bottles—advertisements, labels, fans with perfume advertising, fabrics with perfume images, soaps, perfume trade cards, powders, those little cardboard cutouts that fragrance models hand you in department stores, and many more that I have never thought of.

If you don't collect perfume bottles, it may surprise you to learn that the record price for a perfume bottle at auction is something over $200,000 or that those little sample bottles we used to get for free at perfume counters in the '60s can now bring as much as $300 or $400! It may also surprise you to learn that those miniature bottles are more popular with European collectors than their full-size counterparts or that bottles by American perfume companies are more desirable to European collectors than to Americans, and vice versa. On the other hand, collectors in England seem to prefer Victorian art glass and cut glass with English sterling mounts. It may also surprise you to know that most collectors of commercial perfume bottles will buy empty examples, but those still sealed with the original perfume do carry a premium, and the original packaging can raise the price by as much as 500%! Even a funny (or suggestive) name can increase the price of a bottle.

Collecting perfume bottles is one of those hobbies you can begin with little or no investment. Just ask your friend who wears Shalimar to save you her next empty bottle. But beware! Investment quality perfume bottles can be very pricey! The rules for value are the same as for any other kind of glass—rarity, condition, age, quality of the glass. There are some special considerations with perfume bottles. You do not have an investment quality bottle (one that will appreciate in value over time) unless the bottle has its original stopper and label (if it's a commercial), it is a high quality lead crystal or glass bottle (not a lower end eau de cologne or eau de toilette bottle) and there is no corrosion on any metal part. With commercial perfume bottles, prior to the introduction of those little plastic liners on the dowel end of a stopper in 1979, all stoppers had to be individually ground to match the neck of their specific bottle. Bottles without those liners are to be preferred to those that have them. Perfume bottles with significant chips or with sick glass (which can only be "cured" by a very expensive and time consuming process which essentially involves grinding the glass from the inside of the bottle) lose some, if not most, of their value to collectors.

Some other hints for someone considering collecting perfume bottles as an investment include the fact that men's scent bottles do not usually equal the value of women's perfumes. One exception to the rule that value depends heavily upon rarity is a bottle with widespread sentimental appeal (Evening in Paris is the most obvious example—women of a certain age all remember buying it for their mothers in dime stores or receiving it from their first beau). Another rule has to do with limited edition perfume issues or gift shop type bottles. They are like automobiles—they lose half their value as you take them out of the store and do not regain their original investment for 20 years. This old saying about all modern collectibles has many exceptions in the perfume collecting world, but do remember that you cannot count on collector interest in your bottle in the resale market if every potential buyer could have bought it in its initial offering. Another rule is you make the rules for your own collection! Some miniature collectors will only include a bottle containing 1/8 ounce or less, while another may limit purchases to bottles of less than 3 inches. One collector may insist upon only signed examples while another proudly displays any bottle made by or designed by a certain manufacturer. Some collectors include bottles with figural stoppers in their displays, while others insist that the entire bottle must be made in a figural form (to look like something other than a bottle).

What causes such great differences in the price of the same bottle? The variables in pricing are almost endless. The first is condition, of course. That is followed by location (Is the bottle being sold in Europe or the United States? Is the bottle in an elegant antique shop or a charity thrift shop? Is it in a well advertised auction or a small rural auction? Are two or more bidders determined to own the bottle? If the bottle is in an Internet auction, was it listed in the most logical category and was the description well written?) I am sure you can think of dozens of variables yourself.

PART I

PERFUME BOTTLES: DECORATIVE

The earliest known scent bottles were small stone containers used by the pre-dynastic Egyptians to hold perfumed oil.

Glassmaking has been traced to Sumerian sites in Mesopotamia dating from the 23rd century BC. By the 18th Egyptian dynasty, the very new technique of molding glass was employed for making scent containers. Blown glass was first developed in the Roman Empire approximately 100 BC and increased the ease and speed of producing glass vessels, including scent containers. The Romans also introduced oxides into their soda-lime glass to produce colors such as opaque white and yellow, cobalt and greenish-blue and more.

The Chinese produced excellent opaque and layered glass carved in patterns for centuries before the techniques were used in the West.

Chapter 1

AMERICAN 18TH AND 19TH CENTURY GLASS

The history of American glass really begins in 1738 when **Caspar Wistar** established a glassworks in New Jersey and hired experienced German craftsmen. Today, most South Jersey free blown glass from the 18th and 19th centuries is called by the generic name "Wistar." These are typically in shades of green, aquamarine or amber. After the Revolution, German immigrants were in the forefront of the glass industry. Early glass was mostly simple and utilitarian until after the Civil War. Early scent bottles, called pungents, were free blown in figural shapes like sea horses and musical instruments and could have held either smelling salts or scent. These usually had cork stoppers and were unsigned.

The Boston and Sandwich Glass Company (1825-1888) was known for its colored flint glass (early form of lead glass). It produced pungents with pewter caps and is justly famous today for its large variety of molded and cut glass cologne bottles, often in aquamarine, opaque white, opalescent or other colors. Today, the company is mainly remembered for lacy patterned pressed glass, often referred to generically as "Sandwich glass", but it made several variations of striped and spatter glass in imitation of old Venetian glass.

Yes, there really was a woman named Mary Gregory who worked for the Boston and Sandwich Glass Company. There has been a long controversy over her work at the factory. There is no reliable record that she ever painted scenes of people, usually children, in white enamel on colored glass, even though those items have come to be known as "Mary Gregory glass." Much of what is known by that name was actually made in Europe. My own theory is that the name began when Mary herself started collecting enameled pieces with scenes of children playing with hoops or chasing butterflies and her friends would refer to the style by saying, "Oh, you know, that glass that Mary Gregory likes."

5" green canary cologne with pointed stopper by Boston and Sandwich, ca. 1840-50, $500-650.

"Baron" **William Henry Stiegel** founded his glassworks in the 1760s, His firm was the first to produce cut glass and mold blown glass in the colonies. By 1774, his extravagance forced him to sell out completely. The Stiegel Glassworks was known for colored glass, especially blues, purple and, rarely, amber and for mold blown glass, especially with a daisy pattern. It was also known for enameling, sometimes figural or floral, in primary colors, a style brought to Pennsylvania by Stiegel's German craftsmen and known today as Stiegel-type.

Early American pressed glass was made by pressing liquid glass into metal molds. The technique was developed in America in the 1820s. It was used by a number of different companies, which produced a wide variety of products, including cologne bottles. Colored pressed glass was produced by the 1860s. Later pressed glass was often designed to imitate famous Brilliant Period cut glass patterns.

American Brilliant Period Cut Glass (1876-1915): This era of glassmaking is often dated from the 1876 Centennial Exposition in Philadelphia, which introduced many consumers to a new style featuring very clear glass, intricately cut on thick blanks. The new middle class in America presented a huge market for luxury glassware of all kinds. The prevailing Victorian taste of the period demanded highly decorated pieces that only skilled glassmakers could achieve using hand cutting. The wares were of the finest full lead crystal (with 33% or more lead content; common lead crystal used half as much lead and glass has no lead content). Bottles were often made with silver collars or overcaps, and many of the best examples are in colored or cased glass. The bottles of the time are often unsigned or signed so inconspicuously as to be almost invisible. More often, the silver mounts are signed. By 1920, cutting was getting too expensive and tastes were tending toward

the less ornate. Cut glass was still popular in perfume bottles and other utilitarian items, but the patterns were much less intricate and were less labor-intensive and less expensive to produce.

Christian Dorflinger and Sons of White Mills, Pennsylvania (1852-1921) was renowned for elaborately cut patterns and for being chosen by several first ladies for their White House glassware services. Most pieces had only a paper label.

5" Dorflinger ruby cut to clear cologne in the Hob and Lace pattern, unsigned, c.1880s-1900 $675.

T.J. Hawkes of Corning, New York (1880-1903) was a cutting shop that bought its blanks from the Corning Glassworks. It was one of the few firms that manufactured cut glass and mounted its own pieces in sterling, being careful to mark both glass and silver. The company introduced the most popular American Brilliant Period pattern, called Russian. Later, it was cut by several other companies. In 1903, Hawkes and Fredrick Carder formed the Steuben Company. Some Hawkes pieces are marked with an "H" or a shamrock with two hawks.

7" cologne cut and engraved in the "Rock Crystal" style, signed "Hawkes," sterling stopper by Gorham, ca. 1900, $1,000-1,250.

Mount Washington Glass Company (1837-1894) made cut glass on heavy blanks during the 1870s and '80s for wealthy customers. It also became the leading manufacturer of opal glass and heavily enameled glass. Its Lava glass was the first U.S. art glass, patented in 1878 by F. Shirley of Mount Washington. This was followed by Amberina, which was renamed Rose Amber after a lawsuit by the New England Glass Company. These were soon followed by Burmese and Peach Blow and beautiful acid-etched cameo glass, usually in pink, blue or green on a white base.

Libbey Glass Company of Toledo, Ohio may be known to you as the manufacturer of inexpensive glasses and serving pieces. Actually, it was the successor company of the New England Glass Company which had been a leading art glass manufacturer during the late 19th century. During the Brilliant period, Libbey was the largest manufacturer of cut glass in America. During the Depression period, Libbey continued to produce some of the most elegant and costly cut and engraved glassware in the United States, glassware often sold in the most expensive department and jewelry stores.

T. B. Clark of Honesdale, Pennsylvania produced colognes in several realistic floral patterns after 1900, anticipating the taste for simpler cutting that became known as the Late Brilliant Period.

Late Brilliant Period Glass – This glass reflects the public's simpler tastes and the need glass manufacturers had to lower production costs. Many companies made perfume and cologne bottles with minimal cutting and, often, a central motif like a flower or pattern of swirls.

During this same period, **silver overlay (silver deposit)** techniques were also very popular. The surface of a blown bottle was coated in a desired pattern with a special flux and then electroplated with pure silver. Sometimes the silver was cut and engraved. Most such bottles were clear, but green and cranberry are known. Bottles plated by the Alvin Company and the Gorham Silver Company are often signed on the metal.

Chapter 2

AMERICAN 19TH CENTURY ART GLASS

Satin glass, or Mother of Pearl Satin Ware has a luster finish and has two or more layers of glass over a white core with a pattern caused by internal air traps showing through to the outside. The pieces could be in a single color, one color shading from dark to light, or in several colors forming stripes (called rainbow satin ware). Most of the American production of Mother of Pearl Satin Ware was produced by the **Mount Washington Glass Company.**

Burmese glass shades from yellow at the base to salmon pink at the top. Mt. Washington produced Burmese pieces in both glossy and acid finish and with and without enamel decoration. Cleverly, the company sent a service in the new color to Queen Victoria and she was thrilled with it. Almost immediately **Thomas Webb** in England applied for a license to produce this ware. His wares were called "Queen's Burmese." Forms of Burmese glass were made by several United States manufacturers until at least 1970.

Amberina is a clear amber glass that shades to red or fuschia at the top when fired a second time. Amberina was patented in 1883 for the New England Glass Company. A similar product, called Rose Amber, was made by the Mount Washington Company.

Aventurine, **spangled glass**, **spatter glass** and **Vasa Murrhina** were all types of glass using metallic particles and/or small glass fragments trapped between two layers of glass, the inner one usually opaque to show off the metallic inclusions. These are all variations of glassworking techniques first developed in Venice and France.

Hobbs, Brockunier of Wheeling, West Virginia, inspired by the sale of the Chinese "Peach Bloom" ceramic vase in 1886, developed a cased line of glass with the exterior shading from deep red to amber. It was marketed as "Coral Ware" and today collectors call it "Wheeling Peach Blow." In 1885, **Mount Washington** patented a single layer Peach Blow that shades from dusty rose to bluish gray, which is the rarest version of Peach Blow. The **New England Glass Company** marketed a line of Peach Blow under the name Wild Rose. Theirs was also a single layer glass shading from deep rose pink to white.

Craquelle or Overshot glass was made by applying clear ground glass particles to a hot gather of glass either before or after it has been shaped. Most overshot or "ice" glass came from Europe, but the **Boston and Sandwich** factory produced colognes using this technique. Several other United States glassmakers produced lower quality overshot glass.

Crown Milano is another glass line developed at the **Mount Washington Glass Company**. It is a stain-finished white opal glass that is then painted and enameled in transparent whites, tans and pastels. The mark, when present, is a "C" over an "M" under a crown.

Chapter 3

AMERICAN 20TH CENTURY GLASS

Art Glass:

Steuben Glassworks: Fredrick Carder and T. J. Hawkes founded the Steuben Glassworks in Corning, New York in 1903. Fredrick Carder was the chief designer from 1903 through 1918, when the company was sold to Corning Glass Company. He continued as head of the factory until 1932. Under his leadership, the firm pioneered fabulous innovative colors like **Rosaline, Ivrene** (opaque white glass with pearly iridescence), Jade (a transparent glass produced in white, blue, green, mandarin yellow, amethyst and Rosaline), **Celeste Blue, Verre de Soie** (glass with a silk-like iridescence) and **Aurene** (blue or gold iridescent glass, often marked "Aurene" on the bottom of the bottle). In fact, he created more than 125 different colors! He also developed glass techniques such as **Cluthra** (a bubbled and cloudy glass), **Cintra** (a similar product with a granulated effect),

Oriental Poppy (a pale colored glass with opalescent white stripes and an opalescent luster inside and out). The company also produced **Silverina** (glass flecked with mica and blown into a mold with a diamond pattern), **Reeded** glass (where thin threads of colored glass were coiled by hand around a completed piece) and several colors of opalescent glass. Steuben also produced paperweight colognes made of very thick clear crystal with a "floating" decorated inner layer of Cluthra, Cintra, millefiori or air trap spirals.

In about 1932, the Great Depression caused Steuben to reduce costs by producing only clear glass pieces. Many Steuben pieces are marked with an acid fleur-de-lis logo. Some pieces are signed by Frederick Carder himself. A story, perhaps apocryphal, says that he would carry an etching pen with him at all times, so that when a friend would say, "Why isn't my wife's vase signed, when her sister's is?", he could then sign it on the spot, often on the golf course. Carder continued to be active in the company until his retirement in 1959 at age 96.

Steuben produced more than 200 different scent bottle shapes, and that huge perfume production was enlarged by the work the company did for special orders to be mounted as atomizers by DeVilbiss and to be treated with silver overlay by such companies as Alvin Silver Company.

7.6" Steuben blue Aurene trumpet form perfume bottle with stopper, bottom signed Aurene plus paper label $850

Tiffany Glass: Louis Comfort Tiffany (1848-1933) was a great glass designer known for innovation in many techniques, especially in the Art Nouveau style. In perfume bottles, perhaps his best known examples are in his "**Favrile**" line. Only some Tiffany glass is marked with an engraved signature or etched initials, often with the word "Favrile" and/or with a date or identification number. L. C. Tiffany was the son of the founder of the great New York jewelry retail store, Tiffany's. In 1902, Louis Comfort Tiffany took over the jewelry business and used it as the primary outlet for his glassware designs.

4.25" Tiffany Favrile boule-shaped bottle with ball stopper, decorated with hearts and vines, Signed, ca. 1920s, $750-900

Quezal, named for a colorful Central American bird, was founded by Martin Bach, a former Tiffany employee, in 1904. It produced iridescent glass, sometimes with silver overlay, in imitation of Tiffany's Favrile and Steuben's Aurene. Most Quezal pieces are signed. The firm produced gold iridescent commercial scent bottles for the firm of Melba in Chicago.

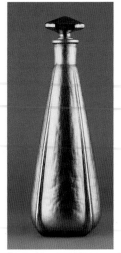

Very rare Quezal trumpet form perfume with four ribs & pointed stopper. Actually a commercial bottle for the Melba Company, bottom marked both "Q" and "Melba," ca. 1920, $1,800-2,000

H. C. Fry Glass Company, founded in 1900, produced perfume bottles in a color called **Foval**, an opaline glass. It was also noted for its Late Brilliant Period Lily of the Valley pattern.

Libbey Glass Company (formerly the New England Glass Company) of Toledo, Ohio, kept up with the changing taste of Americans by converting from elaborately cut crystal of the Brilliant Period to especially fine cut and etched glassware during the Depression.

Elegant Glass of the Depression Era

This is the name used to differentiate the blown or mold blown glass, often engraved or etched, from the inexpensive pressed glassware made during the same period. Generally, colored bottles are more costly than clear. Most of the well known manufacturers of the time were located in the Ohio Valley.

Heisey Glassworks was founded in 1895 in Newark, Ohio. The company made both decorative and commercial perfume bottles for several perfumers. Their bottles are often marked with an elongated diamond, with or without an "H."

Pair of iridescent pale lavender footed perfumes by Heisey, ca. 1930-45, marked with diamond H, pair, $250

Tiffin Glass Company of Tiffin, Ohio made elegant etched glass perfume bottles during the 1920s and later. Its most popular colors were clear and black satin glass.

Cambridge (1901-1954) was known for its high quality blown bottles. When marked, the logo is a C within a diamond.

Fostoria was founded 1887 in Ohio, moved to West Virginia in 1891, and closed in 1986. It made bottles for DeVilbiss atomizer mounts, combination perfume bottles set on powder jars, and elegant gold decorated colognes and perfumes during the period from 1910 to 1950.

Gunderson-Pairpoint (1939-56) produced a wide range of distinctive hand blown scent bottles, some in the paperweight style and often with very large floriform stoppers. During the 1940s and 50s, the **Gunderson Pairpoint** Company produced a version of Peach Blow, shading from pink to white in both glossy and matt finish. Later, pieces in the Peach Blow style were made by several United States companies, making dating and attribution somewhat problematical.

Consolidated Glass Company introduced its unique Ruba Rombic line in 1928. The pieces featured multiangular, cubist rhomboid shapes typical of Art Deco designs popular at that time. Perfume bottles are extremely rare.

Fenton Art Glass Company (1905-present) was influenced by the fine iridescent colors of Steuben and Tiffany. Fenton introduced its inexpensive pressed version of this style of glass in 1907. Today this is called Carnival Glass. Within a short time other American glass factories were also making their version of Carnival glass. Fenton has produced a wide range of scent and perfume bottles during its long history. During the 1930s it also made opalescent hobnail perfume bottles for the Wrisley Company of Chicago to use for their commercial 1930s.

Pair of green & white swirled feather design bottles by Fenton Art Glass, ca. 1953, 5 3/4" h., pr. $225

Imperial Glass Company produced a line of Carnival glass and, a few years later, introduced an iridescent stretch glass called Rainbow Luster. Imperial became a prolific manufacturer of all types of glasswares, including perfume and scent bottles. During the 1920s the company produced fine glass bottles to be used with fancy atomizer fittings made by the DeVilbiss company.

Imperial light blue fading to yellow atomizer with elegant jeweled DeVilbiss mount, signed by DeVilbiss, ca. 1920s, $1,700-2,000

Inexpensive Depression Era Glass

Depression glass is the name commonly used to describe the inexpensive machine made colored glassware of the 1920s through the early 1940s, a time when bad economic conditions necessitated the cheapest production methods. Manufacturers tried to make their products distinctive through the use of bright colors or pretty pressed patterns. Some of the well known companies of that era include:

Hazel Atlas, established in 1885. By the 1930s it was a complex of 15 factories and was the largest glass manufacturer in the world, making machine molded glass. Some of their wares are marked with an A under an H.

Anchor Hocking. Its first products were Royal Ruby in 1939.

Wheaton Glass Company: The T. C. Wheaton Glass Company was founded in 1888 and specialized in bottles for pharmacists and doctors. By the 1930s, the company was making bottles for quality perfume makers, both American and European. The successor firm, the Wheaton Glass Company, was formed after WWII and is still in family control. The firm's logo, a W in a circle, still appears on modern production for such firms as Avon, Estee Lauder, Elizabeth Arden and Houbigant.

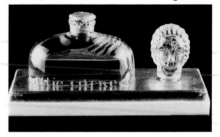

4.25" Carnegie Blue for Hattie Carnegie, mint in box full figural in the form of a lady's head (the stopper) and shoulders (the bottle), c1944 $625-750

Mid-century American pressed glass perfume bottles gained increased acceptance by a newly well off population because cut glass imports, especially from Czechoslovakia, stopped because of the war.

Importers like Irving W. Rice (the Irice Company) had to use domestic bottles. Many of the designs of these pressed bottles by such companies as **Imperial Glass, Duncan and Miller, Fenton and L.E. Smith** were attempts to reproduce cut glass effects using pressed glass methods. American decorative glassware of this period is often referred to as bathroom glassware.

6.2" Pair clear pressed boule shape bottles with oversized stoppers in the form of fire-birds, bottles molded with ribs and facets, unsigned American, c.1940s $175

American colognes and perfumes with Rococo metal mounts were very popular in the 1920s to 1950s. They were identifiable by beveled glass, and ornate filigree mounts made of brass, bronze, gold plated base metal or, occasionally, ormolu. Many had floral themes. Others had figural cherubs or birds as part of the mounts. Many of the largest examples had only a small inner container to hold the actual scent. Most were made in the United States by Apollo, Globe and others and are rarely marked.

10.5" Glass bottle and stopper with rococo metal mounts, long dauber, unsigned c1950s $70

The 20th century Studio Glass Movement

This movement really got started in the United States in the late 1960s and gained its greatest fame in the United States, although there are furnaces in most industrialized countries producing interesting work. Some of the leading innovators working in these studios include:

Harvey Littleton (b.1922) introduced Venetian glassmaking techniques to the Toledo Museum of Art and the University of Wisconsin's art department in the 1960s.

Charles Lotton (b.1935) produces scent bottles in his popular "multi-floral" style with tall pointed stoppers and unusual luster colors. His sons work in his studio and each signs and dates his own production.

7" Lotton atomizer in peach with green, ca. 2000, $550

Orient and Flume of Chico, California was founded in 1972 by Douglas Boyd and David Hopper. Its highly regarded iridescent glass perfumes with Art Nouveau motifs are sought after by collectors.

    Lundberg Studio of Davenport, California was founded by the late James

Lundberg and started making quality paperweights in 1972. This firm is noted for their iridescent and Art Nouveau-style designs.

7.3" Lundberg Studio dark blue glass bottle with white and green flower motif, tall clear stopper with dauber, 1990, signed by Salazar and Steven Lundberg $165

Chapter 4

ENGLISH PERFUME BOTTLES

    Although there was certainly a wide range of perfume and scent bottles produced in glass and ceramics before the Victorian era, the most popularly collected examples date from the last half of the 19th century. A variety of the style of bottles and their manufacturers will be discussed below.

    Stevens and Williams was a major manufacturer of fine English art glass. The company began making specialty glassware in about 1847, when William Stevens bought an existing glasshouse located near Stourbridge. The factory made a number of innovative lines and cased color combinations. Its most easily recognizable pieces feature applied ribbon trim.

Stevens and Williams emerald green engraved to clear bottle with a pinched-in shape (also called the "Kettroff" shape or "glug-glug"). Silver hallmarked for 1897-98, $2,500-$3,000.

English Cameo glass: In the 1870s, John Northwood rediscovered the technique for making cameo glass, which had been lost since Roman times. Cameo glass is made of a body of opaque colored glass cased in white glass. The outer layer is cut away or acid etched away in a pattern to reveal the underlayer. The remaining design on the outer layer stands out in relief. A great deal of hand finishing was necessary for this method. The style is best exemplified by the magnificent, yet still amusing, bird's head bottle made by **Thomas Webb and Sons** in the 1880s. Most other English cameo bottles are of a simple boule (ball) shape and decorated with flowers and vines and stopped with sterling silver.

5" Webb Pefume bottle & stopper, cameo glass, Flattened teardrop form, avocado green ground cased in white & cameo-cut w/triumph-form blossoms on leafy vines. $2400-2750

Double-ended scent bottles: These bottles were extremely popular in the 19th century. One end held smelling salts and the other end was meant for perfume. The ends of the two sections often had different types of lids. The perfume end would commonly have a tiny glass inner stopper covered by a chased silver overcap or a cork lined screw cap. The smelling salt end would usually have a sterling silver screw cap or a spring loaded hinged lid. These bottles could have simple clear faceted glass containers or very

elegant cut and colored glass bodies. Some had finger rings to be carried by the owner at evening functions. Others had fabulously elaborate gold fittings. Cased glass cut back to its clear underlayer was also a Bohemian invention, much copied in England. Many of these creations were then decorated with enamel, a popular style still identified with Bohemian glass. The English also manufactured fine clear cut glass single bottles with sterling silver mounts and caps.

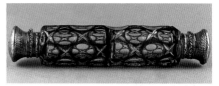

4" Double-ended scent bottle in red cut to clear in a star and punty design with sterling caps and inner stopper on the perfume side, no hallmarks, ca. 1870s. English or possibly American. $350-450

English Porcelains and Stoneware

Chelsea English Porcelains date from the 1750s. They were often made in the form of people, animals or fruit. Rococo bottles with applied flowers and leaves were the firm's most popular products.

3.2" Porcelain bottle molded as a bouquet of pansies, painted dark blue, red and yellow, unmarked, attributed to Chelsea, c1800s, $2500

Girl in a Swing (St. James factory) was a short lived enterprise (thought to have been founded by a partner in the original Chelsea factory. It is known today by the name of one of its most famous figural porcelains.

Wedgwood: Josiah Wedgwood's Jasperware (fine grained stoneware) in a solid color with classical figures in white in relief was used for scent bottles as well as other decorative items.

Other English Porcelain factories made perfume bottles following the decorating techniques in use for other ceramic products. For example, **Coalport** also made perfume bottles with handpainted scenes and lavish gold trim in the 19th century. **Royal Worcester** porcelains were identifiable by their off white backgrounds and handpainted decorations. The **Spode** factory at Stoke-on-Trent pioneered in the development of bone china in 1800 and in transfer printed china in 1785.

4" Royal Worcester creamy porcelain bottle with enameled flowers and a silver cap, late 19th c., $500

Stoneware Pottery: English stoneware in large variety dates from the late 17th century. The best Staffordshire stoneware was salt glazed white and creamware, a lead-glazed earthenware. Scent bottles from this early period are rare and highly sought after.

Chapter 5

FRENCH PERFUME BOTTLES

Porcelain

The **Sevres** porcelain factory has operated since 1738, and in 1759 Louis XV took over the factory and made it the royal porcelain manufacturer. The fame of Sevres ware came from its classical influences, deep colors and lavish gilding. After the French Revolution, the factory began to shift its production away from monumental pieces for the very wealthy in favor of more modest, although still high quality, pieces for the new middle class, including perfume bottles and dresser sets.

5.8" Pair of porcelain colognes, hand-painted with flowers, Sevres mark, 19th c., $250-450

Other French porcelains have been made in the city of Limoges since the 1830s by 35 different manufacturers including

Haviland, Guerin, Jean Pouyat and others. Prior to that time, faience pottery had been produced in Limoges. A great deal of porcelain is still manufactured in the city, including a vast number of enameled boxes fitted with miniature perfume bottles.

6.5" Set of three porcelain bottles and stoppers, hand painted with flowers, in metal holder, marked France $300-400

One special firm actively encouraged the development of Art Deco and Cubist designers of ceramic works, even sponsoring a competition between 1927 and 1931. The Robj Company did not actually manufacture anything, and production was assigned to many established French firms. Their success with imaginative liquor decanters led to additions of perfume lamps and cologne bottles.

French Enamel on Metal

The city of Limoges also had factories that made perfume bottles in a fabulous enamel on metal technique. The art of enameling on metal has been known in France since the 6th century (it was known even earlier to the Egyptians, Phoenicians, Greeks and other ancients). Limoges has been the premier center of enameling since the 12th century.

2.5 " Limoges enamel over copper with inner glass stopper, with lady in blue dress, $1000

French Art Glass

Etling: If you collect glass, ceramics or bronzes of the Art Deco period, you are likely to see the name Etling marked on some wonderful period designs. In fact, Etling was a retailer of high end modern artisan wares of the period (1909-1939). It contracted works by such luminaries as Demitri Chiparus, Marcel Guillard and Marius Sabino. Most of these pieces are marked with both Etling and the name of the artist.

Emile Galle is the most famous maker of French cameo glass. Although his technique was similar to that of the English cameo glassmakers already discussed, his results were entirely different. He used different colors of overlay, experimenting with opaque and translucent glass. He worked mostly in the Art Nouveau style, often using natural looking flowers, ferns and berries. He was also influenced by 18th century Chinese glass. His work has been imitated, but never equaled, by modern automated methods.

9.7" Galle cameo atomizer in dark red cut back to light yellow in design of leaves and berries, modern replacement mount, signed in cameo, c1920s-30s $550

Daum (1875-present) operated in the city of Nancy, France and was famous for its multilayered acid cut-back cameo glass in scenic patterns. Today it is known for innovative designs in heavy cased glass with figural **pate de verre** (paste of glass) colored stoppers. Daum signatures on cameo glass can be gilded, etched, engraved or in relief, but they usually included the name "Nancy" and the double armed Cross of Lorraine.

6.5" Daum cameo and enameled atomizer with berries and leaves, ca. 1905-15, $2,500-2,750

Legras (1864-1915) produced multilayered acid cut back cameo glass.

Rene Lalique (1860-1945) first gained fame as an Art Nouveau jewelry designer. Around 1893, he began working with glass, making magnificent unique bejeweled perfume bottles, among other glass objects. Around the turn of the 20th century, Lalique purchased a glass factory and began mass producing commercial bottles using blown-molded and pressed techniques. Many of his bottles continued to follow the Art Nouveau style of his earlier jewelry. He continued to make decorative bottles for what is now called "Maison Lalique," creating large numbers of mass produced non-commercial bottles and dresser sets (garnitures de toilette) to be retailed at his own shops. The majority of this production was in demicrystal, which required little hand finishing after it was taken out of the mold. The majority of the company's bottles are clear and/or frosted, but red, black, green, blue and opalescent were also produced. Lalique's bottles required a great deal of hand finishing—staining, polishing and enameling, among other techniques. Most bottles designed by Rene Lalique and made during his lifetime are signed with some variation of "R Lalique." Those made after his death in 1945 usually have the "Lalique" signature, whether designed by Rene before his death, or by his son, Marc, or granddaughter, Marie Claude, both of whom succeeded Rene as chief designer for the house of Lalique.

3.8" "Telline" frosted bottle and stopper in form of a seashell with light blue stain, signed in mold R Lalique, c1930s, $2500

3" "Amelie" molded with bands of overlapping leaves, light blue stain, signed R. Lalique, c1930s, $2000

Baccarat was established in 1764, making window glass and other utilitarian products. In 1816, it began making luxury glass. By 1907, it was making over 4,000 perfume bottles a day! In addition, Baccarat is justly famous for its sulphides, made by molding and firing white clay into the desired shape (often a famous person or landmark) and then inserting it into hot glass. The firm also made the finest quality French opaline glass, in such colors as pigeon's blood, pale green, blue, pink coral or red. These colors were used for both decorative and commercial perfume bottles. Other French glassmakers of the 19th and early 20th centuries were also noted for their opaline glass.

Baccarat also made a huge range of dresser items in a version of Amberina called **Rose Tiente**, shading from pale amber to rose. Baccarat signatures were sporadic until 1936, when an effort was made to standardize the placement of the firm logo (a carafe and two glasses) either by acid etching or on a paper label, easily lost over time.

3.75 Baccarat white opaline glass with fold filigree shoulders and turquoise stones, gold hinged top, $3,000

Cristallerie de St. Louis, founded in the late 18th century, was known for its latticino in pseudo-Venetian revival style. During the late 1800s and early 1900s, it also created thinly cased and acid cut back articles, easily confused with similar pieces by Baccarat and Val St. Lambert. They produced some layered semi-opaque cameo glass with elaborate floral and scenic designs, but signed these products **"D'Argental."**

4.12" St. Louis latticino perfume bottle in pseudo-Venetian revival style, ca. 1850-1860, $375-425

Almeric Walter, established 1859, was famous for a process called pate de verre (paste of glass) whereby ground glass was mixed with a liquid and heated in a mold. Pieces are signed "A. Walter, Nancy."

4.5" Almeric Walter pate de verre travel-style atomizer in shades of blue, ca. 1900-1910, $4,000-4,200

Le Verre Francais/Schneider/Charder: The Schneider brothers established Le Verre Francais in 1913. The firm produced Art Deco cameo glass signed "Le Verre Francais" in relief. They also made the pieces which were signed "**Charder**" (for Charles Schneider).

Sabino made a line of opalescent molded perfume bottles in the 1920s and '30s. Production began again in the 1960s until Ernest Sabino's death in 1971. The molds were sold to an American company, which continues to produce glass in France today. Most pieces are signed "Sabino" in raised lettering.

Chapter 6

EUROPEAN BOTTLES

Czechoslovakia, Germany, Austria & Bohemia

Bohemian glass: Bohemia was an historic region in central Europe, what is now the western two-thirds of the Czech Republic. It was bordered by Germany, Poland, Austria and the Czech historical region of Moravia. From the 13th century, Bohemian glassmakers began to experiment with new glassmaking techniques, many of them having wide influence over other countries' glass industries. One of their signature techniques, still being made today, is clear glass coated with a thin layer of colored glass, often as many as three layers of colored glass, and then cut back to reveal the clear base, which is then enameled. Another standard Bohemian product was clear glass cased in red and cut or etched in a stylized pattern, such as deer or castles or trees. Perfume bottles in these patterns are fairly plentiful. In the 1820s, a Bohemian factory first marketed a style of glass called "lithyalin," which is a glass made in imitation of natural stone. The earliest pieces were in opaque brownish-red

with veining resembling agate. Later, good imitations of natural malachite, lapis lazuli and other stones were developed. The technique was produced by a complex surface staining process.

4.5" Bohemian Rubina cologne with enameled decoration and crown top, ca. 1875-1900, $165-225

9" Harrach amber cologne with enameled flowers and applied salamander with lily-form stopper with applied glass rigaree and lady bugs, ca. 1890 $750-1,000

In 1835, **Joseph Riedel** pioneered green or yellow uranium glass (annagrun), which was copied by many others firms, including the Boston and Sandwich Glass Company in this country. It was named for his wife "Anna."

In the period from about 1928 until 1939, Czechoslovakia produced literally thousands of perfume bottle designs. Most were of cut full lead crystal, often beveled at the edges. The stoppers were usually the focal point of the more elaborate designs featuring deeply etched figures or flowers. Different area manufacturers offered a wide variety of colors, often different colors for the base and its companion stopper. Spatter glass bottles were also made. Czech glassmakers also made bottles for commercial perfume companies, such as Elizabeth Arden. Another uniquely Czechoslovakian style is known as "**Tango**." It consists of very brightly colored pieces—yellow, orange or lime green, for example—decorated with simple black details in the Art Deco style.

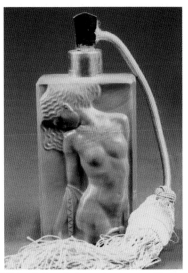

7.2" Lapis lazuli glass atomizer molded with a nude in high-relief, unsigned Czechoslovakian, ca. 1930s $750

6.7" Clear crystal bottle and stopper in the shape of a scimitar, dauber, Czechoslovakia label, c1920s-30s $200-300

7.3" Pink cut crystal bottle with clear and frosted nude stopper, signed Czechoslovakia, c1930s $750-900

Sought after by serious collectors of Czech perfume bottles are the fabulous creations combining full lead (over 40%) cut crystal bottles with elaborate stoppers mounted with lacy metal filigree, sometimes with glass or semiprecious jewels. This work was usually done in Czechoslovakia, but also in **Austria** during the same period—1920s and 1930s.

5.7" Clear cut crystal bottle and stopper, stopper cut with flowers, signed Czechoslovakia, c1920s-30s $150

The firm of **Ludwig Moser and Son** was founded in the mid-19th century and is still making excellent glass items today. It began as an engraving studio, but later developed a technique for producing glass that was as hard as lead crystal. Their early work is often unsigned.

3" pair of crystal bottles with metal collars in gilt metal faux jewel mounted caddy, c1920s, marked Austria $350

Heinrich Hoffman (1875-1939) was a master glass craftsman and designer in the area that became Czechoslovakia in 1918. He made Art Nouveau style molds for perfumes, most signed intaglio in the molds with a butterfly. In the late 1920s, his daughter married **Henry Schlevogt,** who had worked in the jewelry making trade. With Hoffman's help, he founded the **Ingrid Company** (named for Schlevogt's daughter). The new company developed many new processes for making lithyalin glass (in imitation of many natural stones—malachite, lapis lazuli, quartz, etc.) and produced the sought-after perfume bottles with nude daubers, with and without elegant metal filigree mounts with faux jewels. They remain the best loved bottles by collectors.

8" Moser purple urn shape bottle with gold band of women warriors, conforming stopper with dauber, unsigned $750

6.3" Hoffman smoke colored crystal bottle with upright stopper with dauber, stopper etched with lady climbing hill, marked with Hoffman butterfly logo, c1930s $950

5.6" Hoffman lapis lazuli glass bottle and stopper molded as two open chrysanthemum blossoms, signed Ingrid, Czechoslovakia $1200

The American firm of **Irving W. Rice (Irice)** was the leading importer of Czech perfume bottles during the period. The company imported thousands of different designs, often marking them with the Irice logo alongside the "Made in Czechoslovakia" mark. These imports ranged from the simplest glass bottles to the most elaborate metal and jeweled creations. The firm also bought little dram bottles (one-eighth ounce) in cut or pressed glass and topped with a lacy metal screw cap, sometimes with a glass dauber and sometimes topped with a faux jewel. The most unusual of these had tiny figural glass items, people or fruit or hearts, etc., dangling from the cap on little chains. The company is still in business today, importing its vanity bottles from the Far East. Many of the bottles listed in other Czechoslovakian sections were probably imported by Irice, but the paper labels have been lost over time.

4.8" Blue crystal bottle and stopper, bottle mounted with jeweled metal filigree medallion, Irice paper label, signed Czechoslovakia $300-400

2.6" Cut glass with metal and Bakelite cap with dauber, dangling boy and girl black and white charms on chains, ca.1920s-30s, marked by Irice c1920s-30s $135

Czech frosted glass, made by a technique of acid etching, was inspired by the glass popularized by Rene Lalique in the 1920s. It was widely imitated in Czechoslovakia by several companies, sometimes so carefully that it can be confused with Lalique's production.

Many German glass factories also produced literally hundreds of thousands of **"throwaway colognes"** or **"attar of roses"** bottles in the 18th and 19th centuries. These are hand blown, long and narrow bottles, seven or eight inches long, often made as rectangles, meant to hold very small amounts of scent and then meant to be thrown out. They usually had tiny glass stoppers and were clear glass, although colored examples are known. They were often cut in simple geometric designs and then gilded by hand.

Another popular German export was the mercury glass perfume laydown made by the thousands in the 1920s and 1930s. They were usually enameled in abstract swirl patterns.

7.5" Throwaway cologne bottle painted with gold and white enamel with small glass stopper, c19th century $75-100

German Ceramic Bottles

The **Meissen Porcelain Works** dates from the 18th century, when it was established to try to develop hard paste porcelain in imitation of the very expensive Chinese imports. In the early 18th century, the special clay necessary for this process was discovered nearby. Perfume bottles have been produced by the Meissen factory since that time, but in such limited quantities that they are still very sought after.

5.5" Porcelain atomizer in the form of a black boy with an urn, hand painted, with crossed swords mark for Meissen, c.early 20th century $250-300

German crown-top porcelain bottles were on the most popular style in the 1930s. They were small (usually holding less than 1/3 ounce) porcelain figural bottle with a metal and cork crown-shaped stopper. Most of us have seen at least one version of the "Kewpie doll" bottle, but there are figures ranging from elegantly dressed 18th century ladies to orange dogs and fat Buddhas. Most of these bottles are marked "Germany" or "Made in Germany" (after 1920), with or without a mold number. Some of these perfumes came with sets including trays or powder boxes. Some are combinations of perfume bottles sitting atop powder boxes. Those pieces which have a factory signature, like Sitzendorf, are the most sought after. Also highly collectible are the "naughty" figurals, like the little boy peeing.

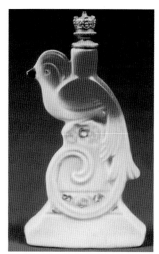

2.3" crown top Art Deco lady head bottle, marked Germany c1920s-30s $165

3.6" Crown top perfume in the form of a bird with a long tail, c1920s-30s, molded Germany mark, $175

Chapter 7

OTHER EUROPEAN BOTTLES

Holland, Denmark and Belgium:

Dutch perfume containers of the 18th and 19th centuries were often inspired by the trade between the Orient and Holland. The Chinese trade led to many unique bottles—Chinese porcelains mounted in the Netherlands with metal caps and cork stoppers, each one-of-a-kind creation mounted by hand. The Dutch were already known throughout Europe for their sophisticated silver and gold work and elaborately cut glass. Dutch engravers excelled at diamond point engraving and stippling. There were also extremely luxurious gold mounted cut rock crystal examples and simpler Delft style ceramic bottles. Until the second quarter of the 19th century, almost all Dutch perfume bottles had cork stoppers with silver or gold pull knobs or full precious metal overcaps. (Lack of the original cork does not affect prices because all cork dries out and falls apart over time.)

4.1" Three Dutch Schoonhoven crystal bottles with sterling collars, bases and overcaps, two with inner glass stoppers, on hallmarked with dagger, c1900 $100-125 each

The Belgian glass firm of **Val St. Lambert** began making cased glass perfume bottles in the 19th century. They were usually clear cased in a single color, most commonly violet, yellow-amber or cranberry, and acid cut back to clear, leaving a pattern of leaves and flowers. These bottles were often sold as part of dresser sets including several sizes of perfume and cologne bottles, powder jars and pin trays.

8" crystal bottle in red acid cut back to clear in a pattern of leaves and branches, facet cut stopper, attributed to VSL, c1920s-30s $150

The Danish porcelain firm of **Royal Copenhagen** is officially the Danish Royal Porcelain Factory, established in 1775 and best known around the world for its Flora Danica dinnerware.

Sweden:

Orrefors has been a glassmaking firm since 1898. It developed a process for cased glass with controlled bubbles called Ariel. Their most popular perfumes, still in production, are boule shaped with tall stick-like ground glass stoppers and engraved figures. Most are signed "Orrefors" or "Of," with or without the date or the designer's name.

Kosta Boda: The Boda Glassworks was founded in 1864 and the Kosta Glassworks was founded in 1742. The two merged to form Kosta Boda in 1970.

Italy:

The terms Venetian and Murano are synonymous for glassware manufactured since the Middle Ages on the island of Murano near Venice. The island of Murano has been a great glassmaking center ever since. During the 16th and 17th centuries, the Venetians developed many new techniques for decorating glass, including latticino (spiral threads) and millefiori canes, and their gold and silver foil techniques are still in use today, sometimes causing confusion when trying to date a particular piece. Early pieces often had finely blown figural swans or dragons as part of the design, usually on the stem of a piece. However these animals did not lend themselves to perfume bottles. Several new glass techniques were developed in the 20th century such as sommerso, that uses a brightly colored bottle, sometimes with a second color overlay, and then cased in an extremely heavy layer of clear glass. Some of the great modern firms of Murano sign their products. Among them are Barovier and Toso, Venini, Cenedese and Barbini.

4.75" Murano clear perfume bottle with unusual encased fish, ca. 1950s, $275-300

Chapter 8

OTHER FOREIGN PERFUME BOTTLES

Ireland:

Waterford Glass Ltd. was founded in 1783. It closed before the mid-19th century. The present company was opened in 1951. It produces a variety of cut crystal scent bottles, most signed with the company's clover logo.

Japan:

Japan has a centuries-long tradition of ceramic and glass manufacturing. Very early pieces were rarely marked. Exports intended for the American market were usually marked Nippon (the Japanese word for Japan, not denoting any particular factory) from 1891 to 1921. When pieces were marked Nippon plus Japan, they are later products. From 1921 to 1945, the mark for exported wares was "Made in Japan" or simply "Japan." During the American occupation of Japan after World War II, from 1945 to 1952, the mark "Occupied Japan" was used.

During the occupation, there was a concerted effort to produce goods that would appeal to the Western market and bring in needed currency. Perfume bottles in the style of Meissen, Staffordshire, prewar-Czechoslovakia and Old Paris porcelain were exported by the thousands.

Mexico:

Mexican silversmiths have produced thousands of different perfume bottles in solid sterling silver, sterling over glass and silver deposit. They are difficult to date since the same designs that were introduced in the 1920s have been in constant production ever since. Those signed by the famous silversmiths are, of course, most costly. Also exported from Mexico are hand carved hardstone bottles.

2.5" Clear glass with sterling overlay decorated with flowers and leaves, marked sterling and Mexico, c1940s-60s $60

Egypt:

In the last 15 years or so, huge numbers of lightweight blown bottles with flashed colors, gold trim and, usually, flame stoppers with long daubers, have been produced and exported from Egypt. Most are based on classical designs, but some are figural animals. They are too abundant to be of much value but they are very attractive.

Russia:

Anyone trying to identify glass or enamel on metal perfume bottles from Russia during the 18th or 19th century may be forgiven for confusing them with French pieces. The two countries traded extensively and freely borrowed designs from each other. After 1900 the French Art Nouveau style of Galle was very popular.

3" silver-gilt scent bottle with stippled background and decorated with brilliant translucent enamels on the bottle and top, Russian hallmarks, ca. 1880, $1,750-2,000

Chapter 9

SPECIALTY PERFUME BOTTLES

Souvenir bottles:

The growth of the tourism industry in the 19th century prompted many manufacturers to produce bottles with the names of towns or resorts on them. This type of bottle could be made of fine hand painted porcelain, an inexpensive ceramic or pressed glass. In France, opaline bottles with views of famous monuments printed on paper and set under glass on the lid were popular with ladies making their "grand tour." German bottles with names of spas painted among flowers were common. Some souvenir bottles were unmarked, but sold in cases with identifying marks. Glass bottles were also used as souvenirs, with their identification cut or etched into the glass surface. Thousands of bottles of all types and in many different materials were issued to commemorate Queen Victoria's Golden Jubilee in 1887, for instance.

2" Blue glass boule shape bottle with clear inner stopper and metal overcap and finger ring, enameled with gold flower and leaves, inscribed "Venise" (the French spelling of Venice) $250

Purse bottles came from many countries, used a variety materials and are found from all eras, from the 18th century to today. They were popular in England, France, Germany and Italy as early as the 1700s. These countries were noted for their tiny luxury bottles made in various materials from colored and cut glass to striped Venetian examples. Even ceramic

and fine porcelain examples are found. Most were made with metal screw caps or had tiny inner glass stoppers with metal overcaps to keep the contents safe within a lady's handbag.

Atomizers:

These are perfume bottles mounted with a pump that sprays the perfume inside as a mist. There were several noted companies that produced these.

Marcel Franck inherited a French company from his father that made all-metal pump-type travel atomizers invented by his father. Under Marcel's direction, the company contracted the glass from such famous glassmakers as Daum, Baccarat, Lalique and others. Most mounts were brass or silver plated, some were gold plated and even solid gold examples are known. Later mounts were chrome plated and are often made for purse or pocket. Often the glass is marked by the maker and most mounts are marked "Marcel Franck," sometimes with the name of the patented mount type, like Le Kid, Le Weekend, L'Escale, or Le Parisien. Other markings include "Brevete" or "SGDG," which mean "patented," or "Depose," which means "registered."

7.3" Rene Lalique "Le Parisien" frosted glass atomizer with nudes and garlands, metal signed SGDG, glass signed R Lalique, c1920s $650

5.5" boule atomizer in multicolor glass, mount signed Marcel Franck and Brevete SGDG $75-100

DeVilbiss was established in Toledo, Ohio in the early 1900s. The company was the leading American manufacturer of atomizers. It purchased the glass bottles from leading glasshouses such as Steuben, Durand, Daum, Imperial and others and mounted its own hardware, hoses and rubber bulbs. Even the Lenox China Company made at least two bottles for DeVilbiss, a comical penguin-shaped bottle and a two-piece circular bottle with the atomizer mounted in the lower half. The hand-crocheted bulb covers were, I am told, made in a "cottage industry" fashion by Ohio housewives working at home. The great years for DeVilbiss were the 1920s and 1930s. The company also made dresser sets including powder jars, trays and perfume bottles with long glass daubers. World War II and changing tastes led to simpler shapes with less hand decoration. The company discontinued atomizer production in 1969. Most DeVilbiss production was signed in gold or engraved "DeV" without any signature of the glassmaker.

4.2" DeVilbiss pink enameled dauber bottle with gold trim, unsigned, $70

5" DeVilbiss violet glass atomizer with gold plated mount with a faux jewel finial, signed DeVilbiss c1930s $90

Etling (1909-1939) was a French company that sold French cameo glass atomizers and perfume bottles signed "Richard" at its Paris shop. It also contracted with another established glassmaker, probably Loetz of Austria. It did not make glass perfume bottles themselves.

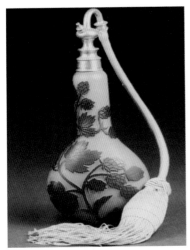

8.7" cameo atomizer in red cut back to orange with motif of leaves, signed Richard, mount unmarked, c1930s $475

Volupte was another American atomizer maker. Many of its designs are very similar to DeVilbiss products.

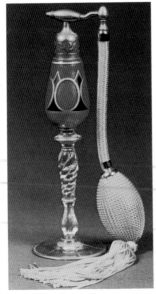

7" Clear bottle w/twisted stem, orange and black enamel trim, paper label "24 kt gold plated," signed Volupte $520

T. J. Holmes and Company made atomizer mounts and bought the glass from several other manufacturers. They are usually marked "Holmspray" on the metal.

Pyramid is a marking found on other atomizer mounts.

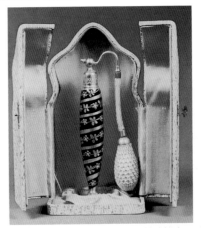

7.4" mint in box tall atomizer with black and gold enamel with orange roses in silk lined display case, mount signed Pyramid $1100

Paperweight scent bottles:

These bottles feature extra heavy bases, usually with distinctive inclusions, and have been made in both Europe and America.

St. Clair Glass Company of Elwood, Indiana was founded by five of the six St. Clair brothers, most notably Joe. The company produced numerous paperweight scent bottles, most with flower inclusions. The company made sulphides and exceptional controlled bubble paperweight scent bottles. In the 1960s, the St. Clair factory was able to reproduce chocolate glass, similar to the color made by the Indiana Tumbler and Glass Company of Greentown, Indiana, to use for its floral inclusions. St. Clair glass signatures vary from etched to raised from "JSC" to "St Clair to Joe St Clair." Some are unsigned.

6.5" Pair of paperweight scent bottles with turquoise flowers rising from pink bases, signed by Joe St. Clair, ca. 1945-70, $750 pr.

Whitall Tatum & Company of Millville, New Jersey, made paperweight scent bottles (or inkwells) with lilies or roses inside the heavy glass bases.

Gunderson-Pairpoint (1939-56) produced a wide range of perfume bottles in the styles of elegant Depression Glass, Mid-century Modern and paperweights.

Perfume Lamps:

These are small lamps that featured an indentation in the top of the shade for perfume or perfumed oil. The heat of the light bulb caused the perfume to evaporate and fill the room with scent. They are often simple frosted glass, but wonderful figural lamps made of ceramic material were also popular in the 1920s, 1930s and 1940s. Due to safety concerns, modern rewiring of these lamps is considered only a minor defect.

6" Fulper (New Brunswick, NJ) perfume lamp with molded dancer, rewired, signed Fulper $600

8.5" DeVilbiss perfume lamp in light to dark orange glass internally painted with nude fairies and foliage in elaborate metal mount, c1930s $500

Perfume Burners: The word perfume comes from the Latin word meaning "to burn." The earliest uses of scents were to burn them as part of religious ceremonies. Incense burners date back at least to ancient Egypt. Perfume burners are usually in the form of glass perfume bottles with long cloth wicks and metal covers that are filled with special perfumed oil. When lighted, they give off scent just like a scented candle does today.

6.7" Sirenes, a clear and frosted burner w/conforming cover, amber stain, molded signature R Lalique $2750

Perfume jewelry, like other jewelry, can take any wearable form. It can mean any jewelry with a well or pierced back to accommodate filling with actual scent or, more recently, can mean any jewelry with a bottle motif or jewelry issued by commercial perfume companies, usually in imitation of that company's perfume bottles. The range of perfume jewelry is enormous, from antique pure gold perfume pins and rings to modern plastic pins that hold tiny miniature bottles.

Dresser sets and boxed sets: During the 18th and 19th centuries, handsome and highly decorative small chests or caskets were made in England and on the Continent to hold matched sets of scent bottles for travel or for protecting the expensive contents at home. The boxes themselves were often made of luxurious imported woods or caskets of glass and metal with or without semiprecious stones. Sets were also made for racks with locks called "Tantaluses." Novelty sets were made in infinite forms, including cruet sets and carts pulled by "coolies." Colognes and toilet waters are less expensive to produce and do not last as long as perfume. Therefore, cologne bottles can be differentiated from perfume bottles because they are larger. Sets for the dresser usually contain cologne and lotion bottles and powder jars, and sometimes even candlesticks and hair receivers, as well as perfume bottles.

DeVilbiss dresser set of four matching pieces: two 6.7" perfume bottles, an atomizer and a dauber bottle in teal blue with gold enamel on gold metal foot and stem with matching powder box and 11" tray, c1930s $1900

Powder Jars: Some powder jars were sold separately. Others were designed to be part of dresser sets with matching perfume and cologne bottles. They range in value from Depression Era examples, which sell for less than $25, to Lalique and Galle examples, which are extremely costly.

1.6" Green crystal powder box, the cover intaglio cut with cupids, on jeweled metal base, marked with Hoffman butterfly, c1930s $700

Perfume Buttons: These are buttons meant to be sewn onto clothing. They are usually metal with pierced designs. A scented cloth is inserted into the back of the button and the perfume wafts through the holes in the button.

Novelties

Schuco, a German manufacturer of stuffed toy animals, made darling monkeys and bears of mohair with movable limbs, whose heads came off to reveal a long tube with a cork stopper for holding perfume.

As early as 1820, English manufacturers delighted in making novelty shaped bottles, with and without silver mounts. Some were the porcelain variety already discussed. Others were in the form of nuts, fruit, eggs, shells, musical instruments, shoes or hands. Creative artisans even used natural nuts and shells topped with metal mounts to cater to the Victorian curiosity about nature.

1.62" English glass perfume bottle in the shape of a strawberry, brass cap and chatelaine ring, ca. 1890-1900, $375

Related Collectibles:

Pomanders: These grew out of the belief that strong fragrances could ward off disease. Therefore, the wealthy carried oranges pierced with cloves when they left home. From these came the first silver boxes, often shaped like oranges, to hold medicinal scents like cloves, ambergris and cinnamon. They were in wide use during the period of the Great Plague of 1665-1666.

Vinagrettes: supplanted pomanders by the late 18th century. These tiny containers, often extremely intricate and expensive, had a space for a cloth or sponge soaked in vinegar or another strong scent and held in place with a decorative inner grill. They were useful when encountering strong odors or to revive a lady from a swoon.

Part II

COMMERCIAL PERFUMES

Commercial perfume design has some important considerations lacking in the design of decorative bottles. One of these is the relationship between the name of the scent and the design of the bottle. Not all perfumes named Rose have a rose on the bottle or the box, of course, but many do. Not all boxes made for holding perfume bottles are decorative or conform to the theme of the bottle's design, but many do. Even the color of the liquid scent itself is considered by some to be an element of the design of the complete perfume package. My personal apology about the headings under this category: This was even more difficult than the decorative section -- does a Rene Lalique bottle for D'Orsay with a nude on the bottle go under the figural heading, the D'Orsay section or the Lalique section? You see what I mean. Most of the dates given are for the introduction of the scent, not the release of the bottle. It is almost impossible to provide the discontinuation date for any bottle or scent. The perfume companies are reluctant to give that information, so as to leave open the possibility of a relaunch or just because they don't like to admit that their product was not particularly successful.

Chapter 10

FIGURALS & DIME STORE NOVELTIES

Figurals

Perfume bottles which are called figural can be any one of three different kinds. First is the full figural bottle where the stopper and the bottle combine to make any form other than a perfume bottle (human, flower, seltzer bottle—anything). Second is one where only the stopper is a figure (a flower or a girl sitting atop a cushion). Next is the type of bottle where the figural element is impressed or cut into the front of the bottle. Last is the kind where the display holding the bottle is the only figural element (Max Factor's colorful cats under domes holding small bottles).

2.5" Suivez Moi by Tre Jur in frosted figure of a lady, with long dauber, c1925 $150-200

9" Au Soliel for Lubin in a bottle with a molded snake chasing the fly on the stopper, c1912 $1100-1300

2.6" Tryst by Villon in its red opaque skyscraper bottle with black glass stopper and good label. This bottle was used for other scents by other companies, including Duska by Langlois, ca.1946 $90-110

3.62" Souvenir d'un Soir by Mary Chess is a replica of the Plaza Hotel fountain in New York, c1956 $310-590

Dime store novelties: The period from the 1920s through the 1950s saw a tremendous expansion in the sale of perfume, including inexpensive colognes and toilet water. Many were marketed in imaginative yet inexpensive figural containers. A vast collection could be made of bottles and/or stoppers in the form of flowers.

2.2" Old Colonial by United Toilet Goods Co. mini in hurricane lamp presentation, good label c1940-60s $25

2" Floral Quintuplets by Karoff , set of 5 with wood heads wearing ruffles at the neck, box c1940s $80-110

3.8" The Duke by Erte in the form of a man with a cane, details in enamel, in glass dome with label, c1930s $60

Chapter 11

FRENCH BOTTLE DESIGNERS

In addition to the tremendous contributions made by Lalique and Baccarat, there were a number of less well known firms that produced quality glass designs.

Brosse: Verreries Brosse was an established glassmaker in France from its founding in 1854, but in the 1920s, the entire production of the factory was converted to perfume bottles. Still in the business of making fine hand finished perfume bottles, the company's trademark is "VB" or "BR." Today's customers include Hermes and Chanel.

5" Coup de Chapeau by Gilbert Orcel in white glass as a figural lady's head and shoulders with gold enameled details, Brosse bottle, c1954 $125

Pochet et du Courval: This venerable company has been making high quality perfume bottles since the early 17th century. Since 1930 the firm's entire business has been the manufacture of commercial perfume bottles for such distinguished parfumeurs as Dior, Jean Patou and Molinard. Many of the company's bottles bear the "HP" mark.

7.25" Vol deNuit eau de cologne in donut bottle with pointed glass stopper and dot label, c1937, marked HP $65

Saint Gobain Desjonqueres: This glassworks was founded in France in the 17th century. They acquired the Desjonqueres factory, which had been destroyed during World War II, after it had been rebuilt and modernized under the Marshall Plan. Today this is the largest maker of perfume bottles in the world. Some of their bottles are marked with the firm's "S" or "SGD" mark.

Julien Viard: Viard was a sculptor as well as designer and part owner of the glassmaking firm of C & J Viard and Viollet le Duc. Many of his designs featured stained or enameled details or wonderful figural stoppers. Often unsigned, bottles may be sometimes found with the "J. Viard" or "J. Villard" signature.

3.1" Fete de Nuit by Agnel in black glass bottle in the form of a bell, sealed, by J Viard c1920 $1250

Sue et Mare: Louis Sue was a famous French architect and interior designer. André Mare trained as a painter but turned to design. They began working together in 1914. Their work encompassed every facet of Art Deco design, from interior wall panels to wallpaper to perfume bottles. Their partnership ended in 1928. Louis Sue or the firm of Sue et Mare designed all of Jean Patou's perfume bottles and boxes and several bottles for other perfumers, notably the popular bottle for D'Orsay's "Le Dandy." He designed the unique "Normandie" presentation for Patou in 1935 to celebrate the ocean liner by that name.

3" Normandie by Jean Patou, mint in box reissue of the original Louis Sue bottle, c1980s $635-900

Chapter 12

THE GREAT PERFUME HOUSES

Elizabeth Arden, whose real name was Florence Nightingale Graham, opened a beauty salon in New York City in 1910. Her first product was a cleansing cream. She began marketing her own perfumes in about 1915.

Bourjois was established in 1863. The firm began marketing perfume in 1903. "Evening in Paris" was introduced in 1928 in its signature cobalt blue bottle. It soon became a hugely popular and inexpensive line presented in holders shaped as shoes, shells, hotel doors, famous landmarks, boats, wheelbarrows, ashtrays, and other designs.

6.5" It's You for Elizabeth Arden in clear figural hand holding a bottle with a blue ring and blue flower stopper, sealed with hang tags, Baccarat signed and numbered, lacking dome, c1938 $1200-1500

2.75" Evening in Paris by Bourjois in cobalt bottle with silver triangular label and frosted upright stopper with its star shaped box, c1928 $75-100

1.8" Blue Grass in its replica miniature bottle with two labels, c1934 $110-125

2" Evening in Paris cobalt mini with silver triangle label in blue Bakelite owl case, c1928 $100-225

Caron was founded in 1903, and its famous scent, "Narcisse Noir," was introduced in 1912.

3.75" Voeu de Noel by Caron is in opalescent white crystal molded with flowers on the front, c1939 $165-225

Ciro was founded in the United States in 1921, but all its perfumes were made and bottled in France.

1.3" Rue de la Paix by Corday set of three miniatures in a metal lamppost with a "cobblestone" ashtray base, minis with good labels, c1952 $188-510

7.5" Chevalier de la Nuit by Ciro in the form of a knight in clear and frosted glass, c1923 $175

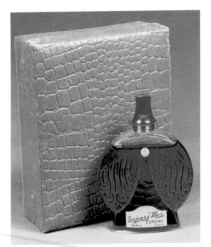

3" Toujours Moi by Corday, mint in box bottle and stopper with impressed flowers, with brown stain and deluxe box c1934 $155

Corday was founded in 1921. Its famous scent, "Toujours Moi," was used in churches in Paris as incense. In 1923 it was first marketed as a commercial perfume. It is thought that Corday originated, in the 1930s, the selling of perfume in tiny one-eighth-ounce miniature bottles that were replicas of the larger Corday bottles.

Coty was founded by Francois Sportuno, who later changed his name to Coty, in 1904. Soon thereafter his firm began to commission Rene Lalique to create labels and then bottles for his early floral scents. Coty was the first to consistently offer his scents in luxurious crystal bottles and expensive presentation boxes.

4.36" L'Effleur was probably Rene Lal-ique's first collaboration with Francois Coty. The label with the raised female figure is actually molded into the glass, brown stain, c1908 $4500-4750

5.12" Ambre d'Orsay is a black glass Rene Lalique design with four draped classical female figures molded on the corners, stopper with stylized flowers, c1913, this version signed Lalique in the mold, $800-900

Guerlain was established in 1828. Now in the hands of the fifth generation of the Guerlain family, the company has created over 200 different perfumes. The Guerlain bottles have been made by several companies, Baccarat, Pochet et du Courval, Saint Gobain–Desjonqueres, Romesnil and Brosse. In addition to beautiful full-sized bottles, Guerlain began producing sample and tester bottles before 1900.

6.25" L'Or by Coty in teardrop bottle and stopper, good gold lettering, marked Baccarat, c1916 $225

D'Orsay was founded in 1830 by Count Alfred D'Orsay, a renowned bon vivant with a talent for creating perfumes. He was a sculptor, painter and writer. His interest in perfume was supposedly inspired by his mistress, Lady Blessington. From then on creating scents became his sole preoccupation.

6.3" Shalimar by Guerlain winged bottle with small blue fan stopper, label and faded velour case, marked Baccarat, c1921 $100-165

6.5" L'Heure Bleu by Guerlin eau de toilette bottle in the teardrop shape with all glass onion dome stopper, good label, c1912 $55-70

2.2" Champs Elysses by Guerlin in limited edition bottle with fountain label, sealed, c1904 $250-330

Richard Hudnut was established in 1880, making this the first major American perfume and cosmetic company. His first scent was "Violet Sec." His most sought-after bottles were designed by Julien Viard.

2.5" Le Debut Noir by Richard Hudnut in a distinctive squat bottle of black glass with a gold raspberry stopper, with bottom label c1927 $175-250

Lancome was founded by a former employee of Coty Perfumes in 1935. His scents were presented in bottles designed by Lalique, Baccarat and other great glass designers.

4.5" Magie by Lancome in its clear twisted bottle with inner glass stopper and glass overcap in its deluxe presentation box, unsigned Baccarat design c1949 $150-250

Lentheric was founded in 1885 by Guillaume Lentheric. He began marketing perfumes in the United States in the 1920s, opening a very lavish salon at the Savoy Plaza in New York.

1.5" A Bientot by Lentheric, mint in box replica with gold ball cap, c1930 $40-50

Prince Matchabelli was founded after the Russian Revolution by Prince Georges Matchabelli. His first venture in the United States was a boutique where he sold custom blended scents, among many luxury items. These scents were so successful that he formed a perfume company in 1926. All his early products were sold in bottles shaped as crowns. Many, but not all, of the names he gave his scents related to royalty.

1.75" Wind Song by Prince Matchabelli in green crown with screw cap in velvet box, c1953 $45-75

2.6" Royal Gardenia by Prince Matchabelli in clear crown with gold and black trim, gold cross stopper, mint in heavy plastic cube c1930 $170

Chapter 13

FRENCH COUTURIERS

French couturiers, beginning with Coco Chanel in 1923, began to market their own scents in elegant bottles, ending the practice of selling perfume in simple containers meant to hold the scent only until it could be decanted into the customer's own bottle. In the next few years, Paul Poiret, Worth, Jean Patou, Elsa Schiaparelli and Lanvin introduced their own scents in elegant bottles that followed the design trends of their fashion houses.

Christian Dior opened his couture house in 1946 and his perfume business in 1947. His most famous perfume presentations were designed by Baccarat.

3.5" Arpege by Lanvin, mint in box, in the Lanvin signature black boule with the gold logo on the front and the (older) raspberry stopper, c1927 $220

Lucien Lelong opened his couture shop in 1919. He began producing perfume in 1921. The first scents were called simply A, B, C and N.

7" Miss Dior in clear with blue enamel amphora with glass stopper, good lettering, marked Baccarat c1933 $525-700

Lanvin: Jeanne Lanvin made hats until her designs for dresses for her own daughter were "discovered" and women began to buy her dresses for themselves and their daughters. She began marketing perfumes in 1923. Paul Iribe designed the famous Lanvin logo which shows Jeanne and her daughter.

6.75" Indiscret by Lelong in beautiful draped bottle with glass bow stopper and label, c1935 $100

Nina Ricci and her son, Robert, opened her couture house in 1932. In 1946, Robert launched the first Nina Ricci scent, "Coeur Joie," in its Marc Lalique-designed open heart bottle.

2.12" Zut by Schiaparelli replica mini of woman's lower torso, empty, good bottom label c1949 $500-600

12.8" L'Air de Temps for Nina Ricci with double dove stopper (called Flacon aux Colombes) was designed by Marc Lalique in 1947. It is often mistaken for a giant factice, but it held eau de toilette. $1250.

Elsa Schiaparelli opened her shop on the Rue de la Paix, Paris in 1929. Her first perfume was "Salut" in 1934, but she is best remembered for "Shocking," released in 1937 in a bottle shaped like a dress manikin. The story has it that she was inspired when walking past the dress dummy she used when designing for Mae West.

Worth was a couture house established in 1858 by Charles F. Worth. He began to market perfume in 1924, all in Lalique-designed bottles.

6.2" Requete for Worth, mint in its box, is a clear footed urn with blue enamel scallops, marked Lalique,c1944 $2000-2500

6" Shocking in its dressmaker dummy bottle with glass flowers around stopper, tape measure around neck and S label, in glass dome c1936 $350

Chapter 14

OTHER PERFUME SPECIALTIES

Factices

"Factice" is the French term for a dummy or display bottle. They may be any size from tiny to one ounce to really huge. The only necessity is that they not contain real scent but, usually, a special colored liquid that will not stain the bottle and that mimics the color of the true scent. Some collectors include small factices among their normal size bottles. Others specialize in the giant size display bottles.

12.5" Vicky Tiel giant factice, used for several of her scents, with shell stopper and molded nudes $400

Miniature Perfume Bottles

Miniatures are an extremely popular specialized collection. It is relatively easy to display a large number of "minis" in a small space. Years ago, perfume companies gave away miniature versions of their full-sized bottles filled with real scent to encourage customers to try their products. Today that has changed and the perfumers give away tubes of scent attached to advertising cards (which are also collectible), while the miniature reproduction bottles, when available at all, are sold. Many companies today make miniatures that have no corresponding full-sized bottles, some in costly limited edition figural bottles.

2.4" Moment Supreme by Jean Patou, mint in box in the Baccarat "bumpy" bottle with gold cap in its deluxe case, c1929 $135

8.5" Prince Matchabelli clear giant crown with gold trim and gold cross stopper, no label; used to advertise the whole line of Prince Matchabelli scents, c1940s-60s $650-725

2" Chi Chi by Renoir mint in box replica of heart bottle with bakelite arrow cap, c1942 $125-150

2.36" Heaven Sent by Helena Rubenstein in form of a frosted angel with metal cap, empty, c1941 $40-60

Miniature boxed sets come in several different versions. There are the sets that were designed so that you could test several of a single company's scents. There were sets composed of several different companies' scents. These are hard to price, since the miniature bottles are often only different by one or two from another set, and it is hard to know which miniatures affect the price of the set. Other box sets include miniature perfumes with other

beauty products, such as soap, lotion or bath powder. Beware of sets composed of one or more companies' scents, which have no corresponding full-sized bottles since there was a Midwestern company that made hundreds of different sets with several different company names, using stock bottles with some generic scents.

1.5" Set of 4 Marquay scents, mint in box replica minis with glass stoppers and individual velvet pouches c1950s $125

2.4" Set of 6 by Rose Valois, mint in box hat manikins wearing different hats (Rose Valois was a haute couture hat designer), c1950 $1000-1100

Testers

"**Tester**" is a term that has come to mean any small (usually one-eighth ounce or less) sample bottle with a label and a long dauber to apply the scent. The most highly prized testers come as sets from a single company and include many of its scents, and are either boxed for sale or sitting on a display base for use at perfume counters. Of course, testers can also be modern spray bottles used at perfume counters to test new scents.

Men's Scents

Men's scent bottles are not nearly as collectible as women's, but there are many exceptions, especially for figural bottles, such as the large military figures made for Canoe and Royal Leather.

15" Canoe by Dana, in giant ceramic bottle in the form of a French sailor, full, signed Dana c1946 $75-100

Chapter 15

SOLID PERFUMES

Estee Lauder: The Lauder Company has been issuing at least one, and often many more, limited edition solid (cream) perfume compacts every year since 1967. Most contemporary ones are figural, that is, made in the shape of something other than a simple compact. They are always well made and usually beautiful. The large number of vintage and contemporary solids makes them ideal for a single company collection. They even lend themselves to theme collections—cats, dogs, circus, produce, hearts, people, etc.

1.8" Estee Lauder Cinnabar Imperial solid perfume foo dog from the Imperial Series (composition figures made to resemble ivory), empty, no label c1979 $350

Corday has been making solid perfumes since approximately 1970. Many of them are figural and several feature the company's signature unicorn.

Molinard: This French company is justly famous for introducing tiny solid perfumes, called "concretas," in containers made of hand-decorated Bakelite. Flowers were the most common decoration, but outdoor scenes and people are the most sought after. They were filled with what the company called "wax of the flower."

1.7" Lauder Youth Dew Cameo Dancers, mint in box, in the form of a cameo with coral background with three dancing figures c1982 $130

7.5" Two Molinard concretas with hand-painted girl smoking, full, labels $20-35 each

Helena Rubenstein opened her first beauty products shop in Australia in 1902. She opened a chain of beauty shops in London, Paris and the United States. She began to market perfumes in 1934.

Lauder (Estée), "Cinnabar," an oval gilt metal box compact with the top mounted by a faux ivory model of a cat scratching its neck, from the Ivory Series, labeled, used, ca. 1982, 1 3/8" h. $150

1.6" Helena Rubenstein Heaven Sent solid perfume in the form of a toad, used, in its box, c1941 $30

Lauder (Estée), "Dazzling," a model of the Statue of Liberty in gold, statues holds lipstick, mint in box, ca. 2000, 3 2/3" h. $79

Chapter 16

CURRENT PRODUCTION PERFUMES

These perfume bottles may be considered future collectibles, however, some of them are purchased for display as soon as they are released. The limited editions of Jean Paul Gaultier are a prime example.

6" Classique by Jean Paul Gaultier in updated version of the original torso spray bottle, c1990s $55

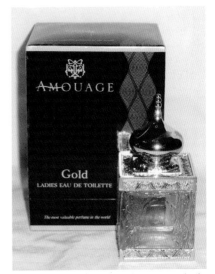

5.12" Amouage Gold by Amouage mint in box bottle with gold domed stopper (also available in limited edition with genuine malachite and lapis bottles), c1983 $175

Chapter 17

SPECIALIZED COLLECTIONS

Lamps related to commercial perfumes are rare. Most were used as perfume counter displays.

Flowers
Hearts
Games/gambling
Nudes
Human figures
Animals
Architecture
Clothing
Crowns
Art Nouveau
Art Deco
Powder Boxes and Tins
Mid-century modern
Single Parfumeurs
Single color
Perfume jewelry

3.2" Indiscret body powder by Lucien Lelong in large cream box with sunburst motif, c1935 $35-45

Paperweights
Related Collectibles
Advertisements
Labels
Soaps
Perfume trade cards
Fans
Powder Boxes and Tins

Books

Crossover collectible themes—e.g.—cars, hands, elephants, dogs, shoes.

Compacts: Some collectors include powder compacts in their perfume bottle collections when they are part of a series. For instance, Richard Hudnut made compacts that matched some of their scent bottles. Estee Lauder still releases compacts as part of its series of solid perfumes.

Awards and samples given by perfumers to perfume counter salespeople. These included pins, plaques, glassware, etc.

Dealer Signs

1" Le Golliwogg pin by Vigny in the form of a smiling black Golliwogg face, c1919 $250-350

Future Collectibles

Celebrity brand scent bottles: perhaps these bottles which bear the name of movie and music notables should be considered current collectibles (they accounted for $140 million in sales in 2006).

New figurals will also be appealing to collectors.

Chapter 18

SOME GENERAL RULES

1. There are no rules! Every rule has exceptions!

2. Specialize! Specialize!

3. Until you have studied the market and handled many, many bottles, you should only buy from a reputable dealer who will guarantee his/her merchandise.

4. Always remember that identification of glass manufacturers can be a problem because workers moved from factory to factory, even from country to country, taking with them every technique they had learned. Also, signatures can be forged.

5. The importance of labels and packaging cannot be overstated when collecting commercial perfume bottles.

6. The importance of rarity is more difficult to quantify. Buy something rare, but not obscure.

7. The secondary market places great importance on signed/documented pieces.

8. Condition is all important. Check carefully for any signs of sick glass, chips, repairs, mismatched stoppers, false signatures and torn labels. The exception is those little rubber bulbs on atomizers. Because they dry out over time, replacements or missing bulbs are not considered flaws. Missing a tiny inner stopper under a silver or gold cap or ornate stopper cover is considered a minor flaw.

9. With some bottles, a "marriage" between a bottle and a stopper made for an identical bottle is considered a minor flaw.

However, with cut glass or silver deposit bottles, the stopper must match the pattern of the bottle exactly.

10. Prefer something by a famous glassmaker or porcelain manufacturer.

11. Prefer something by a famous perfume house over an unknown one.

12. Buy a complete presentation whenever possible.

13. Buy a perfect example whenever possible.

14. Prefer crystal to glass.

15. Prefer examples where the stopper is ground to match its individual bottle over examples with plastic stopper liners on the tongue of the stopper (post-1979).

16. Buy a perfume bottle over cologne or eau de toilette.

17. Buy the best quality you can afford.

18. Size matters. Some commercial scents are rare in large sizes (2 ounces or larger) but fairly common in miniatures—or vice versa.

19. If you absolutely love it, buy it.

20. Of course, be wary of reproductions, but some designs, especially Czechoslovakian and Murano bottles, have been in almost continuous production for many, many years, so that their recent products cannot be considered reproductions.

CREDITS

Penny Dolnick is a past president of the International Perfume Bottle Association and a dealer in collectible perfume bottles since 1987. She is the author of the Penny Bank Commercial Perfume Bottle Price Guide, 8th Edition, the Penny Bank Miniature Perfume Bottle Price Guide, 3rd Edition and the Penny Bank Solid Perfume Bottle Price Guide, 4th Edition. She is willing to help you identify and date your bottles, but will not appraise them. You can email her at alpen@gate.net.

The International Perfume Bottle Association is an organization of 1,500 perfume bottle collectors in several countries. It fosters education and comradeship for collectors through its gorgeous quarterly full-color magazine, its regional chapters and its annual convention. For information or a membership application, go to www.perfumebottles.org.

Every year, the IPBA convention plays host to the Monsen and Baer Perfume Bottle Auction, featuring approximately 400 perfume bottles and related items. Back issues of the full color hard-bound catalogues are available. For more information, email Monsen and Baer at monsenbaer@errols.com .

Special thanks to Frank and Elizabeth Creech, Joan Walter and Madeleine France for bearing with me and continuing my education.

Thanks to all my friends in the International Perfume Bottle Association for answering my endless questions.

Photos courtesy of

Al Dolnick

Randall Monsen and Rod Baer

Frank and Elizabeth Creech

Joan Walter

Madeleine France

Shirley Hanick

Amelia Chatham

Connie Linne

Barbara Miller

Helen Farnsworth

Shari Hopper

Marsha Crafts

Anne Conrad

Joyce Geeser

Sabra Brae

Teri Worth

Cathy Weiss

PERFUME, SCENT & COLOGNE BOTTLES

Ancient Perfume Containers

Ancient Roman Glass Perfume Dropper

Perfume dropper, blown glass, aqua w/natural iridescence, Rome Empire, 2nd to 4th century A.D., 3 3/4" h. (ILLUS.)..... **$400-500**

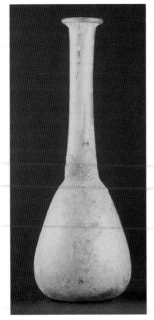

Early Roman Glass Scent Holder

Scent holder, blown aqua glass w/a long neck, Roman Empire, 2nd to 4th c. A.D. (ILLUS.) **$300-400**
Unguent holder, terra cotta, in the form of a small amphora, 6th or 7th century B.C., 5" l. (ILLUS., top next column) **$650-700**

Rare Early Phoenician Unguent Holder

Perfume Bottles Around the World

Austria

Dressing table set: cologne bottle, cov. jar & atomizer; each in black glass in a shapely tapering cylindrical shape trimmed w/narrow gilt-trimmed panels set w/faux blue jewels, round-footed bronze bases & fittings, ca. 1920s-30s, tallest 7" h., the set (ILLUS., top next page) **$4,500**

Perfume Bottle, Jar & Comb From an Ornate Six-Piece Egyptian Revival Dressing Table Set

Dressing table set: perfume bottle w/stopper, cov. dresser jar, hand mirror, brush & clothing brush; each in the Egyptian Revival style, the perfume bottle in cobalt blue cut to clear domed crystal shape w/an ornate scrolled gilt-metal neck & bulbous filigree stopper set w/blue glass cabochons the matching cylindrical glass jar w/a low domed gilt-metal cover w/matching designs & blue glass cabochons, a long comb w/a narrow matching mount, the other brushes & mirror w/matching backs set w/blue glass cabochons, signed "Austria," 1920s, bottle 5 1/2" h., the set (ILLUS.)............. **$4,500-5,500**

Three-Piece Black Glass Austrian Dressing Table Set

Amber Austrian Perfume Bottle

Austrian Cut Crystal Perfume Bottle

Perfume bottle & stopper, amber crystal in an oblong upright shape w/a low angled shoulder to the short neck fitted w/an amber facet-cut stopper, mounted in a gilt-metal base w/a decorative plaque on the side, paper label reads "T&B Austria," ca. 1920s, 8 1/2" h. (ILLUS.).............. **$3,000-4,000**

Perfume bottle & stopper, clear cut crystal in a short cylindrical shape, panel- and lobe-cut lower bands below a wide strawberry diamond-cut upper band, panel-cut shoulder & neck, paneled silver stopper inset on the top w/an ivory miniature portrait of a lady wearing a coronet, mid-19th c., 3 3/4" h. (ILLUS., top next column) **$500-600**

Pale Amethyst Austrian Perfume Bottle

Perfume bottle & stopper, pale amethyst crystal, narrow long ovoid shape w/sharply tapering paneled sides w/a small neck & a pointed stopper, resting on a narrow gilt-metal band trimmed w/white enamel, metal stamped "Austria," ca. 1920s, 7" h. (ILLUS., previous page)............................... **$1,500-2,000**

Austrian Bottle Set in a Frame

Perfume bottles & stoppers, a pair of small upright square crystal body w/gilt-metal enclosed necks & clear facet-cut stoppers, mounted in a gilt-metal frame trimmed around the base w/faux jewels & w/an arched overhead faux jewel-set handle, signed, ca. 1920s, 3" h., the set (ILLUS.)... **$350**

Belgium

Fine Belgian Cameo Perfume Bottle

Perfume bottle & stopper, cameo glass w/a cylindrical body & wide shoulder to the short neck w/flared rim, crystal overlaid in red & acid-cut w/a design of vines & leaves against a frosted clear ground, clear facet-cut stopper, attributed to Val St. Lambert, ca. 1920s-30s, 8" h. (ILLUS.) **$150**

Bohemia

Enameled Rubina Bohemian Cologne

Cologne bottle & stopper, bell-shaped Rubina glass body enameled in yellow of fancy scrolls & small flowers, metal collar & small crown-shape stopper, late 19th c., 4 1/2" h. (ILLUS.)........................... **$165-225**

Bohemian Amber-Flashed & Cut Cologne

Cologne bottle & stopper, cylindrical clear glass w/a rounded shoulder & short neck, flashed in amber & ornately cut overall w/tall almond-shaped panels alternating w/block & fan panels, amber facet-cut stopper, ca. 1860, 6 3/4" h. (ILLUS.)... **$400-500**

Cologne bottle & stopper, green glass h.p. in white enamel in the Mary Gregory style w/a chicken & foliage, late 19th c., 8 1/2" h. **$250**

Elaborate Harrach Enameled Cologne

Cologne bottle & stopper, mold-blown square amber bottle w/optic ribbing & a stepped shoulder to the short flaring neck, heavily & ornately enameled overall w/colorful flowers & leaves, one side applied w/a large salamander, the tall ribbed & lily-form stopper w/an applied rigaree rim band & applied lady bugs on the sides, Harrach factory, ca. 1890, 9" h. (ILLUS.) **$750-1,000**

Fine Ruby-Flashed & Cut Cologne

Cologne bottle & stopper, ruby-flashed on clear glass, tall slightly tapering cylindrical shape w/a narrow shoulder & cylindrical ringed neck, the sides cut w/three bands separating faceted panels in alternating clear & ruby engraved w/stylized leaves, a tall paneled ruby stopper etched w/vertical squiggly bands, ca. 1890-1910, 5" h. (ILLUS.) **$250**

Rare Green Silver-Overlay Cologne

Cologne bottle & stopper, silver-overlay glass, squatty bulbous lower body below slender tapering cylindrical upper body w/a short flaring neck, bulbous pointed stopper, dark green overlaid w/ornate sterling scrolls & flowers w/lattice panels up the neck, solid silver neck, silver overlaid stopper, Bohemia, 8" h. (ILLUS.)...... **$4,320**

Cobalt Blue Squared Squatty Cologne

Cologne bottle & stopper, squatty cobalt blue glass shape w/four projecting tiered oval panels below a curved shoulder & short flaring neck, ornately trimmed w/gilt flower & leaf sprigs, large squared mushroom stopper, possibly Bohemia, ca. 1900-20, 4 2/3" h. (ILLUS.) **$150-175**

Ruby Perfume Atomizer with Portrait

Perfume atomizer w/fittings, deep ruby bell-shaped body enameled w/a dotted body band & leafy sprigs w/an oval reserve enameled in white w/the profile of a young woman, unusual metal pump fittings, southern Bohemia, ca. 1865-75, 4" h. (ILLUS.) **$375-450**

Riedel Annagrun Enameled Perfume

Perfume bottle & stopper, annagrun uranium bulbous ovoid bottle tapering to a short neck w/flattened rim, enameled around the shoulder w/leafy scrolls & blossoms, bulbous pointed stopper, Joseph Riedel, ca. 1850-60, 4 1/2" h. (ILLUS.) **$250-275**

Ornately Cut Annagrun Glass Perfume

Perfume bottle & stopper, annagrun uranium glass in a cylindrical shape deeply cut around the sides w/diamond panels, silver collar & fancy hinged cap w/glass inner stopper, Joseph Riedel, mid-19th c., 4 1/4" h. (ILLUS.) **$450-500**

Leaf & Acorn-decorated Chatelaine Perfume

Perfume bottle & stopper, chatelaine-style, flattened milky opal teardrop-shaped small bottle ornately enameled in color w/clusters of oak leaves & gold acorns on slender branches, brass collar w/short chain & ring, twist-off domed cap, Moser, ca. 1880-90, 3 1/8" l. (ILLUS.)........ **$300**

Turquoise Gold-trimmed Moser Perfume

Perfume bottle & stopper, chatelaine-style, turquoise blue round teardrop-shaped small bottle ornately enameled in gold w/stylized flowers & leaves & panels down the shoulders, brass collar w/chain & ring below the domed hinged cap, Moser, ca. 1880-90, 3 1/8" l. (ILLUS.). **$300-450**

Ornately Gilded Bohemian Perfume

Perfume bottle & stopper, cylindrical cobalt blue glass bottle w/rounded shoulders & short cylindrical neck, the upper half of the body covered in gold forming points & further highlighted w/raised gilt stylized florals, the lower body decorated w/delicate gold flowers, gold-covered knob stopper, ca, 1865, 5 1/4" h. (ILLUS.) **$350-450**

Elaborately Decorated Cranberry Perfume

Perfume bottle & stopper, cylindrical cranberry glass cased in clear w/a short neck w/a flaring rim, the sides decorated w/a wide center band ornately enameled in color w/leafy scrolls & flowers, flanked by bands decorated w/gold lappets, cranberry ball stopper w/gold lappet design, probably the Myers-Neffe factory, ca. 1885, 6 3/4" h. (ILLUS.) **$1,250-1,500**

Fancy White to Blue Cut-Overlay Bottle

Perfume bottle & stopper, cylindrical cut-overlay glass w/rounded shoulder & small cylindrical neck, blue opaline cased in while & cut w/trefoils & quatrefoils w/the white layer ornately trimmed w/gilt, gold neck & ball stopper, ca. 1860s, 4 1/4" h. (ILLUS., previous page)........ **$300-400**

Moser Gold-decorated Perfume Bottle

Perfume bottle & stopper, domed cylindrical cranberry glass bottle h.p. w/heavy gold shoulder panels above lily-of-the-valley decoration, gilded knopped stopper, Moser, ca. 1900-20, 3 1/2" h. (ILLUS.)..................................... **$650**

Perfume bottle & stopper, green cut to clear crystal waisted bottle w/a tall pointed stopper, heavy gold floral enamel trim, attributed to Moser, 6" h. **$450**

Early Bohemian Milk Glass Bottle

Perfume bottle & stopper, oval milk glass bottle w/a color h.p. scene of trees & a village, silver mounts, ca. 1800, 2 1/3" h. (ILLUS.)... **$600**

Extraordinary Jet & Malachite Glass Bottle

Perfume bottle & stopper, round graduated ring design black glass bottle w/a large figural malachite glass stopper carved as the head of a woman, ca. 1920s-30s, 6" h. (ILLUS.).......... **$10,000-15,000**

Moser Squatty Bulbous Bottle on Base

Perfume bottle & stopper, squatty bulbous clear bottle painted overall in pale orange trimmed w/yellow leaves & blue & white flowers accented w/nine small round windows, raised on a gilt-brass footed base, brass collar w/pointed knop brass stopper, signed by Moser, ca. 1920s, 5 1/2" h. (ILLUS.) **$550**

Scarce Red Lithyalin Perfume Bottle

Perfume bottle & stopper, squatty bulbous red lithyalin glass w/tapering paneled sides & a ringed neck, paneled mushroom stopper, F. Egermann, ca. 1830-40, 4 1/2" h. (ILLUS.) **$1,200**

Purple Moser Gold-Banded Perfume

Perfume bottle & stopper, tall slender footed dark purple urn-shaped bottle w/a tall knopped neck, etched around the shoulder w/a wide gold band of women warriors, slender upright stopper w/matching gold band, w/dauber, unsigned Moser, 8" h. (ILLUS.) **$750**

Bohemian Malachite Glass Perfume Bottle & Matching Atomizer

Perfume bottle & stopper & perfume atomizer w/fittings, Malachite glass, each w/a bulbous shape heavily molded w/figures of cherubs, bottle w/large molded flower spray stopper, atomizer w/gilt metal fittings, tube & bulb, ca. 1930s, 4 1/2" h. & 6 1/2" h., the set (ILLUS.).................... **$450-550**

Small Moser Cranberry Scent Bottle

Scent bottle w/original brass cap & finger ring, tusk-form, cranberry decorated around the top w/a wide band of gold enameled w/tiny blossoms, the sides decorated w/gold fern leaves, Moser, some gold wear, 3" l. (ILLUS.) **$546**

Czechoslovakia

Czech Cameo Glass Atomizer

Perfume atomizer w/fittings, cameo glass, flaring base tapering sharply to a slender cylindrical body in black cut to red, w/flowers, original fittings & tube & bulb, unmarked, ca. 1920s, 9" h. (ILLUS., previous page).. **$500**

Czech Orange & Spatter Atomizer

Perfume atomizer w/fittings, footed blown glass bottle w/swirled red & white spatter around the base & a dark orange upper body, gilt-metal fittings w/original tube & bulb, unsigned, ca. 1930s, 7 1/2" h. (ILLUS.)..................................... **$210**

Czech Red Atomizer with Nudes

Perfume atomizer w/fittings, footed ovoid bottle w/a dark red ground & relief-molded bright red female nudes, gilt metal fittings, no bulb, unsigned, ca. 1930s, 7 1/2" h. (ILLUS.) **$900**

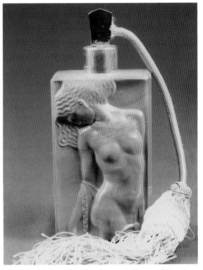

Czech Molded Lapis Lazuli Glass Atomizer

Perfume atomizer w/fittings, upright rectangular lapis lazuli glass molded in high-relief w/an Art Deco nude woman, original fittings, tube & bulb, unsigned, ca. 1930s, 7 1/4" h. (ILLUS.)........................... **$750**

Pink Bottle with Harem Dancer Stopper

Perfume bottle & stopper, a low squared pink cut crystal bottle fitted w/a tall frosted clear figural stopper of a harem dancer w/dauber, signed, 1930s, 5 7/8" h. (ILLUS.) **$450**

Clear Arched Czechoslovakian Bottle

Perfume bottle & stopper, a Prochaska bottle by J. Viard in clear crystal w/enamel & brown patina, a long low arched container w/molded & colored borders, squatty stopper w/a molded half-figure of a child, ca. 1926, 3 1/4" h. (ILLUS.) **$3,000**

Czech Red Perfume & Clear Stopper

Perfume bottle & stopper, a red crystal base w/a paneled base divided by buttress feet below the tiered sides & short neck, tall flat clear stopper etched w/a scene of a woman & child w/flowers, w/dauber, signed & silver original silver-leaf label, ca. 1930s, 5" h. (ILLUS.) **$700**

Czech Bottle with Figural Nudes

Perfume bottle & stopper, amber crystal molded as a pair of seated nude young maidens on an oblong base & flanking a gilt-metal filigree-framed oval black cameo jewel w/the head of an elegant lady, mounted on a thin filigree base raised on small scroll feet, a flower-molded mushroom-shaped stopper, unmarked, 1920s, 5 3/4" h. (ILLUS.) **$3,200-4,000**

Peach Cut Bottle with Nude on Stopper

Perfume bottle & stopper, arched & facet-cut peach crystal bottle w/a large round flat clear stopper etched w/a kneeling female nude & large blossoms, signed, ca. 1930s, 6 1/2" h. (ILLUS.)............................ **$400**

Unusually Cut Black & Clear Bottle

Perfume bottle & stopper, black cut crystal bottle w/an asymmetrical ziggarat-style design accented w/cut thistles, flattened pointed clear stopper etched w/a standing classical maiden, w/dauber, ca. 1930s, 6 1/3" h. (ILLUS.)............................ **$300**

Black Fanned Bottle with Green Mount

Perfume bottle & stopper, black glass fanned shape w/blocked ends, ornate gilt-metal filigree decorated w/small pale green jewels & a flower-carved oval jewel, the tall flat crystal stopper w/a narrow

fanned center flanked by etched floral panels & ending in dauber stub, stenciled oval "Made in Czechoslovakia," 1920s, 6 3/4" h. (ILLUS.) **$1,100-1,600**

Bell-shaped Black Bottle with Mount

Perfume bottle & stopper, black glass flattened bell-shaped body mounted w/a long filigree-bordered panel enclosing a floral-carved green plaque, tall crystal notched asymmetrical stopper w/dauber, stenciled oval "Made in Czechoslovakia" & metal tag reading "Czechoslovakia," 1920s, 5 1/2" h. (ILLUS.)................. **$850-1,200**

Black Bulbous Perfume with Red Mount

Perfume bottle & stopper, black glass flattened bulbous body mounted on the front w/a delicate scrolling filigree enameled metal plaque fitted w/a coral red round flower-decorated plaque, tall crystal flattened & pointed plume-style stopper complete w/dauber, stenciled oval "Made in Czechoslovakia," 1920s, 6 3/4" h. (ILLUS.) **$1,100-1,600**

Black Paneled Morlee Czech Perfume

Perfume bottle & stopper, black glass paneled bell-form shape w/a cylindrical neck w/a flattened faceted oval stopper etched w/a scene of seated lovers complete w/dauber, the neck & shoulders decorated w/gilt-metal filigree jewel-mounted bands w/a long front panel enclosing a long oval pale green flower-molded jewel, stenciled oval "Made in Czechoslovakia" & metal tag w/"Czechoslovakia - Morlee," 7 1/4" h. (ILLUS.)
.... **$1,300-1,600**

Black Perfume with Jeweled Filigree

Perfume bottle & stopper, black glass w/ringed foot decorated w/gilt-metal filigree bands trimmed w/red jewels, the flaring paneled sides below the filigree-trimmed neck, tall plain crystal spear-point stopper w/dauber stub, stenciled oval "Made in Czechoslovakia," 1920s, 5 1/4" h. (ILLUS.) **$900-1,700**

Fan-shaped Bottle with Nudes on Stopper

Perfume bottle & stopper, clear crystal flattened fan-shaped body fitted w/a pierced frosted clear stopper molded w/draped nudes, unsigned, 1930s, 5 5/8" h. (ILLUS.) **$1,200-2,100**

Long Low Crystal Czech Filigreed Bottle

Perfume bottle & stopper, clear crystal in a long low form w/a gently curved &

ribbed bottom, the wide shoulder & neck trimmed w/enameled gilt-metal filigree trimmed w/red jewels, tall clear oblong stopper etched w/a large cockatoo on a flowering vine, ending in dauber stub, metal tag marked "Czechoslovakia," ca. 1920s, 5 3/4" h. (ILLUS.)............... **$1,000-1,500**

Fine Flower-form Czech Perfume Bottle

Perfume bottle & stopper, clear crystal squatty domed shape resembling a pet-aled daisy, the tall clear oblong stopper etched w/a tall nude flying female fairy, stenciled oval "Made in Czechoslovakia," 1920s, 8 1/2" h (ILLUS.).......................... **$1,560**

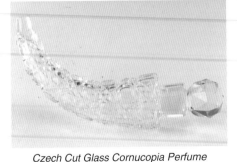

Czech Cut Glass Cornucopia Perfume

Perfume bottle & stopper, clear cut glass lay-down type, in the shape of a cornuco-pia w/a facet-cut stopper, ca. 1910, 4 1/4" l. (ILLUS.)... **$200**

Fine Czech Pyramidal Perfume & Blue Stopper

Perfume bottle & stopper, clear cut glass pyramidal bottle w/a small neck, fitted w/a tall flat rectangular stopper w/an inta-glio design of a troubador, ca. 1920-30s, 5 1/2" h. (ILLUS.) **$240-275**

Clear Czech Bottle with Fililgree & Rose

Perfume bottle & stopper, clear faceted crystal w/a flattened & sharply tapering form & wide shoulders, mounted w/gilt-metal enameled filigree trimmed w/red jewels & centered by a carved white rose, the tall flat spade-shaped crystal stopper etched w/branches of roses & ending in a dauber stub, metal tag marked "Czecho-slovakia," 1920s, 5 1/2" h. (ILLUS., previous page) **$950-1,400**

Clear & Black Scroll-decorated Bottle

Perfume bottle & stopper, clear flattened & arched crystal bottle w/an etched scroll design, tall flat arched black glass stopper etched w/a large gilt-trimmed scroll, signed, ca. 1930s, 4" h. (ILLUS.) **$135**

Czech Scimitar-shaped Perfume Bottle

Perfume bottle & stopper, clear glass bottle in a scimitar shape w/overall cut-style decoration, large flat fanned stopper w/dauber, original paper label, ca. 1920s-30s, 6 3/4" l. (ILLUS.) **$200-300**

Clear Bottle with Dancing Nudes Stopper

Perfume bottle & stopper, clear upright cut fan-shaped bottle w/a very tall flat oblong stopper etched w/two dancing female nudes, signed, ca. 1930s, 7 1/2" h. (ILLUS.) **$1,000**

Clear Perfume with Bird of Paradise Stopper

Perfume bottle & stopper, crystal flat-sided oblong ribbed shape on short feet, overlaid w/ornate gilt-metal enameled filigree bands set w/blue jewels, tall flat crystal shaped oblong stopper etched w/a flying bird-of-paradise & ending in a dauber stub, stenciled oval "Made in Czechoslovakia" & metal tag w/"Czechoslovakia," 1920s, 7 1/4" h. (ILLUS.).............. **$1,600-2,100**

Clear Squatty Perfume & Cupid Stopper

Perfume bottle & stopper, crystal footed squatty tapering form w/fluting down the sides, decorated w/fancy gilt-metal enameled & jeweled filigree leafy scroll mounts, tall flat crystal oblong stopper etched w/a scene of cupid, a bird & flowers ending in dauber stub, stenciled in oval "Made in Czechoslovakia" & w/metal tag reading "Czechoslovakia," 1920s, 5 1/2" h. (ILLUS.) **$750-1,100**

Pyramidal Perfume with Figural Stopper

Perfume bottle & stopper, dark blue faceted pyramidal shape raised on a filigree-trimmed metal base w/ball feet & wrapped around the neck & shoulders w/enameled & jeweled leaf & blossom mounts, tall crystal stopper molded in the shape of a stylized lady wearing a pleated gown & holding a bouquet of flowers, complete w/dauber, stenciled oval "Made in Czechoslovakia," 1920s, 6" h. (ILLUS.).............. **$3,900**

Long Low Cut Czech Perfume Bottle

Perfume bottle & stopper, crystal, long low bottle of cut yellow crystal on a fitted filigree metal base trimmed w/a large porcelain plaque, clear glass arched & fanned openwork flat stopper w/a figural design & dauber, stenciled "Made in Czechoslovkia," 1920s, 5 3/4" h. (ILLUS.)... **$1,300-1900**

Bulbous Blue Filigree-mounted Perfume

Perfume bottle & stopper, dark blue flattened bulbous bottle flaring at the base, wrapped w/a filigree metal base band & a fancy enameled & jeweled filigree side panel, tall flattened & pointed blue openwork stopper etched w/large stylized flowers, w/dauber stub, metal tag reading "Czechoslovakia," 1920s, 8 1/2" h. (ILLUS.) **$1,900-2,400**

Pink Pyramidal Czech Perfume Bottle

Perfume bottle & stopper, dark pink faceted pyramidal shape raised on a filigree-trimmed metal base w/square feet & mounted on one side w/an enameled & jeweled filigree scroll mount centered w/a long jewel framed w/seed pearls, tall rectangular pink stopper etched w/the figure of a tall lady in a garden, complete w/dauber, stenciled oval "Made in Czechoslovakia," 1920s, 6 1/2" h. (ILLUS.)
.... **$1,900-2,500**

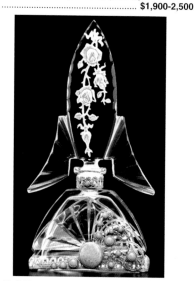

Tall Czech Perfume with Filigree Trim

Perfume bottle & stopper, domed & flattened clear crystal fluted form mounted

w/enameled gilt-metal mounts & opaque green jewels, the tall clear spearpoint stopper w/flared, pointed lower wings & etched w/cascading roses, ends in a dauber stub, stenciled "Made in Czechoslovakia," 1920s, 8 3/4" h. (ILLUS.) **$1,700-2,500**

Black & Crystal Starburst-cut Perfume

Perfume bottle & stopper, flattened black crystal bottle cut in a starbrust design, a tall clear flattened diamond-shaped starburst-cut stopper w/dauber, signed, 5 3/8" h. (ILLUS.) **$350-400**

Black Tapering Paneled Czech Perfume

Perfume bottle & stopper, footed black glass form w/flattened paneled & flaring sides tapering to a short neck, ornate filigree metal neck band & enameled & jeweled side panels centering a rectangular floral-carved plaque, tall arched crystal stopper etched w/a stylized rose & w/daub-

er stub, metal tag marked "Czechoslova-
kia," 1920s, 4 1/4" h. (ILLUS.) **$420**

Oblong Blue Diamond-cut Bottle

Perfume bottle & stopper, footed low oblong pale blue bottle cut w/an overall design of diamond points, clear diamond-
shaped   starburst-cut   stopper
w/dauber, ca. 1930s, 5 1/8" h. (ILLUS.) **$175**

Footed Clear Bottle & Floral Stopper

Perfume bottle & stopper, footed squared
clear tier-cut bottle w/a very tall flat rectangular stopper etched along one side
w/an arching stem of flowers, signed, ca.
1920s-30s, 5 3/4" h. (ILLUS.) **$150**

Unmarked Green Metal-trimmed Bottle

Perfume bottle & stopper, green crystal
w/flattened sides & angled shoulders,
jeweled metal band on neck, high arched
flattened stopper complete w/dauber,
mounted w/a filigree metal triangular side
panel w/enamel & a rectangular green
center jewel, unmarked, 1920s, 5 1/4" h.
(ILLUS.).. **$1,100-1,800**

Czech Perfume Bottle by Ingrid

Perfume bottle & stopper, lapis blue crystal, flattened rounded upright shape
w/molded blossom-form sides, large
arched blossom-form stopper, marked
"Ingrid," shallow edge chips on end of
stopper, ca. 1930, 5" h. **$900**

Fine Long Czech Bottle with Fancy Filigree

Perfume bottle & stopper, long low clear crystal shape w/flattened sides & angled shoulders, decorated around the lower half w/ornate gilt-metal triple-arched filigree trimmed w/green jewels, the rounded clear faceted stopper etched w/a scene of seated lovers & ending in a dauber, unmarked, 1920s, 5 3/4" h. (ILLUS.)............ **$2,160**

Fine Czech Lapis Lazuli Glass

Perfume bottle & stopper, lapis lazuli glass bulbous bottle molded in high-relief w/stylized bluebells, the tall stopper w/matching bluebells, signed, ca. 1930s, 6 3/4" h. (ILLUS.) **$1,100**

Light Blue Crystal Czech Perfume

Perfume bottle & stopper, light blue crystal w/flattened line-incised sides & a high plain fanned stopper w/dauber, fitted w/filigree metal neck, side & foot bands accented w/enamel & jewels, stenciled "Made in Czechoslovkia," 1920s, 4 1/2" h. (ILLUS.) **$750-1,000**

Black & Crystal Glass Irice Bottle

Perfume bottle & stopper, low arched & faceted black glass body mounted w/a filigree neck band joined to a filigree metal panel centered by a long oval pink jewel, the tall openwork frosted clear stopper molded w/flowers & complete w/dauber, stenciled oval "Made in Czechoslovakia" & an "Irice" label, 1920s, 6" h. (ILLUS.) .. **$1,800**

Black Glass Perfume in Ornate Stand

Perfume bottle & stopper, low flattened black glass bottle w/an arched & beveled top, fitted into an ornate gilt-metal scroll-pierced stand set w/opal-like cabochons & small pearls, on four leafy-scroll feet, a matching pierced neck band & a flaring metal filigree stopper set w/a domed & faceted opal-like stone, ca. 1920s-30s, 3 7/8" h. (ILLUS.) **$2,000**

Red Frosted & Smooth Irice Perfume

Perfume bottle & stopper, low flattened & flaring red crystal bottle molded w/a smooth V-form panel & frosted rose panels, arched tiara-form stopper w/matching decor, no dauber, Irice label & signed, ca. 1920s-30s, 3 1/2" h. (ILLUS.) .. **$300**

Low Pink Crystal Bottle w/Tall Stopper

Perfume bottle & stopper, low, long & slightly arched facet- and fan-cut bottle w/a tall Gothic arch-form flat clear stopper w/a half-length figure of a nude woman, signed, 7 1/3" h. (ILLUS.) **$750-900**

Czech Crystal & Pink Cut Perfume

Perfume bottle & stopper, low flattened crystal bottle cut w/fanned ends flanking a center diamond, the small neck w/an oversized flattened pink cut crystal stopper w/a Daisy & Button-style design, signed, ca. 1920s-30s, 7" h. (ILLUS.) **$250**

Czech Miniature Clear Square Bottle

Perfume bottle & stopper, miniature clear upright square footed bottle w/a flattened dark green stopper w/dauber, signed, part of a series made to resemble famous commerical bottles, ca. 1930s, 2 1/2" h. (ILLUS.)... **$100**

Black Miniature Bottle with Filigree

Perfume bottle & stopper, miniature, cylindrical black glass w/the upper body in a diamond point design, the lower body decorated w/a gilt metal filigree band

trimmed w/faux jewels, the cylindrical cap mounted w/similar filigree & jewels, signed, ca. 1930s, 2 1/8" h. (ILLUS.)......... **$375**

Fine Moser Black Crystal Bottle

Perfume bottle & stopper, Moser black crystal bottle, rounded foot below the tall slender tapering bottle w/a thin pointed stopper, gilt intaglio figural bands, w/dauber, marked by Moser & w/Moser labels, in deluxe fabric box, ca. 1920s, 6 3/4" h. (ILLUS.).................................. **$3,900**

Blue Bottle with Figural Nude Figures

Perfume bottle & stopper, oval upright blue crystal bottle resting on gilt-metal feet, each side of the bottle molded w/a full-figure seated nude woman flanking a tall gilt-metal mount framing a small oval white porcelain plaque h.p. w/a courting couple, blue molded pointed button-form stopper, ca. 1930s, 7" h. (ILLUS.).. **$1,500-1,750**

Czech Malachite Glass Floral Perfume

Perfume bottle & stopper, ovoid malachite glass deeply molded overall w/poppy-like blossoms & w/a blossom-form stopper, unsigned, ca. 1920s-30s, 6 7/8" h. (ILLUS.) **$525**

Blue Czech Perfume in Fancy Stand

Perfume bottle & stopper, pale blue crystal, oblong notched container fitted on a fancy gilt-metal pierced & jeweled stand w/ball feet, large flattened & notched stopper, ca. 1920s, 5" h. (ILLUS.) **$1,800**

Blue Molded Flower & Butterfly Bottle

Perfume bottle & stopper, pale blue crystal bulbous shape molded as a flower blossom, fitted w/a figural butterfly stopper w/dauber, unsigned Irice, Czechoslovakia, 1920s, 5 3/4" h. (ILLUS.) **$2,200-3,400**

Czech Labeled Morlee Perfume Bottle

Perfume bottle & stopper, pale blue & crystal, the blue tapering & faceted bottle mounted w/a large floral-molded panel above the thin metal filigree enameled & jeweled base band, jeweled & enameled neck band, tall clear rectangular flat stopper etched w/Cupid & complete w/dauber, stenciled oval "Made in Czechoslovakia" & original foil label reading "Morlee," 1920s, 3 3/4" h. (ILLUS.) **$480**

Blue Bottle & Tall Clear Floral Stopper

Perfume bottle & stopper, pale blue footed & waisted cut crystal bottle w/a tall flat clear pointed stopper etched w/large flowers & vines w/cut-out portions, dauber missing, marked, ca. 1920s-30s, 6 1/4" h. (ILLUS.) **$255**

Green Czech Perfume in Fancy Stand

Perfume bottle & stopper, pale green crystal, flattened rectangular form w/beveled corners & short neck fitted w/a tall flattened spearpoint stopper, resting on a fancy jeweled openwork gilt-metal stand decorated w/dragons & classic masks,

marked "Czechoslovakia," ca. 1920s, 5 1/2" h. (ILLUS.) **$1,500-2,000**

Labeled Pale Purple Czech Perfume

Perfume bottle & stopper, pale purple arched & fanned bottle fitted w/filigree metal decorated w/enamel & jewels, flat plain fanned stopper w/dauber, stenciled "Czechoslovakia" & w/metal tag reading "Czechoslovakia, Aristo," 1920s, 3 1/4" h. (ILLUS.) **$840**

Jewel-mounted Purple Perfume Bottle

Perfume bottle & stopper, pale purple crystal w/flattened angled sides, metal band on neck, wide flat diamond-form stopper etched w/a kneeling maiden, complete w/dauber, a large enameled & jeweled metal plaque on the side centered by a large green jewel, stenciled "Made in Czechoslovakia" & metal tag reading "Czechoslovakia," 1920s, 3 7/8" h. (ILLUS.) **$1,100-1,800**

Yellow Perfume of Overlapping Discs

Perfume bottle & stopper, pale yellow crystal molded as graduated overlapping flattened discs w/the outer two ribbed, matching stopper w/overlapping ribbed discs & ending in a dauber, unsigned, 1930s, 6" h. (ILLUS.)..................... **$1,800-2,500**

Pink Czech Bottle with Bird on Stopper

Perfume bottle & stopper, pink crystal w/a short neck wrapped in metal filigree, tall almond-shaped stopper molded w/a bird, filigree leaf sprig & blossom on the side, filigree metal base band, stenciled oval "Made in Czechoslovakia," metal tag marked "Czechoslovakia," 1920s, 5" h. (ILLUS.)................................. **$900-1,600**

Pink Shell-shaped Perfume Bottle

Perfume bottle & stopper, pink crystal molded in a shell form & mounted on the side w/filigree enameled metalwork centered by a pink flower-molded jewel, tall flat clear spearpoint stopper etched w/flowers & complete w/dauber, stenciled oval "Made in Czechoslovakia" & metal tag w/"Czechoslovakia," 1920s, 5 3/4" h. (ILLUS.) **$960-1,600**

Czech Block-Cut Crystal Perfume Bottle

Perfume bottle & stopper, rectangular block-cut clear crystal bottle w/a small neck w/a large flattened block-cut red crystal stopper, no dauber, signed, ca. 1920s-30s, 4 3/8" h. (ILLUS.) .. **$285**

Perfume bottle & stopper, square pale purple body w/the wide shoulder centered by a small metal filigree-wrapped neck, wide plain purple chevron-shaped stopper w/dauber, resting on a square filigree metal base & w/a large oval filigree metal side mount centered by a flower-molded pale green jewel, raised on four small ball feet, stenciled "Made in Czechoslovakia," 1920s, 5 1/8" h. **$800-1,200**

Square Pink Czech Perfume Bottle

Perfume bottle & stopper, square pink body w/the wide shoulder centered by a small metal filigree-wrapped neck, wide plain pink chevron-shaped stopper w/dauber, resting on a square filigree metal base & w/a large oval filigree metal side mount centered by a flower-molded pink jewel, raised on four small ball feet, stenciled "Made in Czechoslovakia," 1920s, 5 1/8" h. (ILLUS.)............................ **$900**

Czech Malachite Perfume with Nude

Perfume bottle & stopper, upright flattened tapering malachite glass bottle molded w/a seated nude female holding a garland of flowers, the tall flattened almond-shaped stopper molded w/a bird & flowers, signed, ca. 1930s, 6" h. (ILLUS.) .. **$750**

Black Glass & Filigree Czech Bottle

Perfume bottle & stopper, wide low pyramidal black glass bottle w/block-molded panels decorated w/gilt metal filigree bands trimmed w/a large green triangular stone & faux pearls w/small jewel-set bands around the base & neck, tall flat clear rectangular stopper w/beveled corners etched w/a scene of Leda & the swan, signed, ca. 1930s, 6 1/4" h. (ILLUS.) **$800-900**

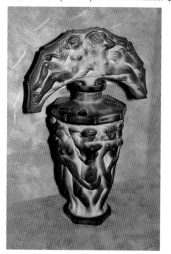

Czech Malachite Perfume with Nudes

Perfume bottle & stopper, tapering cylindrical malachite bottle molded w/draped nude ladies, the arched tiara-style stopper further molded w/nudes, unsigned, ca. 1930s, 7 3/8" h. (ILLUS.)................ **$1,400-1,600**

Perfume bottles & stoppers, bright orange bulbous Tango-style Art Deco bottles w/black glass button stoppers, signed "Czechoslovkia," ca. 1920s-30s, 3" h., pr. **$150-200**

Denmark

Danish Royal Copenhagen Bottle

Perfume bottle & stopper, pink porcelain in a footed, flattened & squared shape molded w/a kneeling nude woman, tiny cylindrical neck w/ball stopper, Royal Copenhagen paper label, early 20th c., 4 7/8" h. (ILLUS.) **$150-200**

Egypt

"L'Armes de Nuit" by Kesma Bottle

Perfume bottle & stopper, "L'Armes de Nuit" by Kesma, clear tapering double-ruffle skirt-shaped bottle w/tall frosted stepped stopper, labeled, in a black cylindrical satin-lined box, bottom label reads

"Formule Legrain - Made in Egypt," 1950s, 5" h. (ILLUS.)............................. **$2,040**

Egyptian "Lotus Flower" Perfume Bottle

Perfume bottle & stopper, "Lotus Flower" by Ahmed Soliman, cylindrical crystal Czechoslovakian bottle w/dauber in a fitted Ivorine case w/label, in original velvet-line box, 1920s, 4 3/4" h. (ILLUS.) **$2,200-2,700**

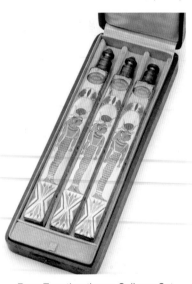

Rare Egyptian-theme Soliman Set

Perfume bottles & stoppers set, Ahmed Soliman set w/three very long, slender squared bottles each enameled in color w/an ancient Egyptian goddess, jeweled metal screw caps, in original green leather box, ca. 1920s, 7 1/2" l., the set (ILLUS.) **$2,160**

Soliman "Sandalwood" & "Attar of Roses" Set

Perfume bottles & stoppers set, "Sandalwood" & "Attar of Roses" by Ahmed Soliman, three long slender squared clear bottles w/jeweled screw caps, two enameled in color w/ancient Egyptian figures, the third w/a gilded figure, in original red leather box, labeled, 1920s, 7 1/2" l.,the set (ILLUS.) **$2,200-3,000**

England

Pretty Swirled Rainbow Ribbed Atomizer

Perfume atomizer w/fittings, spherical form w/molded ribs in swirled shades of blue, peach & yellow cased in clear, original white metal atomizer fittings missing original bulb, late 19th c., 5 3/4"h. (ILLUS.) **$518**

Perfume bottle & stopper, "April Violets" by Yardley, clear glass bottle w/upright stopper & floral label, mint in box, ca. 1938, 4 3/4" h. **$140-175**

Fine Royal Worcester Perfume Bottle

Perfume bottle & stopper, asymmetrical scroll-molded porcelain bottle in cream h.p. w/delicate flowering leafy stems issuing from a blue scroll, heavy gold trim, répoussé sterling silver hinged cap, Royal Worcester, late 19th c., 4" h. (ILLUS.) **$500**

Round Webb Citron Cameo Glass Perfume

Perfume bottle & stopper, boule-shaped cameo glass bottle, citron cased in white & cameo-carved w/large flowers & buds w/on leafy stems, hinged sterling silver cap w/hallmarks for Birmingham, 1891-92, 3 1/2" h. (ILLUS.) **$1,800-2,200**

Unmarked English Porcelain Perfume

Perfume bottle & stopper, boule-shaped white porcelain bottle h.p. w/red & pink blossoms on green leafy stems, sterling silver collar & cap hallmarked for Birmingham, 1893, 3" h. (ILLUS.)................. **$125**

English Cameo Lay-down Perfume Bottle

Perfume bottle & stopper, cameo glass teardrop-shaped lay-down bottle in white cased in pumpkin & cameo-carved w/large blossoms on leafy branches, unsigned, silver hallmarked for 1885 (ILLUS.) **$1,500**

English Mother-of-Pearl Satin Perfume

Perfume bottle & stopper, bulbous tapering ovoid pink mother-of-pearl satin glass in the Diamond Quilted patt., trimmed w/gilt flowers, sterling silver collar & hinged répoussé cap w/glass inner stopper, ca. 1880, 4 7/8" h. (ILLUS.)... **$750-850**

Perfume bottle & stopper, cameo glass lay-down style, flattened teardrop shape in Prussian blue overlaid in white & cameo-carved w/a leafy stemmed flowers & ferns, hallmarked sterling silver collar & rounded cap, ca. 1880, 4" l. **$940**

Early Chelsea Pansy Bouquet Perfume

Perfume bottle & stopper, Chelsea porcelain molded as an upright colored bouquet of pansies in dark blue, red & yellow, unmarked, 18th c., 3 1/4" h. (ILLUS.)...... **$2,500**

Chelsea Basket-form Perfume Bottle

Perfume bottle & stopper, Chelsea porcelain, upright bulbous molded basket-form lower body w/a molded gold chain around the middle w/a shield-shaped tag inscribed "eau de senteur," tall tapering neck h.p. w/a colorful bouquet of flowers, metal collar & stopper w/tall porcelain finial molded as a model of a butterfly atop a blossom, ca. 1765, 4" h. (ILLUS.) **$3,000**

Wedgwood Jasper Ware Perfume Bottle

Perfume bottle & stopper, dark blue Jasper Ware tapering ovoid body decorated w/white relief classical figures w/Pegasus, sterling silver collar & nickel-plated sprinkler top, Josiah Wedgwood, hallmarked for London, 1913, 3 1/4" h. (ILLUS.)... **$650**

Squatty Viard Bottle Made For Dubarry

Perfume bottle & stopper, Dubarry bottle by J. Viard & made by Depinoix, clear wide squatty round shape molded overall w/a repeating wave design & multicolored patina, the upright figural frosted stopper w/a kneeling nude, flea bites to stopper plug, ca. 1920s, 3 1/2" h. (ILLUS.).. **$3,000-4,500**

English Porcelain Figural Perfume Bottle

Perfume bottle & stopper, figural porcelain, modeled as a seated man in fancy patterned costume above colorful applied flowers, domed & molded base, ca. early 19th c., bottom marked w/a gold anchor, 3 1/4" h. (ILLUS., previous page)... **$1,500**

Unusual English Pitcher-form Perfume

Perfume bottle & stopper, flattened ruby red pitcher-form bottle, flattened round bottle mounted on a round sterling silver foot & a silver collar, spouted neck, cover & S-scroll handle, London hallmarks for 1872, 4 1/2" h. (ILLUS.) **$400-500**

Perfume bottle & stopper, "Heart's Delight" by Dubarry, a figure of a green Pierrot on a matchbox holding a simple miniature, ca. 1920, 2" h. **$203**

Rare Early Anchor-shaped Perfume

Perfume bottle & stopper, model of an anchor, the stem in paneled green glass forming the bottle w/the anchor base & top in stamped silver & brass mounts w/a chain wrapped around the bottle, small period photos of a lady & gentleman at the bottom sides, unknown manufacturer, ca. 1850-60, 3" h. (ILLUS.) **$3,000**

English Tiger Eye Perfume Bottle

Perfume bottle & stopper, novelty-type, flattened oblong real tiger eye agate w/metal collar & hinged cap, glass inner stopper, ca. 1875, 3" l. (ILLUS.).......... **$350-400**

English Strawberry-shaped Perfume

Perfume bottle & stopper, novelty-type, mold-blown glass in the shape of a strawberry painted red, cream & green, brass collar w/chain & finger ring & hinged cap, ca. 1890-1900, 1 2/3" h. (ILLUS.)....... **$375**

English Purse-sized Cut Glass Perfume

Perfume bottle & stopper, purse-sized, clear cylindrical cut glass w/dented screw-on sterling silver cap marked for Birmingham, 1894, 2 7/8" h. (ILLUS.) **$45**

Fine English Cut-Overlay Small Perfume

Perfume bottle & stopper, purse-sized, cut-overlay, red, cut to white cut to clear, cylindrical body deeply cut w/cross designs & vesicas, paneled

neck & red & white stopper, ca. 1860-80, 4 1/2" l. (ILLUS.) **$900-1,000**

Grouping of Three Satin Glass Perfumes

Perfume bottle & stopper, satin glass, dusty pale blue w/a ring of bluish violet at the base, swelled ovoid body tapering to a short gilded neck w/gilt & blue ball stopper, highlighted overall w/gold beads, late 19th c., 5 3/4" h. (ILLUS. upper right with two Stevens & Williams satin glass perfume bottles, listed on page 175)......... **$259**

Short Blue Panel-Cut Perfume Bottle

Perfume bottle & stopper, short cylindrical dark blue panel-cut design w/fancy silver-gilt hinged cap & inner glass stopper, sterling w/hallmarks for Birmingham, 1916, 1 2/3" h. (ILLUS.) **$175**

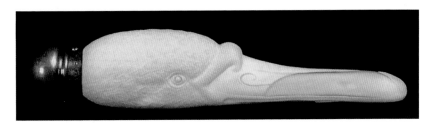

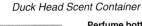

Duck Head Scent Container

Perfume bottle & stopper, upright squared shape w/rounded shoulders, cameo glass in citron cased in white & cameo-carved w/long leafy stems of blossoms, sterling silver collar & hinged bulbous chased cap, silver w/Birmingham hallmarks for 1896-97, 5 1/2" h. (ILLUS.) **$1,400-1,750**

Perfume bottle w/cap, cameo glass, lay-down style, figural engraved duck head in overlay colors of white over yellow, original silver cap marked underneath, 8 3/4" l. (ILLUS., top of page).................. **$4,600**

Perfume bottle w/cap, satin glass, spherical shape in the mother-of-pearl swirled band design, shaded green to yellow, marked sterling silver collar & scroll-embossed cap, ca. 1900, 5" h. (ILLUS. right with Thomas Webb green cameo glass perfume, page 176).................................... **$538**

Pungent bottle, clear blown glass, dolphin- or mermaid-shaped pungent-type, applied clear rigaree, engraved "Eliz-h Richardson" on one side & a sprig on the other, American or English, early 19th c., small rough spot on rigaree, 3" h. (ILLUS. second from left with other blown & pattern-molded pungent bottles, bottom of page) **$44**

Upright Squared Webb Cameo Perfume

Group of Four Blown & Mold-Blown Early Pungent Bottles

Short Panel-Cut Clear Scent Bottle

Scent bottle & stopper, clear short panel-cut cylindrical shape w/hinged sterling silver cap & glass inner stopper, silver marked for Birmingham, 1897, 1 3/4" h. (ILLUS.).. **$180**

Lovely Yellow English Cameo Scent Bottle

Scent bottle & stopper, English cameo glass, spherical body in amber-yellow ground overlaid in white & cameo-carved w/a design of flowering branches around the sides, marked sterling silver collar & spherical cap, missing interior stopper, late 19th c., 3 3/4" h. (ILLUS.)................. **$1,265**

Scent bottle & stopper, pottery, Gardenia patt., black curled handle, Motto Ware, "A thing of beauty is a joy Forever - Gardenia Eau de Cologne - Toogoods - London - England," pink gardenia on blue ground, brass crown-form stopper, Watcombe, Torquay Pottery, ca. 1930s, 5" h............. **$30-50**

Scent bottle & stopper, pottery, Lavender patt., "Hill's English Lavender," marked "Genuine Devon Pottery - Made in En-

gland," Torquay Pottery, still sealed, ca. 1930s, 2 1/2" h. **$30-50**

English Blue & White Cameo Scent

Scent bottle w/cap, cameo glass, cylindrical form in white cut to blue w/a flower & leaf design, silver cap & base band, England, late 19th c., 2 3/4" h. (ILLUS.) **$690**

Pretty Wedgwood Jasper Scent Bottle

Scent bottle w/cap, Jasper Ware, flatted teardrop shaped body in blue jasper centered by a long oval olive green reserve framed by a ring of small white relief blossoms & enclosing a scene of a classical woman seated on a chair w/cupid in her lap, the reverse scene shows a woman walking w/cupid leading the way, w/original fitted case, Josiah Wedgwood, bottle 3 1/4" l. (ILLUS.)...................................... **$1,035**

Scent bottle w/cap, lay-down style, long dagger shape in dark red cut to clear, plain sterling silver cap & inner glass stopper, hallmarks for Birmingham, 1890, 7 1/2" l. **$375**

Ruby Cut to Clear Double-ended Scent

w/hallmarks for Birmingham, 1897, 8" l.
(ILLUS.).. **$350**

Loop-decorated Satin Glass Scent Bottle

Scent bottle w/cap, satin glass & silver,
bulbous form w/long slender neck, an
engraved & hallmarked silver band at
base of neck w/silver chain extending
from it to embossed silver floral cap,
w/overall pink & cream loop decoration,
6 1/2" h. (ILLUS.)....................................... **$575**

Scent bottle w/caps, double-ended style,
emerald green facet-cut bottle w/plain silver stopper at each end, sterling mark for
London, 1899, 3 7/8" l. **$375**

Scent bottle w/caps, double-ended style,
long cylindrical shape in dark red cut to
clear w/a star & punty design, sterling
caps & inner stopper on the perfume
side, probably English, ca. 1870s, 4" l.
(ILLUS., top of page)........................... **$350-450**

Scent bottle w/caps, double-ended style,
long cylindrical shape w/bottle encased
in spiraling sterling silver mounted w/a
monogram, spring-loaded hinged cap on
perfume end, screw-on silver cap on
smelling salts end, w/original case from
Gass & Co., London, England, silver
marked by Samson Mordan, ca. 1882,
4 1/2" l. (ILLUS., top next page).... **$1,250-1,500**

Cut Glass Lay-down Scent Bottle

Scent bottle w/cap, lay-down type, long
tapering conical form w/overall elaborate cutting, sterling silver hinged cap
w/hallmarks for London, 1884, 5 1/2" l.
(ILLUS.) **$150**

Short Cobalt Blue Double-ended Scent

Scent bottle w/caps, double-ended style,
short oblong facet-cut cobalt blue bottle
w/gadrooned silver caps at each end, unmarked, probably English, ca. 1880s,
3 1/2" l. (ILLUS.)................................. **$250-300**

Long Cut Vaseline to Clear Scent Bottle

Scent bottle w/cap, long slender tapering
shape in vaseline shading to clear fancy
cut glass, sterling silver screw-on cap

Sterling Silver-Encased Double-Ended Scent Bottle

Europe - General

Coquilla Nut Carved Perfume Bottle

Building-Shaped Clear Cologne Bottle

Cologne bottle, mold-blown clear glass, designed as a building w/a domed cupola, neck w/flared lip, pontil scar, ca. 1840-60, 5 1/8" h. (ILLUS.) **$224**

Perfume bottle & stopper, novelty-type, ornately carved coquilla nut, the acanthus leaf foot supporting a swelled cylindrical container carved down the sides w/inverted fruit-filled cornucopias joined by swags, leaf-carved flared rim w/an urn-shaped neck w/loose ring handles & a figural swan stopper, Germany or Switzerland, ca. 1830, 3 3/4" h. (ILLUS., top next column)....... **$1,200**

Perfume bottle & stopper, paperweight-type, clear squatty ovoid bottle w/facet-cut panels & enclosing a millefiori paperweight base, matched domed stopper, unsigned, unknown date, 6" h. (ILLUS., bottom next column)........................... **$175-200**

Fine Facet-cut Paperweight Perfume

European Blue & Yellow Blown Scent

Scent bottle, free-blown glass, flattened teardrop form in cobalt blue w/olive yellow overlay in a herringbone design, sheared & ground lip, polished pontil, ca. 1840-60, 2 1/2" h. (ILLUS.) **$134**

Unusual Scent Holder Tower Box

Scent holder, Bessamin box or spice tower, silver, a domed foot & slender stem support a bulbous tower-form container set w/colored stones below the pierced neck, conical cover, middle European, 19th c., 6" h. (ILLUS.) **$1,200-1,500**

Polish Silver Scent Holder Tower Box

Scent holder, Bessamin box or spice tower, silver, a tall tapering stem supporting a bulbous tower-form container set w/colored stones & w/a pierced band around the middle, conical cover w/flag finial, Poland, 19th c., 7 1/4" h. (ILLUS.)..... **$1,500-2,000**

France

Large Mold-Blown Cathedral Cologne

Cologne bottle, mold-blown clear glass, designed as a paneled cathedral, embossed "PD" on side at base, tall neck w/rolled lip, pontil scar, some milky interior stain, ca. 1840-60, 10 1/2" h. (ILLUS.)... **$269**

Sevres-marked Porcelain Perfumes

Cologne bottles & stoppers, square upright porcelain w/beveled corners, wide shoulder to short flared neck & tall button stopper, white ground h.p. around the sides w/pink & colored blossoms between gold-trimmed dark blue bands, gilt trim on shoulder, neck & stopper w/lighter blue banding, Sevres mark on the bottom, late 19th c., 5 7/8" h., pr. (ILLUS.)......................... **$250-450**

"Prince Douka" Bottle with Costume

Factice bottle & stopper, "Prince Douka" by Marquay, large clear glass bottle w/a frosted stopper in the shape of a man's head wearing a turban, bottle trimmed w/a cream satin cape decorated w/red,

blue & green rhinestones, feather in turban, full & sealed w/original box, ca. 1951, 6 1/2" h. (ILLUS.) **$325-400**

French Figural Rose & Butterfly Atomizer

Perfume atomizer w/fittings, a figural French porcelain container in the shape of a large red rose resting on green leaves, fitted w/a gilt-metal figural butterfly atomizer w/original cord & bulb, in fitted box, marked "Artyse - Made in France," ca. 1925, 4 1/4" h. (ILLUS.) **$2,400**

Signed French Cameo Perfume Atomizer

Perfume atomizer w/fittings, cameo glass, frosted white cased in amethyst & cameo-carved w/a design of berry clusters hanging from leafy stems, the side signed in cameo "G. Raspiller," late 19th-early 20th c., 7" h. (ILLUS.)........................ **$748**

Lavender to Clear Ribbed Atomizer

Perfume atomizer w/fittings, footed bulbous ovoid optic-ribbed bottle shading from lavender to clear & enameled around the shoulder w/an orange scrolling band, plated fittings w/a black bulb, ca. 1900-20, 6" h. (ILLUS.)............... **$325**

Perfume atomizer w/fittings, porcelain shell-shaped bottle w/a gilt-bronze mount in the shape of a baby, ca. 1880-1890, 6 3/4" h. **$1,000**

French Frosted Atomizer with Butterfly

Perfume atomizer w/fittings, slender tapering cylindrical frosted glass bottle hand-enameled w/a large butterfly in

dark blue & orange, signed "AM," ca. 1930s, 7 1/2" h. (ILLUS.)..................... **$350-450**

Perfume bottle & stopper, "A Votre Ordres" by Forvil, clear glass tiered bottle, no label, signed by Verreries Brosse, ca. 1930, 4 3/4" h. **$75**

Figural "Adorée" by Eroy Bottle

Perfume bottle & stopper, "Adorée" by Eroy, clear & frosted glass w/the low round base supporting the tall frosted figure of a kneeling nude lady, w/label, sealed, w/box, 1940s, 4 3/8" h. (ILLUS.).... **$900**

Rosine "Aladin" Arched Metal Bottle

Perfume bottle & stopper, "Aladin" by Rosine, arched flat-sided metal bottle embossed on each side w/mythical animals, chain handle suspended from shoulder, domed cork stopper, molded label along front bottom rim, ca. 1919, 2 1/2" h. (ILLUS.)...................................... **$400**

"Ambre Antique" Bottle by Arcy

Perfume bottle & stopper, "Ambre Antique" by Arcy, tall slender slightly tapering square form w/a tall faceted gold-painted stopper, original paper label w/applied carved shell cameo, ca. 1920, 6 1/4" h. (ILLUS.) **$1,300-2,000**

"Ambre de Delhi" by Babani Bottle

Perfume bottle & stopper, "Ambre de Delhi" by Babani, upright flattened disc-form clear glass bottle covered in gold enamel & decorated w/black scrolls, gold faceted stopper, signed on the bottom, ca. 1920, 2 2/3" h. (ILLUS.) **$1,500**

"Ami" by Silka Black & Gold Perfume Bottle

Perfume bottle & stopper, "Ami" by Silka, tall flattened rectangular black glass bottle w/a small neck & clear ball stopper, the sides decorated in gold w/very thin overall herringbone design & a tall narrow center vertical band w/a rockwork design, gilded labels, ca. 1925, 7 3/4" h. (ILLUS.).. **$480**

Perfume bottle & stopper, "Apogée" by Veolay, squat clear glass bottle w/a metal overcap, two labels, ca. 1932, 2" h. **$68**

Rare "Bermuda Angel Fish" Bottle

Perfume bottle & stopper, "Bermuda Angel Fish" by Peniston-Brown, figural opalescent glass fish stopper on short glass bottle base, base marked "A. Jollivet - Made in France," ca. 1937, 4 1/2" h. (ILLUS.).................................... **$3,500**

Victorian Blue Opaline Perfume Bottle

Perfume bottle & stopper, blue opaline low cylindrical bottle w/rounded shoulder, fitted on a gilt-brass base w/leaftip feet, openwork metal geometric mounts suspending metal beads around the shoulder, gilt-brass collar & pointed stopper, probably French, late 19th c., 5" h. (ILLUS.) **$225**

"Carnet de Bal" Brandy Snifter Bottle

Perfume bottle & stopper, "Carnet de Bal" for Revillon, clear glass designed to resemble an inverted brandy snifter, disc-form thick stopper, mint in box, ca. 1935, 2 3/8" h. (ILLUS.) **$75-125**

Perfume bottle & stopper, "Casque" by Jean d'Albert, clear glass urn-form bottle w/shield-shaped label, mint in box, ca. 1957, 1 3/4" h... **$55**

Sabino Leaf-molded Perfume Bottle

Perfume bottle & stopper, bulbous ovoid milky opalescent glass molded overall w/stylized leaves, tapering tiered stopper, signed by Sabino, date unknown, 5 1/2" h. (ILLUS.) **$150**

"Cassandra" by Weil Ionic Column Bottle

Perfume bottle & stopper, "Cassandra" by Weil, clear glass model of an Ionic column w/the scrolled capital forming the stopper, mint in original box, full & sealed, gold label, ca. 1935, 3" h. (ILLUS.) **$375-400**

"Christmas Bells" Bell-shaped Perfume

Perfume bottle & stopper, "Christmas Bells" by Molinard, flattened black glass model of a bell w/gold screw-off cap, mint in fitted red box, ca. 1926, 2 3/4" h. (ILLUS.) **$150**

Figural "Chu Chin Chow" Pefume Bottle

Perfume bottle & stopper, "Chu Chin Chow" by Bryenne, figural glass in the shape of a very fat seated Oriental man w/a gold head & body & wearing a blue-dotted robe, holding a blue fan w/product name in gold, atop a low square striped pillow-form base, head & wide collar form stopper w/small chips, some gold wear, ca. 1918, 2 1/2" h. (ILLUS.)............................ **$1,800-2,400**

"Circé" Black Glass Bottle with Figures

Perfume bottle & stopper, "Circé" by Moiret, domed black glass bottle molded in relief w/a figure of the crouching sorceress, a lion & a dog, flaring button stopper, ca. 1930, 3 1/2" h. (ILLUS.).......... **$350**

Early French Glass & Silver Perfume Bottle

Perfume bottle & stopper, clear columnar glass bottle mounted on a flaring silver base cast w/swags & floral designs, a silver collar & silver stopper cast as a sculpted bust of Bacchus, inner glass stopper, ca. 1840, 6" h. (ILLUS.)... **$3,000-3,500**

French Cut Crystal Medal-shaped Bottle

Perfume bottle & stopper, clear cut crystal bottle in the shape of a cross-form military medal, the center cut w/a fine diamond point design, ca. 1840-50, 2 3/4" h. (ILLUS.).. **$450-550**

French Clear Craquelle Glass Perfume

Perfume bottle & stopper, clear squatty bulbous base tapering to a tall slender neck w/flattened rim, craquelle glass w/a cranberry snake applied around the neck, clear craquelle mushroom stopper, ca. 1850-70, 6 1/2" h. (ILLUS.) **$275-350**

"Coup de Chapeau" Bottle by Brosse

Perfume bottle & stopper, "Coup de Chapeau" by Gilbert Orcel, a white opaque figural glass bottle by Verrieries Brosse, in the shape of the stylized bust of a woman wearing a hat, gilt trim, empty, ca. 1954, 5" h. (ILLUS.) **$125**

Bienaimé "Cuir de Russie" Bottle & Box

Perfume bottle & stopper, "Cuir de Russie" by Bienaimé, clear glass oval three-tier bottle w/scalloped edges, matching stopper, original label, full & sealed, w/original drop-front box, ca. 1950, 2 3/4" h. (ILLUS.) **$110**

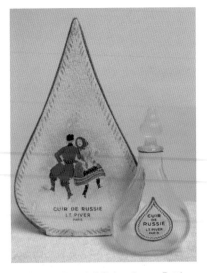

"Cuir de Russie" Onion Dome Bottle

Perfume bottle & stopper, "Cuir de Russie" by L.T. Piver, bulbous tapering clear glass bottle w/pointed stopper representing an onion dome on a Russian church, in matching box, ca. 1991 (ILLUS.) **$240**

French Cut-Overlay Perfume Bottle

Perfume bottle & stopper, cut-overlay glass in clear cased in white & turquoise blue, rounded notch-cut base tapering to six cut oval panels each enameled w/flowers or leaves below tall cut neck panels w/matching decoration, panel-cut & enameled acorn-shaped stopper, ca. 1870-80, 4 1/4" h. (ILLUS.) **$253**

Pretty Limoges Enamel Perfume Bottle

Perfume bottle & stopper, cylindrical Limoges enamel over copper decorated bottle h.p. w/an elegant lady in a blue dress against a dark red ground, gilt trim, metal fittings, 19th c., 2 1/2" h. (ILLUS.) . **$1,000**

"Debutante International" Perfume Bottle

Perfume bottle & stopper, "Debutante International" by Jean Desprez, upright flattened tapering clear glass bottle w/a frosted glass flame-shaped stopper, original label, in original damask-covered box, a limited edition for Daggett and Ramsdell, ca. 1960, 3 2/3" h. (ILLUS.)......... **$65**

Scarce Hermès "Doblis" Bottle & Box

Perfume bottle & stopper, "Doblis" by Hermès, clear upright square glass bottle w/rounded edges & green glass mushroom-shaped stopper, w/original label, in a paper box replica of the Hermès building in Paris, ca. 1955, 3 1/2" h. (ILLUS.) **$2,700**

Figural "Ecarlate" by Suzy Perfume

Perfume bottle & stopper, "Ecarlate" by
Suzy, clear figural glass bottle in the
shape of a stylized woman's head, the
stopper formed by a red-enameled hat,
w/original box, ca. 1939, 3" h. (ILLUS.)
.... **$350-800**

"Escarlate de Suzy" Manikin Bottle

Perfume bottle & stopper, "Escarlate de
Suzy" by Suzy, clear glass manikin head
wearing a red-enameled hat & name at
the base, ca. 1940, 4 1/2" h. (ILLUS.)........ **$340**
Perfume bottle & stopper, "Essence Rare"
by Houbigant, glass iceberg-shaped bottle, "HP" mark of Pochet et de
Courval, ca. 1929, 1 3/4" h..................... **$25-30**
Perfume bottle & stopper, "Femme" by
Rochas, small purse-sized flattened oval
white opaline bottle covered in black
lace, gilt-metal hinged cap, w/dauber,
pouch & box, special Christmas
Edition, ca. 1944, 2 3/4" l. (ILLUS., top
next column)... **$475**

Small Purse-sized "Femme" Bottle

Rochambeau Grape Cluster Perfume

Perfume bottle & stopper, figural clear
blown glass cluster of grapes w/fabric
leaves, Rochambeau, w/labels & orignial
decorative   rectangular   box,   1920s,
4 1/2" l. (ILLUS.).. **$600**

Figural Baby Enamel on Metal Perfume

Perfume bottle & stopper, figural enamel
on metal, in the shape of a small baby

wearing a pale yellow gown decorated w/red roses, gilt-silver mounts at neck, head forms cap, possibly French, ca. 1820-40, 3" h. (ILLUS.) **$2,800**

Crystal Perfume with Napoleon Sulphide

Perfume bottle & stopper, flattened oval crystal bottle w/notch-cut sides & enclosing a sulphide bust of Napoleon, decorative silver cap, ca. 1840-50, 3 1/4" l. (ILLUS.) **$2,000**

Clichy Twisted Filigrana Glass Perfume

Perfume bottle & stopper, flattened violin-shaped glass body in red, pink & white twisted filigrana decoration, cylindrical silver cap, Clichy factory, second half 19th c., 4 1/4" h. (ILLUS.) **$750-1,000**

Figural Windmill Perfume Bottle by Deroc

Perfume bottle & stopper, "Gai Monmartre" by Deroc, figural red-painted glass windmill w/a pointed metal cap & enameled windmill blades, partial label, ca. 1926, 4 3/4" h. (ILLUS.) **$2,200-3,200**

Perfume bottle & stopper, "Gardenia" by Valois, clear glass bottle w/amber glass floral stopper, w/original box, ca. 1936 .... **$54**

Perfume bottle & stopper, gently swelled cylindrical cut crystal bottle in a honeycomb design, a cylindrical silver base mount & collar & ornate cap, ca. 1880, 4" h. **$350-400**

Perfume bottle & stopper, "Golden Laughter" by Suzy, clear glass manikin head wearing a green-enameled hat, w/label, ca. 1941, 4 1/3" h. **$300-425**

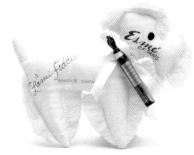

Poodle Sachet & Perfume Bottle by Esmé

Perfume bottle & stopper, "Green Eyes" by Esmé, small slender cylindrical clear glass bottle w/metal hand-shaped cap, labeled, tied to a stylized white poodle cloth sachet marked "L'ami fidèle - Poodle Sachet - Esmé of Paris," ca. 1946, bottle 3 1/4" h., the set (ILLUS.) **$650-950**

Tall Green Opaline Perfume Bottle

Perfume bottle & stopper, green opaline
bottle w/a footed squatty bulbous base
tapering to a very tall, slender neck w/a
flared rim, a gilt-trimmed band wrapped
around the lower neck, tall double-knop
blown stopper, overall leaf & vine gilt decoration, France, second half 19th c.,
9 3/4" h. (ILLUS.) **$350**

Perfume bottle & stopper, "Guy Six" by
Jeannette Renard, curved clear glass
bottle, mint in box, ca. 1930s, 1 1/2" h.
.... **$110-120**

Perfume bottle & stopper, "Hallo! Coco!"
by Jovoy, designed by Brosse as a bird-
cage enclosing an enameled glass container w/a figural parrot stopper, cord
seal, w/original box, ca. 1924, bottle 4" h.
(ILLUS., bottom of page)...................... **$15,600**

Figural Early Telephone Perfume Bottle

Perfume bottle & stopper, "Hop 6010" by
Pascall, figural clear glass candlestick-
style telephone w/a metal head & handle,
metal bicycle bell ringer, bottom molded
"C.T.G.," 1920s, 6 1/2" h. (ILLUS.)...... **$550-950**

Perfume bottle & stopper, "HRH" by Chevalier Garde, clear glass bottle w/a frosted
double-eagle stopper, worn label, ca.
1937, 5 3/4" h..................................... **$130-205**

Rare "Hallo! Coco!" by Jovoy Display Bottle

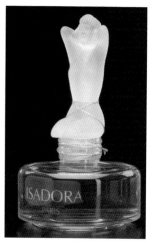

Rare Limited Production "Isadora" Bottle

Perfume bottle & stopper, "Isadora" by Isadora, factice bottle from a Pierre Dinand design, squatty cylindrical clear glass bottle printed in gold, a tall frosted clear figural stopper showing a seated female nude w/her hands behind her head, extremely limited Czechoslovakian production, ca. 1990, 12" h. (ILLUS.)...... **$3,750**

Perfume bottle & stopper, "Jasmin" by Giraud Fils, simple clear glass bottle w/flowers on stopper, labeled, original box, ca. 1920, 4" h. **$85**

"Jasmin" Figural Lady Perfume Bottle

Perfume bottle & stopper, "Jasmin" by Lander, figural frosted yellowish green glass in the shape of a standing lady, her torso forming the stopper w/cork tip, original label on the bottom, ca. 1945, 4 1/3" h. (ILLUS.)........................... **$175**

"Jasmine d'Or" by La Valliere Bottle

Perfume bottle & stopper, "Jasmine d'Or" by La Valliere, footed squatty disk-shaped bottle in clear glass enameled around the edge w/a band of blue leaves & white & yellow blossoms, the shoulder enameled w/a random webbing design, large flattened flower-form stopper, ca. 1922, 2 1/4" h. (ILLUS.) **$540**

Perfume bottle & stopper, "Joy" by Jean Patou, eau de parfum in a simple clear glass flat rectangular bottle w/a gold cap & label, full, marked "BR" for Verreries Brosse, ca. 1931, 3 1/4" h............................ **$55**

Watch-form "L'Heure Est Venue" Bottle

Perfume bottle & stopper, "L'Heure Est Venue" by de Marcy, a flattened round clear glass bottle in the shape of a pocket watch w/the paper label designed as the watch dial, yellow ribbon around neck, small gilt metal stopper, fitted in flattened oval red box w/satin lining, ca. 1930s, 2 3/4" h. (ILLUS.) **$150**

Perfume bottle & stopper, "La Boheme" by Arly, clear glass wing-shaped bottle w/black stopper, labeled, ca. 1915, 4 1/8" h. **$200-245**

"Le Chic Chic" Bird-shaped Perfume Bottle

Perfume bottle & stopper, "Le Chic Chic" by Vigny, clear bulbous ovoid body w/gold-painted wings at the side, figural metal bird head cap over an inner stopper, full, ca. 1920, hairline in bottle, 3 1/2" h. (ILLUS.) **$375-500**

"Le Diamant Noir" by Lydes Bottle

Perfume bottle & stopper, "Le Diamant Noir" by Lydes, an A. Jollivet clear glass disk-form bottle w/a small pointed black glass stopper, original center label, in original box w/tassel, c. 1926, 3 1/2" h. (ILLUS.) **$2,800-3,500**

"Le Golliwogg" by Vigny Figural Bottle

Perfume bottle & stopper, "Le Golliwogg" by Vigny, bulbous frosted glass bottle w/a white disk-form collar, the stopper in the form of the Golliwogg head enameled in black & red & w/real seal fur hair, original foil label w/printed hands, in original black box w/drop-front, based on English character, ca. 1919, 5 1/2" h. (ILLUS.) **$480-675**

Smaller 3" "Le Golliwogg" Bottle

Perfume bottle & stopper, "Le Golliwogg" by Vigny, bulbous frosted glass bottle w/a white disk-form collar, the stopper in the form of the Golliwogg head enameled in black & red & w/real seal furn hair, original foil label w/printed hands, empty, no box, based on English character, ca. 1919, 3" h. (ILLUS.) **$110-210**

Black Glass "Le Prestige" Bottle

Perfume bottle & stopper, "Le Prestige" by Moiret, flattened ovoid black glass bottle w/an overall fish scale design, black beaded ball stopper, no label, ca. 1930, 4 1/8" h. (ILLUS.) **$30**

"Le Roy Le Veult" Crown-form Bottle

Perfume bottle & stopper, "Le Roy Le Veult" by Marcel Buerlain, squatty clear glass figural crown bottle trimmed w/gold, figural fleur-de-lis stopper frozen in place, labeled, in original box, ca. 1927, 3 1/8" h. (ILLUS.) **$2,800-3,500**

Perfume bottle & stopper, "Les Fleurs" by Ybry, a clear glass bottle w/a square lower half & cylindrical upper half, short neck & clear ball stopper suspending a gold silk cord & enameled metal tag, ca. 1928, 3 1/2" h. (ILLUS., top next column) **$1,800**

"Les Fleurs" by Ybry Perfume Bottle

"Les Sylvies" Bottle with Dragonflies

Perfume bottle & stopper, "Les Sylvies" by Violet, Lucien Gaillard bottle in a clear flattened rectangular shape molded w/large dragonflies decorated w/multicolor patina, molded "LG" in circle mark on the bottom, w/original box, 1920s, 3 1/2" h. (ILLUS.) **$3,600-4,100**

Early "Madelon" by Depinoix Bottle

Perfume bottle & stopper, "Madelon" by Depinoix, a Boissard J. Viard bottle in clear & frosted glass, footed squatty disk-form bottle w/a colorful enameled patina band around the sides, the tall figural stopper w/further color trim, ca. 1919, 4" h. (ILLUS., previous page) **$2,400**

"Maharadjah" by Paul Poiret Bottle

Perfume bottle & stopper, "Maharadjah" by Paul Poiret (Rosine), cylindrical clear glass bottle w/black glass mushroom stopper, on a three-legged green glass stand, w/original label, ca. 1926, 4" h. (ILLUS.) **$4,500**

Perfume bottle & stopper, "Maharajah" by Rosine, glass bottle w/green glass stopper, mint in original box featuring pretty graphics, ca. 1922, 2 3/4" h. **$338**

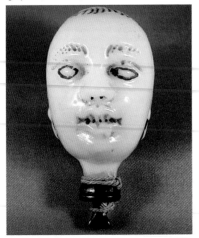

Rare Early Glass Human Head Perfume

Perfume bottle & stopper, mold-blown milk white glass in the form of a human head w/painted trim, attributed to Bernard Perrot, ca. 1680, 2 3/4" l. (ILLUS.).. **$1,200**

Perfume bottle & stopper, "Narcisse Bleu" by Mury, upright flattened clear glass octagonal bottle molded w/flowers, blue patina, Art Deco style label, original worn box, ca. 1925, 3 1/2" h. **$210-220**

Perfume bottle & stopper, "Niki" by Niki de St. Phalle, first edition, square black glass bottle w/square gold cap decorated w/the artist's signature colorful entwined snakes, ca. 1980s, 3" h. **$55-75**

Rare Boxed "Niradjah" by Marquis Bottle

Perfume bottle & stopper, "Niradjah" by Marquis, a Depinoix spherical black glass bottle w/original round color sticker w/the name & head of an exotic lady, red cased in clear ball stopper, original presentation box, 1920s, 3 3/4" h. (ILLUS.). **$7,200**

Scarce Mademoiselle Chanel "No. 1" Bottle

Perfume bottle & stopper, "No. 1" by Mademoiselle Chanel, clear cylindrical glass bottle w/rounded shoulder & short cylindrical neck, upright clear glass disc stopper w/red & white paper label, red & white paper label wrapped around bottle, molded mark on the bottom, w/scarce original box, ca. 1940, 4 1/8" h. (ILLUS.)... **$2,500-3,000**

Rare Inlaid Tortoiseshell Perfume Bottle

Perfume bottle & stopper, novelty-type, a carved tortoiseshell teardrop-shaped container w/tiny overall inlaid gold stars & an ornate filigree collar, tall bulbous engraved cap over the interior glass bottle, ca. 1849, 4 3/4" l. (ILLUS.) **$2,000**

Tall Bottle with Molded Lizard & Fly

Perfume bottle & stopper, novelty-type, "Au Soliel" for Lubin, frosted clear bottle w/a wide squatty bulbous base tapering to a very tall slender cylindrical neck molded w/a gold lizard climbing the side

to reach a small molded fly on the pointed stopper, ca. 1912, 9" h. (ILLUS.)... **$1,100-1,300**

Contemporary French Figural Perfume

Perfume bottle & stopper, novelty-type, figural porcelain model of a man in 18th c. costume, head stopper chained to body, marked "Hand-painted in France," contemporary, 5 1/4" h. (ILLUS.) **$75**

Purse-shaped Perfume Bottle by Lubin

Perfume bottle & stopper, novelty-type, "Ouvrez-Moi" by Lubin, figural black glass purse w/metal rim & black glass button stopper, original black silk cord strap, original label on strap, ca. 1937, 3 1/2" h. (ILLUS.) **$1,100-2,000**
Perfume bottle & stopper, novelty-type, "Ouvrez-Moi" by Lubin, molded black

glass bottle & stopper in the shape of a
purse, ca. 1936, 3" h. **$600-825**

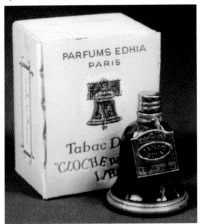

Novelty Liberty Bell Perfume Bottle

Perfume bottle & stopper, novelty-type,
"Tabac Doux" by Parfums Edhia, cobalt
blue glass bottle in the shape of the Liberty Bell w/original hang tag & mint in
box, probably a tribute to the United
States after the Liberation of France in
World War II, ca. 1946, 2" h. (ILLUS.)........ **$125**

"Offrande" by Cheramy Perfume Bottle

Perfume bottle & stopper, "Offrande" by
Cheramy, upright tall clear bottle w/black
glass stopper, labeled, in original triangular drop-side box decorated w/a flower &
spider web design, ca. 1925, 5 1/2" h.
(ILLUS.).. **$800-1,400**
Perfume bottle & stopper, "Ondine" by Su-
zanne Thierry, clear glass bottle w/point-
ed stopper, mint in box, ca. 1954,
4 1/4" h. **$131**

Unusual Cut Crystal & Vermeille Perfume

Perfume bottle & stopper, panel-cut clear
crystal bottle on an ornate vermeille over
silver base mount & similar scrolling
shoulder & neck mounts, crown-style
matching cap over inner glass stopper,
19th c., 4" h. (ILLUS.).............................. **$4,500**

Duckling & Snail Novelty Perfume Bottle

Perfume bottle & stopper, "Parfum Narcissus" by Hetra, blown glass figural of a
yellow duckling looking down at a colorful snail, on a clear base, w/original label, two lines in base, 1920s, 2 1/2" l.
(ILLUS.) **$400-550**

Lionceau "Parfum pour Blondes" Bottle

Perfume bottle & stopper, "Parfum pour Blondes" by Lionceau, upright flattened oval turquoise green opaque glass w/molded scrolls trimmed w/tan stain, small cylindrical matching stopper, small faded oval label, signed on the bottom, ca. 1920, 3 1/8" (ILLUS.)........ **$200-225**

Perfume bottle & stopper, "Parfum pour Brunes" by Lionceau, upright flattened oval turquoise green opaque glass w/molded scrolls trimmed w/tan stain, small cylindrical matching stopper, no label, ca. 1920, 3 1/8" h. **$375-400**

Perfume bottle & stopper, "Platine" by Dana, clear bottle w/silver off-center label & metallic flake floating in bottle, mint in box, ca. 1939, 2 1/4" h. **$50**

"Replique" by Raphael Perfume Bottle

Perfume bottle & stopper, "Replique" by Raphael, short square clear glass bottle

w/rounded shoulder, upright flattened tulip-shaped stopper w/letter "R," red wax seal tag around neck, w/original box, ca. 1940s, 3 1/8" h. (ILLUS.)........................ **$40-50**

"Rose d'Ispahan" Bottle by Coryse

Perfume bottle & stopper, "Rose d'Ispahan" by Coryse, clear frosted tapering ovoid bottle w/molded roses tinted pink around the shoulder & on the button stopper, w/original label, sealed, 1920s, 6 3/4" h. (ILLUS.) **$1,202**

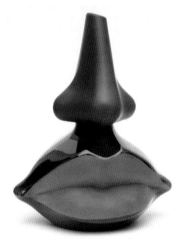

Figural Salvador Dali Factice Bottle

Perfume bottle & stopper, "Salvador Dali" black (dark blue) glass factice bottle designed as a pair of full lips below a tall nose forming the stopper, based on Dali's 1981 painting "Apparition du Visage de l'Aphrodite de Cinde dans un Payage," ca. 1983, 12 1/2" h. (ILLUS.) ... **$1,200**

Miniature "Sculptura" by Jovan Bottle

Perfume bottle & stopper, "Sculptura" by Jovan, miniature square black glass pedestal-style bottle w/a gold stylized nude female torso sculptural stopper, ca. 1970, 2 3/4" h. (ILLUS.) **$25-30**

Langlois "Shari" Octagonal Bottle & Box

Perfume bottle & stopper, "Shari" by Langlois, slender upright clear glass octagonal bottle w/frosted flattened disc stopper, original label, tall silk-covered octagonal box decorated w/Oriental florals, ca. 1925, 3 1/2" h. (ILLUS.) **$45-55**

Perfume bottle & stopper, "Side Glance" by Anjoi, clear glass diamond faceted bottle w/glass stopper, labeled, original box, ca. 1952, 4" h. **$50**

Figural Glass "Suivez Moi" Perfume

Perfume bottle & stopper, "Suivez Moi" by House of Tre-Jur, figural frosted clear glass, the bottle in the shape of a wide layered crinoline dress, the tall stopper in the shape of the upper torso of a lady w/head tilted & wearing a hat, w/long dauber, ca. 1925, 2 1/2" h. (ILLUS.) **$150-200**

Perfume bottle & stopper, "Sweet Pea" by Renaud, green opaque glass tubular bottle w/screw-off cap, gold label, in original leatherette case, ca. 1930, 4" l **$85**

Square "Tigress" by Fabergé Bottle

Perfume bottle & stopper, "Tigress" by Fabergé, upright square clear glass bottle w/upright clear glass disc stopper, original pink banner label, in original box, ca. 1938, 3 1/8" h. (ILLUS.)................. **$35**

"Triomphe" Arc de Triomphe Bottle

Perfume bottle & stopper, "Triomphe" by Leon Laraine, clear & frosted glass stylized model of the Arc de Triomphe in Paris, tall flattened rectangular red glass stopper w/engraved name, unmarked Czech bottle, ca. 1940s, 6 3/8" h. (ILLUS.) **$230**

"Tryst" byVillon Red Skyscraper Bottle

Perfume bottle & stopper, "Tryst" by Villon, figural red opaque bottle in the shape of a skyscraper w/a black glass stopper, original paper label, bottle used for other scents by other companies including Duska by Langlois, ca. 1946, 2 2/3" h. (ILLUS.) **$90-110**

Square French Perfume with Swans

Perfume bottle & stopper, upright square porcelain shape w/a figural small molded gold swan at each bottom corner w/a gold corner band up to a gold palmette at each corner each joined by a low palmette band in gold, the side panels centered w/h.p. floral bouquets within scalloped green bands, tapering shoulder w/further designs below the gold neck & large molded & gold-trimmed button stopper, unmarked, 19th c., 9" h. (ILLUS.)............. **$450-550**

Perfume bottle & stopper, "Votre Main" by Jean Desprez, Sevres porcelain figural hand bottle w/applied flowers, original label, ca. 1939, 7 1/4" h. **$762**

Disc-form White Opaline Perfume Bottle

Perfume bottle & stopper, white opaline disc-shaped bottle w/fancy gold shoulder mounts & cap w/basse taille enameling, mid-19th c., 3" l. (ILLUS.).............. **$2,000-2,500**

"Ze Zan" with African Princess Case

Perfume bottle & stopper, "Ze Zan" by Tuvache, gilded ceramic bottle within a figural carved wood African princess case, ca. 1938, 7 1/2" h. (ILLUS.) **$900-1,400**

Perfume bottle & stopper, "Zibeline" by Weil, clear glass upright flattened oblong bottle w/gilded sides & logo-form stopper, ca. 1927, 3 1/2" h. **$75**

Perfume bottles & stoppers, dime store novelty-type, set of three bottles each in the shape of a puppy, mint in cellulois tent box, by Manon Freres, ca. 1940s, 2 3/4" h., the set **$45-50**

Perfume bottles & stoppers, "Prince Douka" by Marquay, small clear bottles w/frosted head stoppers, each wearing a different colored satin cape, mint in cellulois box, ca. 1951, 3" h., the set **$650-700**

Triple Set of French Porcelain Bottles

Perfume bottles & stoppers, three porcelain upright wedge-shaped bottles forming a cylinder, each h.p. w/pale yellow bands w/colored florals flanking a wide white middle band w/colorful floral bouquet, short cylindrical neck w/gold rim & tall pointed stopper h.p. w/red & blue stripes on a white ground, held in a slender gilt-metal frame, bottoms marked "Made in France," 6 1/2" h., the set (ILLUS.) **$300-400**

Perfume bottles & stoppers set, "Cuir de Russie," "Petite Fleur Bleue," & "Sous-Bois" by Godet, each in an upright flattened oval dark red glass bottle w/a pointed black glass stopper, original labels, sealed, in original presentation box, 1930s, 3" h., the set (ILLUS., bottom of page) **$720**

Godet Three-Bottle Gift Set & Original Box

Rare Early Mold-Blown French Scent

Scent bottle w/cap, mold-blown yellowish amber glass, flattened tapering bulbous form molded w/a heart & fleur-de-lis design, original pewter crown cap, pontil scar, ca. 1750-1800, 3 1/2" h. (ILLUS.)...... **$728**

Germany

Long Glass Throwaway-type Cologne

Cologne bottle & stopper, clear glass throwaway-type, long slender square laydown style w/a tiny glass stoper, the bot-

tle enameled in gold & white, late 19th c., 7 1/2" l. (ILLUS.).................................... **$75-100**

Dressing table set: a pair of tall cologne bottles & a cov. powder box; each piece in porcelain w/a dramatic angular Art Deco style body decorated in light & dark green triangular design, figural Flapper head stoppers, w/daubers, probably German, ca. 1930s, 6 1/4" h., the set (ILLUS., bottom of page).............. **$950**

Figural Dutch Girl Atomizer

Perfume atomizer w/fittings, figural ceramic bottle in the shape of a seated Dutch girl holding a large urn w/metal fittings & mesh-covered bulb, light blue glaze, gold label on the front base "Ketma," probably German, ca. 1900-20, 3" h. (ILLUS.) **$175**

Art Deco Three-Piece Dressing Table Set

Perfume atomizer w/fittings, figural porcelain model of a nude lady h.p. in pastel colors, marked "Germany 4390," ca. 1920s-30s, 6" h. **$150-200**

German World Globe Perfume Atomizer

Perfume atomizer w/fittings, footed spherical bottle decorated in color as a world globe w/the wording in German, gilt metal fittings w/mesh-covered bulb, ca. 1920s-30s, 6 7/8" h. (ILLUS.)................................ **$350**

Figural Elegant Lady Perfume Bottle

Perfume bottle & stopper, figural porcelain modeled as an elegant lady wearing a long blue gown trimmed w/a yellow rose, white bow at her waist, upper body forms stopper w/glass dauber, unmarked, ca. 1930s, 5" h. (ILLUS.)................................... **$150**

Germany Porcelain Perfume & Powder Box

Perfume bottle & powder box, porcelain, figural, designed as a lady in 18th c. dress in yellow w/green trim, her upper body lifts off to expose the powder box, her upper body forms the perfume bottle topped by a small metal crown-form stopper, ca. 1930s, 7 1/4" h. (ILLUS.)........ **$525**

Novelty Airplane Perfume from Germany

Perfume bottle & stopper, "Annette," clear blown glass model of an early airplane w/painted tail, wings, propeller & wheels, fitted w/a small bird pilot, sealed w/cork stopper under rear of body, labeled "Made in Germany," 1920s, 4 3/8" l. (ILLUS.) **$400-550**

German Swirl-decorated Glass Bottle

Perfume bottle & stopper, blown milk glass teardrop-shaped bottle decorated w/swirled yellow & blue bands, resting on a round foot, metal cap w/crown-shaped stopper, unmarked, ca. 1930s, 3" h. (ILLUS.) **$75-100**

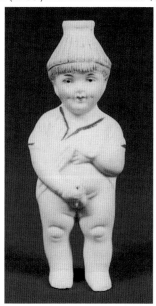

"Naughty" Figural Bisque Bottle

Perfume bottle & stopper, figural bisque porcelain "naughty" design, modeled as a standing little boy ready to urinate, h.p. features & pale blue cap,

probably   German, ca.   1880-1900, 3 3/4" h. (ILLUS.) **$375**

Porcelain Sphinx-shaped Perfume Bottle

Perfume bottle & stopper, figural porcelain designed as the Egyptian sphinx glazed in red, red-painted metal crown-shaped stopper, marked, ca. 1920s-30s, 3 3/8" h. (ILLUS.) **$175-200**

Perfume bottle & stopper, figural porcelain model of a lady wearing a blue & gold court dress & a powdered wig, small metal crown-shaped stopper, marked, 4 3/4" h. **$235-275**

Porcelain Art Deco Lady Pefume Bottle

Perfume bottle & stopper, figural porcelain model of a standing Art Deco lady wearing a full red & yellow gown & holding a white cylinder trimmed w/zigzag lines & topped by a small metal crown-shaped stopper, unmarked, ca. 1920s-30s, 3 1/4" h. (ILLUS., previous page)............... **$150**

Porcelain Red Dog Perfume Bottle

Perfume bottle & stopper, figural porcelain model of a stylized red dog w/large eyes, metal crown-shaped stopper, marked, ca. 1930s, 2 3/4" h. (ILLUS.)............................ **$120**

Porcelain Oriental Lady Head Bottle

Perfume bottle & stopper, figural porcelain model of the head of an Oriental lady w/tall black hair, small metal crown-shaped stopper, ca. 1920s-30s, 3 1/2" h. (ILLUS.)... **$245**

Figural Pierrot Perfume Bottle

Perfume bottle & stopper, figural porcelain modeled as a seated figure of Pierrot wearing yellow, holding up a large white urn w/a molded red rose stopper, w/dauber, marked "Bavaria," ca. 1930s, 5" h. (ILLUS.) **$325**

German Porcelain Baby-form Bottle

Perfume bottle & stopper, figural porcelain, modeled as a seated kewpie-like baby w/hands behind its back, small metal crown-shaped cap, marked, ca. 1920s-30s, 3" h. (ILLUS.).................... **$120-140**

Figural Dutch Boy Perfume Bottle

Perfume bottle & stopper, figural porcelain standing Dutch boy holding a bouquet of pink flowers, his tall cylindrical pink hat topped by a metal crown-shaped stopper, unmarked, ca. 1920s-30s, 4 1/4" h. (ILLUS.)... **$150-200**

German Porcelain Flapper Bottle

Perfume bottle & stopper, figural porcelain stylized head of a 1920s Flapper w/a long earring & white cap, small metal crown-shaped stopper, marked, ca. 1920s-30s, 2 1/3" h. (ILLUS.) **$165**

German Bottle with Molded Face

Perfume bottle & stopper, flattened oval porcelain bottle w/a yellowish iridescent ground, molded w/the head of a Harelquin-like lady, ca. 1920s, 2 3/4" l. (ILLUS.)... **$125**

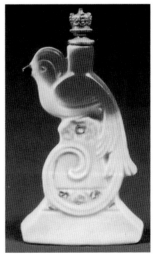

German Porcelain Figural Bird Bottle

Perfume bottle & stopper, flattened porcelain bottle designed as a long-tailed red & yellow bird perched atop a tapering white column, small figural crown metal stopper, molded mark, ca. 1920s-30s, 3 2/3" h. (ILLUS.) **$175**

Perfume bottle & stopper, mercury (silver) glass lay-down teardrop shape w/an orange swirl design & ball stopper w/long dauber, neck marked "Germany," ca. 1920s-30s, 2 7/8" l. **$75**

Perfume bottle & stopper, mercury (silver) glass lay-down teardrop shape w/orange, yellow & green swirls design & ball stopper w/long dauber, neck marked "Germany," ca. 1920s-30s, 2 1/2" l. **$60-75**

Silver-Mounted Dralle Perfume Bottle

Perfume bottle & stopper, "Ora e Sempre" by Dralle, upright square clear bottle within a silvered metal footed frame & w/a hinged domed silvered metal cap opening to the stopper, 1920s, 3" h. (ILLUS.) **$1,560**

Googlie-eyed Figural Girl Head Bottle

Perfume bottle & stopper, porcelain figural head of a googlie-eyed girl w/short black hair, cork stopper, unmarked, ca. 1930s, 2 1/4" h. (ILLUS.) **$90**

Yellow Porcelain Bottle with Flowers

Perfume bottle & stopper, upright squared shape w/rounded shoulders, yellow ground w/a rectangular white reserve on the front h.p. w/roses & flowers enclosed by gilt scrolls, yellow fan-shaped stopper, w/dauber, marked "Dresden - Saxony," ca. 1891-1921, 3" h. (ILLUS.) **$175**

Holland

Dutch Footed Cut Crystal Perfume Bottle

Perfume bottle & stopper, flattened oval panel-cut crystal footed bottle w/an oval diamond point cut side panel, gold hinged overcap & collar, gold inner loop w/original cork, ca. 1794, 4 1/4" h. (ILLUS.) **$500-650**

Early Dutch Tapering Crystal Bottle

Perfume bottle & stopper, tapering ovoid cut crystal bottle w/a gold base mount cut w/lotus leaves, gold hinged overcap & collar, glass inner stopper, ca. 1790-1810, 4 1/4" l. (ILLUS.) **$650-750**

Perfume bottles & stoppers, cut crystal w/a bulbous bottom & tall tapering panel-cut neck w/a silver collar & crown-form stopper, two on a fluted silver foot, two w/glass inner stoppers, one hallmarked w/a dagger, Schoonhoven, Holland, ca. 1900, 4 1/8" h., each **$100-125**

Ireland

Brush tray & scent bottles, Irish Belleek, Thorn patt., turquoise & gilt decoration, D333-I & D335-I (ILLUS., bottom of page) **$2,200**

Early Cut Crystal Irish Perfume Bottle

Perfume bottle & stopper, small oblong crystal deeply cut overall w/a diamond design, silver screw-on cap & glass inner stopper, damage to inner lip, probably Cork, ca. 1820, 3 1/8" h. (ILLUS.) **$300-400**

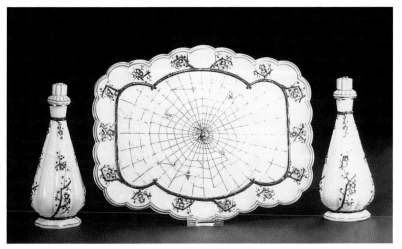

Thorn Brush Tray & Scent Bottles

Italy

Unusual Tall Figural Head Bottle

Factice or cologne bottle, "Egizia" by La Ducale, tall figural ceramic head of an African lady w/a tall pointed hairdo & a tall ringed neck, gold trim & long brass wire earrings, marked "Canova - Canova Italy," missing brass & cork stopper, ca. 1936, 11 3/4" h. (ILLUS.) **$600**

Small Murano Spatter Glass Perfume

Perfume bottle, blown ovoid body tapering to a small flared neck, clear glass enclosing a spatter design in red, yellow & green, Murano, late 19th c., 3 3/4" h. (ILLUS.) **$125**

Colorful Blown Venetian Perfume Bottle

Perfume bottle & stopper, blown glass, footed upright ovoid body tapering to a small cylindrical neck w/a flaring rim composed of white lattacinio & colored twisted bands, slender applied clear loop handles, tall flower-cluster stopper w/clear aventurine leaves, aventurine foot, Venice, late 19th - early 20th c., 7" h. (ILLUS.) **$460**

Perfume bottle & stopper, blown "sommerso" style in light green glass over blue in a heavy teardrop form, paper label for Seguso, Murano, ca. 1960, 4" h. **$175-200**

Murano Encased-Fish Perfume Bottle

Perfume bottle & stopper, flattened upright blown glass disc shape in clear encasing an upright black fish w/white-threaded fins & tail, open mouth forms opening fitted w/a clear ball stopper, Murano, ca. 1950s, 4 3/4" h. (ILLUS.) **$275-300**

Fine Mold-Blown Italian Perfume

Perfume bottle & stopper, mold-blown glass w/a mottled red round foot & stem supporting a tall slender optic-ribbed mottled red baluster-form body, clear stopper w/applied yellow & red blossoms w/curled green leaves, similar band of blossoms & leaves applied around the stem, Murano, ca, 1910-30, 9 1/2" h. (ILLUS.).................... **$800**

Early Italian Carved Coral Perfume

Perfume bottle & stopper, novelty-type, a footed ovoid natural red coral bottle w/a gilt-metal collar & hinged cover set w/a coral cameo, ca. 1790, 1 7/8" h. (ILLUS.)....... **$1,600**

Japan

Cologne bottle w/flower cluster stopper, Noritake china, Art Deco man wearing checkered cape, lustered sides, 6 3/4" h. .. **$470**

Nippon Porcelain Ovoid Perfume Bottle

Perfume bottle & stopper, bulbous ovoid porcelain bottle tapering to a short flaring neck, decorated w/gold vertical band & zigzag band around the shoulder under a black band, gold lines on rim & ball stopper, w/a Nippon mark, pre-1921, 4 1/2" h. (ILLUS.).. **$275**

Mexico

Small Mexican Glass & Silver Perfume

Perfume bottle & stopper, flattened rectangular clear glass container decorated overall w/sterling silver overlay in a design of engraved leafy vines & blossoms, cylindrical silver cap, marked "Sterling - Mexico," ca. 1940s-60s, 2 1/2" h. (ILLUS.) **$60**

Fine Enameled Silver-Gilt Russian Perfume

Perfume bottle & stopper, flattened ovoid fancy silver-gilt body w/a stippled background highlighted w/delicate designs in enamels colored red, blue & white, matching ball-form cap, hallmarked, ca. 1880, 3" h. (ILLUS.) **$1,750-2,000**

Spain

Small Mexican Silver-encased Perfume

Perfume bottle & stopper, upright rectangular sterling silver case w/gently angled & line-incised sides enclosing a miniature glass bottle, marked "Sterling - Mexico," ca. 1940s-60s, 2 1/4" h. (ILLUS.) **$35**

Russia

"Maderas de Oriente" by Myrurgia

Perfume bottle & stopper, "Maderas de Oriente" by Myrurgia, upright slender cylindrical body w/colored enamel label, clear disc-form stopper, w/bullet-shaped wooden box w/a large tassel, ca. 1920, 4 1/3" h. (ILLUS.) **$25-45**

Pretty Enameled Brass Perfume Bottle

Perfume bottle & stopper, enameled brass, lay-down type, tapering eight-paneled brass tube w/each panel decorated w/inlaid colored enamel forming loops & points, glass-lined w/original glass stopper under the brass cap, probably Russian, late 19th c., 3 1/2" l. (ILLUS.) **$1,438**

Sweden

Perfume bottle & stopper, clear crystal faceted bottle & stopper, Kosta Boda, signed "V. Lindstand," ca. 1950, 3 1/2" h. **$65**

1960s Orrefors Perfume Bottle

Perfume bottle & stopper, clear crystal ovoid form tapering to a tiny neck w/a tall cylindrical stopper, signed by Orrefors, ca. 1960s, 5 1/2" h. (ILLUS.)......... **$65**

United States

Blue Satin Glass Chatelaine Bottle

Chatelaine scent bottle & stopper, mother-of-pearl satin glass, flattened ovoid body shaded blue to pale blue in the Diamond Quilted patt., gilt-metal collar, finger chain & cap, ca. 1885-95, 4 1/2" h. (ILLUS.).. **$400**

Rare Amethyst Mold-Blown Cologne

Cologne bottle, amethyst glass, mold-blown ovoid body tapering to a tall neck w/flattened rim, sixteen ribs swirled to the left, tubular pontil scar, probably Pittsburgh region, ca. 1820-60, 6" h. (ILLUS.)............ **$1,904**

Sandwich Blue Mold-Blown Cologne

Cologne bottle, cobalt blue mold-blown glass, tall paneled & waisted sides w/an angled shoulder to the long paneled neck w/a flattened rim, smooth base, Boston & Sandwich Glass Co., mid-19th c., 7" h. (ILLUS.).. **$1,456**

James Garfield Bust Figural Bottle

Cologne bottle, figural bust of James Garfield, clear glass, ground lip, original wooden base w/original gold paint, 95% original label for "The Garfield Cologne," ca. 1880-84, 7 1/4" h. (ILLUS.) .. **$364**

Figural Chinese Man Cologne Bottle

Cologne bottle, figural Chinese man, clear glass, tooled mouth, smooth base marked "C.T.," original paper label

around neck reading "For The Toilet," ca. 1890-1910, 5 1/4" h. (ILLUS.) **$112**

Unusual Opera Glasses Figural Bottle

Cologne bottle, figural opera binoculars, clear glass w/original metal brackets, focusing mechanism & stopper w/screw caps, 98% original neck labels for "Bradley's Opera Bouquet Cologne - New York," ca. 1885-1910, 4 1/4" h. (ILLUS.).... **$224**

Torso of Woman Figural Bottle

Cologne bottle, figural torso of woman, clear glass, ground lip, smooth base, original metal screw-on cap, 85% original faded paper label reading "Santa Clara Cologne," ca. 1890-1910, 6 1/2" h. (ILLUS.)... **$96**

Clear Teardrop Cologne Bottle

Cologne bottle, free-blown teardrop form, clear glass decorated w/alternating blue, white & pink vertical stripes, tooled mouth, pontil, America, ca. 1840-70, 4 3/4" h. (ILLUS.) **$147**

Cologne bottle, medium green mold-blown glass, rectangular w/two recessed label panels, sheared mouth w/applied ring, pontil scar, ca. 1840-60, 2 5/8" w., 6" h...... **$616**

Amethyst Cologne with Original Stopper

Cologne bottle, mold-blown amethyst glass, 12-sided cylindrical shape tapering to a tall round neck w/a rolled lip, original tall pointed ground stopper, smooth base, shallow flake off side of base edge, ca. 1850-80, 7 1/2" h. (ILLUS.) **$336**

Amethyst Paneled Cologne Bottle

Cologne bottle, mold-blown amethyst glass, 12-sided cylindrical shape tapering to a tall round neck w/a rolled lip, smooth base, ca. 1850-80, 4 5/8" h. (ILLUS.) **$134**

Early Labeled American Cologne Bottle

Cologne bottle, mold-blown aqua glass, spherical ribbed basket form, long neck & rolled lip, pontil scar, 100% of original paper label reading "Eau De Cologne - Paris," ca. 1840-60, 3 1/8" h. (ILLUS.) **$78**

Rare Early Labeled American Cologne

Cologne bottle, mold-blown clear glass, designed as a building w/a domed cupola, molded inscription "Morris - Johnson - N-York," neck w/flared lip, pontil scar, some faint interior stain, ca. 1840-60, 6 1/4" h. (ILLUS.) **$672**

Clear Cologne with Dagger & Vine Design

Cologne bottle, mold-blown clear glass, upright rectangular shape w/bulbed neck w/flared lip, molded w/a dagger & scrolling vine design, pontil scar, some light scratches on back label panel, ca. 1840-60, 8 1/4" h. (ILLUS.) **$157**

Violin-Shaped Ship Design Cologne

Cologne bottle, mold-blown clear glass, flattened violin shape molded w/a sailing ship, tooled, flared lip, pontil scar, ca. 1840-60, 4 3/4" h. (ILLUS.) **$134**

Large Cobalt Blue Paneled Cologne

Cologne bottle, mold-blown cobalt blue glass, 12-sided cylindrical shape tapering to a tall round neck w/a rolled lip, smooth base, ca. 1850-80, 7 1/8" h. (ILLUS.) **$246**

Cobalt Blue Paneled Cologne Bottle

Cologne bottle, mold-blown cobalt blue glass, 12-sided cylindrical shape tapering to a tall round neck w/a rolled lip, smooth base, ca. 1850-80, 6 1/8" h. (ILLUS.) **$258**

Paneled Labeled Cobalt Cologne Bottle

Cologne bottle, mold-blown cobalt blue glass, tall 12-sided vertically ribbed form, sheared & rolled lip, smooth base, 85% original paper label reading "Eau de Cologne de Paris," ca. 1860-80, 7 5/8" h. (ILLUS.).. **$157**

Labeled Cobalt Blue Paneled Cologne

Cologne bottle, mold-blown cobalt blue glass, 12-sided cylindrical shape tapering to a tall round neck w/a rolled lip, pontil scar, 90% original paper label on side reading "Eau De Cologne - Reetifiee," ca. 1860-80, 7 5/8" h. (ILLUS.) **$308**

Deep Cobalt Blue Paneled Cologne Bottle

Cologne bottle, mold-blown dark cobalt blue glass, 12-sided cylindrical shape tapering to a tall round neck w/a rolled lip, smooth base, ca. 1850-80, 4" h. (ILLUS.) .. **$112**

Scarce Tall Ribbed Cologne Bottle

Cologne bottle, mold-blown dark cobalt blue glass, 16 vertical ribs in the cylindrical shape tapering to a tall round neck w/a rolled lip, polished pontil, faint interior base haze, ca. 1850-80, 12 1/8" h. (ILLUS.) **$728**

Scarce Cobalt Paneled & Waisted Cologne

Cologne bottle, mold-blown deep cobalt blue glass, eight-sided rounded deeply waisted form w/a tall neck & tooled lip, smooth base, ca. 1850-80, 7" h. (ILLUS.) **$1,344**

Middle-sized Cobalt Paneled & Waisted Cologne

Cologne bottle, mold-blown deep cobalt blue glass, eight-sided rounded deeply waisted form w/a tall neck & rolled lip, pontil scar, ca. 1850-80, 6 1/8" h. (ILLUS.)........ **$784**

Tall Cobalt Blue Tapering Cologne Bottle

Cologne bottle, mold-blown deep cobalt blue glass, gently tapering cylindrical shape w/a tooled & rolled lip, pontil scar base, ca. 1850-1880, 12" h. (ILLUS.)......... **$202**

Scarce Mint Green Cologne Bottle

Cologne bottle, mold-blown fiery opalescent mint green glass, gently tapering cylindrical shape w/a rolled lip & pontil scar on base, ca. 1850-1880, 9 3/8" h. (ILLUS.) **$336**

Scarce Purple Bead & Flute Cologne

Cologne bottle, mold-blown deep purple glass, tapering cylindrical form molded w/vertical ribs & a bead & flute design, tooled mouth, smooth base, ca. 1850-80, 5 7/8" h. (ILLUS.) **$784**

Scarce Fiery Powder Blue Cologne

Cologne bottle, mold-blown fiery opalescent powder blue glass, eight-sided deeply waisted shape w/tall neck & tooled mouth, smooth base, some light inside stain, ca. 1850-80, 4 7/8" h. (ILLUS.) **$616**

Fiery Opalescent Waisted Cologne Bottle

Cologne bottle, mold-blown fiery opalescent glass, eight-sided deeply waisted shape w/tall neck & tooled mouth, smooth base, ca. 1850-80, 4 5/8" h. (ILLUS.) **$560**

Early Figural Elephant Cologne Bottle

Cologne bottle, mold-blown glass, model of a standing elephant w/a fancy blanket on its back, tall swelled neck w/rolled lip in top center, open pontil, clear, ca. 1840-60, 4 7/8" h. (ILLUS.) **$392**

Figural Swan Glass Cologne Bottle

Cologne bottle, mold-blown glass, model of a swan w/wings up supporting a tulip-form bulb w/a cylindrical neck w/flared lip, open pontil, greenish aqua, ca. 1840-60, 6 5/8" h. (ILLUS.) **$448**

Basket of Fruit Clear Glass Cologne

Cologne bottle, mold-blown glass, molded as a tall basket of fruit, tall cylindrical neck w/tooled mouth, pontil, clear, ca. 1840-60, 5 5/8" h. (ILLUS.) **$308**
Cologne bottle, mold-blown glass, molded on one side w/a scene of a mandolin player seated below a tall pointed arch w/a quatrefoil, rolled lip, pontil, clear, ca. 1840-60, 5 3/4" h. (ILLUS., top next column) **$395**

Mandolin Player Clear Cologne

Paneled Grape Amethyst Cologne Bottle

Cologne bottle, mold-blown grape amethyst glass, 12-sided cylindrical shape tapering to a tall round neck w/a rolled lip, pontil scar, ca. 1850-80, 7 1/4" h. (ILLUS.) **$476**

Light Bluish Green Paneled Cologne Bottle

Cologne bottle, mold-blown light bluish green glass, 12-sided cylindrical shape

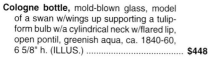

tapering to a tall round neck w/a rolled lip, smooth base, ca. 1850-80, 6" h. (ILLUS.) .. **$202**

Rare Canary Waisted Cologne Bottle

Cologne bottle, mold-blown light canary yellow glass, eight-sided deeply waisted shape w/tall neck & tooled mouth, smooth base, ca. 1850-80, 4 5/8" h. (ILLUS.) **$3,920**

Rare Large Bluish Green Cologne

Cologne bottle, mold-blown medium bluish green glass, 12-sided cylindrical shape tapering to a tall round neck w/a rolled lip, smooth base, crude textured glass w/very tiny seed bubbles, ca. 1850-80, 9 5/8" h. (ILLUS.) **$1,120**

Light Blue Mold-blown Cologne Bottle

Cologne bottle, mold-blown light opalescent blue glass, paneled cylindrical shape tapering to a long neck w/flared rim, attributed to the New England Glass Co., ca. 1870, 5 1/2" h. (ILLUS.) **$300-400**

Lavender Tall Paneled Cologne Bottle

Cologne bottle, mold-blown medium lavender glass, 12-sided cylindrical shape tapering to a tall round neck w/a rolled lip, pontil scar, ca. 1850-80, 7 1/8" h. (ILLUS.) **$308**

Prussian Blue Paneled Cologne Bottle

Cologne bottle, mold-blown medium Prussian blue glass, 12-sided cylindrical shape tapering to a tall round neck w/a rolled lip, smooth base, ca. 1850-80, 4 1/4" h. (ILLUS.) **$258**

Fine Deep Green Paneled Cologne

Cologne bottle, mold-blown medium to deep emerald green glass, 12-sided cylindrical shape tapering to a tall round neck w/a rolled lip, smooth base, ca. 1850-80, 7 1/2" h. (ILLUS.) **$1,008**

Teal Blue Paneled Cologne Bottle

Cologne bottle, mold-blown medium teal blue glass, 12-sided cylindrical shape tapering to a tall round neck w/a rolled lip, smooth base, ca. 1850-80, 4 7/8" h. (ILLUS.)............. **$202**

Paneled Sapphire Blue Cologne Bottle

Cologne bottle, mold-blown sapphire blue glass, 12-sided cylindrical shape tapering to a tall round neck w/a tooled lip, smooth base, ca. 1850-80, 9" h. (ILLUS.) .. **$308**

Rare Mold-blown Blue Cologne Bottle

Cologne bottle, mold-blown sapphire blue glass, flattened corseted shape w/palmette scrolled acanthus w/cross-hatching, inward rolled mouth, pontil scar, America, ca. 1840-60, 5 3/4" h. (ILLUS.) **$2,128**

Teal Blue Paneled-Waisted Cologne

Cologne bottle, mold-blown teal blue glass, eight-sided deeply waisted shape w/tall neck & tooled mouth, smooth base, ca. 1850-80, 4 7/8" h. (ILLUS.) **$308**

Labeled Paneled Teal Blue Cologne

Cologne bottle, mold-blown teal blue glass, 12-sided cylindrical shape tapering to a tall round neck w/a rolled lip, smooth base, 98% original paper label on side reading "Eau De Cologne - Paris," ca. 1850-80, 6 5/8" h. (ILLUS.) **$280**

Hourglass Cologne Bottle

Cologne bottle, mold-blown teal blue glass, eight-sided hourglass form w/long slender neck, tooled lip, smooth base, ca. 1850-80, 4 5/8" h. (ILLUS.) **$840**

Tall Labeled Amber Cologne Bottle

Cologne bottle, mold-blown tobacco amber glass, gently tapering cylindrical shape w/an applied mouth & smooth base, 85% original paper label reading "French's Bay Rum Imported by Geo. C. Goodwin & Co. 38 Hanover St. Boston," ca. 1850-1880, 11 1/2" h. (ILLUS.) **$90**

Scarce Libbey Amberina Cologne

Cologne bottle & stopper, Amberina art glass, tall pedestal base & slender ovoid body tapering to a flared & lobed rim, tall acorn-form stopper, signed by Libbey, ca. 1917, 8 1/4" h. (ILLUS.) **$2,500**

Rare Turquoise Blue Waisted Cologne

Cologne bottle, mold-blown turquoise blue glass, 10-sided slender waisted form w/a tall neck & tooled lip, smooth base, some light interior stain, ca. 1850-80, 6 1/2" h. (ILLUS.) **$1,904**

Boldly Colored Modern Thiewes Bottle

Cologne bottle & stopper, blown boule-shaped bottle w/a bold marbleized design in shiny red, orange, yellow, blue & matte white, signed "George J. Thiewes 1983," 6 1/2" h. (ILLUS.) **$275-300**

Cologne bottle & stopper, clear pressed glass, pink-stained, Banded Portland patt., large size... **$215**

Pretty Engraved American Cologne

Cologne bottle & stopper, clear spherical body nicely engraved w/a floral design, ball stopper, unmarked, ca. 1890 (ILLUS.) **$350-450**

Unusual Modern Robert Levin Bottle

Cologne bottle & stopper, blown deep violet iridescent glass squatty bulbous bottle decorated overall w/amber patches, the cylindrical neck w/applied pointed deep purple handles at the base below a band of purple threading, deep purple knob stopper, signed "Robert Levin 1977," 5" h. (ILLUS.) **$275**

Leaf & Flower Engraved Cologne

Cologne bottle & stopper, clear engraved glass, bell-shaped body decorated w/long leafy stems & engraved daisy-like flowers, the button-form stopper cased in sterling silver & topped by red guilloche enamel, ca. 1920, 4 1/2" h. (ILLUS.)... **$175-200**

Cologne bottle & stopper, clear pressed glass, Banded Portland patt., large size....... **$85**

Cologne bottle & stopper, clear pressed glass, Banded Portland patt., small size **$55**

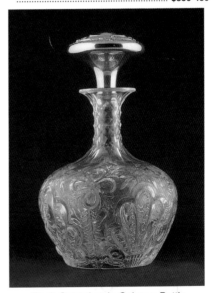

Rock Crystal-style Cologne Bottle

Cologne bottle & stopper, cut & engraved clear glass, squatty bulbous shape w/a tall neck & sterling silver-coated mushroom stopper, in the Rock Crystal style, signed by Hawkes, sterling by Gorham, ca. 1900 (ILLUS.) **$1,000-1,250**

Lovely Ruby Flashed & Cut Cologne Bottle

Cologne bottle & stopper, cylindrical cut glass, clear flashed in ruby & cut overall w/a Cane patt., cut ball stopper, unsigned   Dorflinger, ca.   1889-1900, 7 1/2" h. (ILLUS.) **$850-1,075**

Cologne bottle & stopper, cylindrical cut glass, clear flashed in ruby & cut overall w/a Cane patt., cut ball stopper, unsigned Dorflinger, ca. 1889-1900, 5" h. **$800**

Cut Overlay American Cologne Bottle

Cologne bottle & stopper, cylindrical shape in clear cased in sapphire blue & cut in a strawberry diamond & fan design, clear facet-cut stopper, Cape Cod Glass

Company, Sandwich, Massachusetts, ca. 1860s, 7 3/8" h. (ILLUS.) **$650-750**

Cologne bottle & stopper, Grape & Cable patt. Carnival glass in marigold, Northwood Glass Co... **$150**

Cologne bottle & stopper, Grape & Cable patt. Carnival glass in purple, Northwood Glass Co. **$175**

Cologne bottle & stopper, Hobnail patt. (No. 118), blue opalescent glass, Duncan & Miller **$100**

Pineapple-shaped Cologne Bottle

Cologne bottle & stopper, mold-blown milky clambroth knobby pineapple-shaped body w/an applied green neck w/flaring ruffled rim, matching green tulip-shaped stopper, gilt trim, attributed to Boston & Sandwich Glass Co., ca. 1845-60, 7 3/4" h. (ILLUS.) **$750-850**

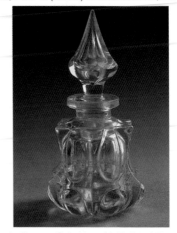

Early Canary Cologne with Pointed Stopper

Cologne bottle & stopper, pressed canary glass, squatty base & paneled patterned sides, fitted w/a pointed stopper, Boston & Sandwich Glass Co., ca. 1840-60, 5" h. (ILLUS., previous page)............. **$500-650**

Canary Star & Punty Pattern Cologne

Cologne bottle & stopper, pressed canary yellow six-sided shape, Star & Punty patt., upright matching stopper, Boston & Sandwich Glass Co., ca. 1850-70, 6 1/2" h. (ILLUS.) **$550-600**

Hobnail Cologne Bottle & Stopper

Cologne bottle & stopper, pressed glass, Hobnail patt., amber, Duncan & Miller, 6 1/2" h., 8 oz. (ILLUS.).............................. **$65**

Cologne bottle & stopper, pressed glass, Star & Punty patt., paneled sides & stopper, yellowish green, Boston & Sandwich Glass Co., ca. 1860, minor flakes, 6 1/8" h. (ILLUS. left with canary Star & Punty cologne, bottom this column).......... **$440**

Cologne bottle & stopper, pressed Hobnail patt. glass, pink opalescent, Hobnail ball stopper, Duncan & Miller Glass, ca. 1940s, 6" h. **$45**

Cologne bottle & stopper, pressed Hobnail patt. milk glass w/cork stopper, Fenton Art Glass, ca. 1930s-40s, 6 1/2" h. ... **$30-40**

Rare Ruba Rombic Cologne Bottle

Cologne bottle & stopper, pressed Ruba Rombic patt. by Consolidated Lamp & Glass Co., silvery dark brownish grey, ca. 1928, 7 1/2" h. (ILLUS.).. **$3,500-4,500**

Two Star & Punty Cologne Bottles

Cologne bottle & stopper, pressed glass, Star & Punty patt., paneled sides & stopper, canary, Boston & Sandwich

Glass Co., ca. 1860, minor flakes, 6 1/8" h. (ILLUS. right with yellowish green Star & Punty cologne) **$286**

Very Rare Royal Flemish Cologne Bottle

Cologne bottle & stopper, Royal Flemish art glass, squatty bulbous body h.p. w/flowers & butterflies, the neck & base of stopper in dark brown trimmed w/heavy gold scrolls, Mt. Washington Glass Co., marked, ca. 1894, 5 3/4" h. (ILLUS.)... **$6,500-8,000**

Footed Ruby Cologne with Acorn Stopper

Cologne bottle & stopper, ruby mold-blown glass, low pedestal foot & bulbous body tapering to a tall cylindrical neck w/flattened rimm, tall acorn-form hollow stopper, attributed to the New England

Glass Co., ca. 1850-75, 9" h. (ILLUS.) **$350-500**

Dorflinger Bulbous Green to Clear Cologne

Cologne bottle & stopper, squatty bulbous cut glass, clear flashed in green & cut overall in the Marlborough patt., cut ball stopper, unsigned Dorflinger, ca. 1890-1910, 6 1/2" h. (ILLUS.) **$6,500-7,500**

Smith Brothers Decorated Cologne

Cologne bottle w/cap upright melon-lobed glass in opal decorated w/dark brown shading to cream & h.p. w/white & yellow daisies on leafy stems, decorated by Smith Brothers, silver collar & hinged cap, ca. 1875-90, 5" h. (ILLUS.).......... **$750-900**

Cologne bottles & stoppers, mold-blown green rim over milk glass Emerald Crest line in the Beaded Melon shape, clear pointed ribbed stopper, clear applied ruffled neck, Fenton Art Glass, ca. 1940s, 4 1/2" h., pr... **$150**

House of Men "Northwoods" Cologne Set

Cologne bottles & stoppers, "Northwoods" by The House of Men, figural bottle in the shape of a man's torso wearing an evening jacket enameled in brown, ivory-colored plastic caps shaped as a squared man's head, labeled, in box labeled "His Elite Duo," ca. 1947, some box scuffs, 6 1/4" h., the set (ILLUS., top of page) **$650-1,000**

Fine American Cut Glass Colognes

Pair of Elegant Ruby to Clear Colognes

Cologne bottles & stoppers, ruby cut to clear glass, a thick round foot & a ringed stem supporting an urn-form body w/a shoulder band, tapering panel-cut neck w/cupped & scalloped rim, tall pointed cut stoppers, foot rim & body cut overall w/punties, probably American, unknown maker, ca. 1845-60, 7" h., pr. (ILLUS.) **$750**

Cologne bottles & stoppers, upright clear fine cut glass w/a shoulder tapering to a ringed neck, bulbous stopper, ca. 1900, 6" h., pr. (ILLUS., top next column) **$125**

Pyramid Atomizer & Perfume Set

Perfume atomizer & matching perfume bottle, each w/a round gold foot below a tall slender swelled body in gold w/long almond-shaped black reserves enameled w/gold & orange blossoms, gilt-metal atomizer fitting w/gold fabric tube & mesh-covered bulb, the perfume w/a flat-topped gilt stopper, marked "Pyramid," 1920s, 7" h. (ILLUS.) **$1,000-2000**

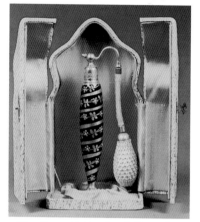

Fine Pyramid Atomizer & Fancy Box

Perfume atomizer w/fittings, a gilded round foot below the tall slender & gently swelled black glass bottle ornately decorated w/a gold spiraling band alternating w/a gold & orange flowering vine design, gilt metal fitting w/gold tube & mesh-covered bulb, mount signed "Pyramid," in original fancy tall arched display box w/hinged front doors, 7 3/8" h. (ILLUS.) **$1,100**

New England Peach Blow Atomizer

Perfume atomizer w/fittings, New England Peach Blow art glass, lobed pear shape in deep pink to light pink, original gilt-metal fitting & pink cocheted tube & bulb covering, ca. 1886-90, 6 1/4" h. (ILLUS.) **$350-500**

Fine Crown Milano Atomizer

Perfume atomizer w/fittings, Crown Milano art glass, footed bulbous ovoid creamy body h.p. w/stylized flowers & leaves & heavy gold trim, gilt-metal top & gold tubing & crochet-covered bulb, ca. 1893, 5 1/2" h. (ILLUS.) **$1,100-1,200**

Fine Wave Crest Perfume Atomizer

Perfume atomizer w/fittings, Wave Crest glass in the Helmschmeid Swirl mold, shaded pink to white ground h.p. overall w/tiny blue blossoms on leafy stems, by C.F. Monroe Co., ca. 1898, 5 1/2" h. (ILLUS.) **$750-900**

Vantines Perfume Bottle-Powder Set

Perfume bottle & face powder gift set, short cylindrical frosted glass bottle w/button stopper w/a cork tip, resting on a silk powder box trimmed in metallic fabric & a Peking glass ring & beads, w/contents, in original square box, Vantines, 1920s, bottle 1 3/4" h., the set (ILLUS. atop box) **$850-1,300**

Clear Bottle with Ornate Brass Filigree

Perfume bottle & stopper, a clear glass boule-shaped bottle encased in ornate pierced flowering leafy vine brass filigree, the tall upright oval stopper w/a border of brass filigree enclosing a large faceted amber glass jewel, ca. 1940s-50s, 5 3/4" h. (ILLUS.) **$250**

"847-A" Figural Bride Perfume Bottle

Perfume bottle & stopper, "847-A" by Eisenberg, frosted clear figure of a standing woman wearing a wedding gown & holding a bouquet, traces of brown patina, label on bottom, ca. 1938, 3 1/2" h. (ILLUS.)... **$245-350**

Scrolled Brass & Glass Perfume Bottle

Perfume bottle & stopper, an upright scrolling oval framework around large oval beveled clear glass panels enclosing a small cylindrical bottle w/a brass filigree covering, the tall pierced & looped stopper centered by a large clear beveled glass panel & a long dauber, unsigned, ca. 1950s, 10 1/2" h. (ILLUS., previous page) **$70**

Perfume bottle & stopper, "Ben Hur" by Andrew Jergens, rounded clear glass bottle w/a frosted stopper & black label, ca. 1904, 5 1/4" h. **$40**

Burmese Hand-Shaped Perfume Bottle

Perfume bottle & stopper, Burmese art glass, glossy finish, long slender ovoid form w/a figural hand at tip, attributed to Mt. Washington Glass Co., ca. 1886-90, 6 7/8" l. (ILLUS.)............................ **$2,750-3,000**

Bottle for "Camelia Noir" by Erte

Perfume bottle & stopper, "Camelia Noir" by Erte, Inc., thin upright rectangular black glass bottle w/small pointed stopper, paper label on side, w/original label & drawer-slide box, stain in box interior, ca. 1925, 3 5/8" h. (ILLUS.).... **$550-800**

Mary Sherman Figural "Can Can" Bottle

Perfume bottle & stopper, "Can Can" by Mary Sherman, frosted clear glass figure of a French cancan dancer, head forms stopper, ca. 1940s-50s, 8 1/2" h. (ILLUS.) **$125**

Hawkes Venetian Pattern Perfume Bottle

Perfume bottle & stopper, clear bulbous cut glass in the Venetian patt. by Hawkes, set on a high scroll-decorated sterling silver base & w/silver mounts by Gorham, ca. 1885-90, 7" h. (ILLUS.) **$1,200-1,500**

Tall Libbey Cut Glass Perfume Bottle

Perfume bottle & stopper, clear cut glass, pedestal base w/tall elaborately cut ovoid body & flared neck, pointed cut stopper w/long dauber, engraved monogram on side, signed by Libbey, ca. 1900, 7 3/4" h. (ILLUS.) **$750-850**

Perfume bottle & stopper, clear elaborately cut boule-shaped bottle w/faceted ball stopper, signed by Hawkes, ca. 1890s, 5 1/2" h. **$150**

Perfume bottle & stopper, clear floral-etched glass, tall conical shape, sterling silver-cased stopper w/long dauber, signed by Hawkes, ca. 1900, 7 1/2" h. **$135**

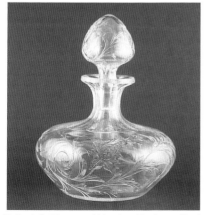

Delicately Engraved Hawkes Perfume Bottle

Perfume bottle & stopper, clear glass delicately engraved squatty bulbous body, matching hollow knob stopper, signed by Hawkes, ca. 1905, 6 3/4" h. **$600-750**

Early Roller Skate Shoe Perfume Bottle

Perfume bottle & stopper, clear glass model of a high-topped shoe roller skate, by Solon Palmer for an unknown scent, metal crown-form stopper, ca. 1900-20, 5" h. (ILLUS.) **$150-200**

Clear Press-Cut American Perfume

Perfume bottle & stopper, clear glass pressed-cut design fanned bottle w/a stylized blossom on each side, a very tall pointed arch & rayed stopper, proba-

bly American, ca. 1940s-50s, 6 7/8" h.
(ILLUS.) **$55-75**

Clear Glass Low Bottle with Tall Stopper

Perfume bottle & stopper, clear pressed
glass low round bottle w/a diamond point
design, the short neck supporting a very
tall pierced stopper in a stylized scrolling
leaves & flower design, ca. 1940s-50s,
6" h. (ILLUS.) **$50-70**

Clear Imperial Bottle Made for Irice

Perfume bottle & stopper, clear pressed
glass w/a step-sided bottle supporting an
oversized frosted clear stopper designed
as a bouquet of sunflowers, glass made
by Imperial for Irice, original paper
label, ca. 1940-60, 6" h. (ILLUS.) **$75-125**
Perfume bottle & stopper, clear squat
pressed glass bottle w/a stopper designed as two birds atop a ball, ca.
1950s, 6" h. **$55**

Perfume bottle & stopper, "Djer Kiss" by
Kerkoff, clear bottle w/pointed glass stop-
per, mint in box, ca. 1908, 4 3/4" h. **$32-36**

Fannie London "Fan Toi" Bottle

Perfume bottle & stopper, "Fan Toi" by
Fannie J. London, hexagonal short clear
bottle decorated w/silver overlay floral
designs, short cylindrical neck w/pointed
disk stopper, ca. 1920, 3 1/2" h. (ILLUS.) .. **$100**
Perfume bottle & stopper, Fenton Burmese art glass, satin finish, bulbous
shaped w/a diamond optic design decorated w/h.p. roses, signed by C.
Griffith, ca. 1990s, 6" h.............................. **$163**

Figural Pocket Watch Perfume Bottle

Perfume bottle & stopper, figural pocket
watch, clear glass, tooled mouth, smooth
base, 100% of original paper labels of a
watch face & "Extract Magnolia," metal
neck band & hanger, original cork
w/some advertising wrapped around
it, ca. 1890-1910, 2 7/8" h. (ILLUS.).......... **$146**

Fine Gold & Black DeVilbiss Perfume

Perfume bottle & stopper, flat-bottomed squatty base covered in gold tapering to the slender black body trimmed w/slender gilt stripes & scrolls, gilt-metal cap fitted w/an upright flat octagonal finial w/black enameled trimmed w/blue & lavender enameled scrolls, long slender gilt-metal rods hanging from bottom sides of finial & ending in small black glass balls, w/dauber, marked "DeVilbiss," 1920s, 4 3/4" h. (ILLUS.) **$4,200**

Perfume bottle & stopper, footed brass filigree enclosing a clear glass bottle w/a large upright prong-set stopper w/a large pink glass jewel, w/dauber, ca. 1930s-50s, 9 1/2" h. **$95**

"Gala Performance" by Rubenstein

Perfume bottle & stopper, "Gala Performance" by Helena Rubinstein, clear

glass in the shape of a woman dancing wearing a long wide skirt (there is a version w/a narrower skirt also), her stylized arms & head form the stopper, ca. 1940, 6" h. (ILLUS.) **$150-185**

Perfume bottle & stopper, "Isadora" by Isadora, low round clear glass bottle w/kneeling nude lady stopper, mint in box, ca. 1979, 3 1/4" h. **$140**

"Jasmine of Southern France" Bottle

Perfume bottle & stopper, "Jasmine of Southern France" by United Drug, a round squatty three-tiered clear glass bottle w/a black cap, fitted in a hinged steel ball holder, ca. 1940s, 1 3/4" h. (ILLUS.) **$140**

Perfume bottle & stopper, "Lov' Me" by Melba, clear bottle w/embossed female nude, full, frozen stopper, ca. 1913, 5 1/4" h. **$89**

Early "May Bloom" Bottle from Palmer

Perfume bottle & stopper, "May Bloom" by Solon Palmer, clear cylinder bottle w/cylindrical neck fitted w/a cloth-wrapped ball stopper, original label & box w/pretty floral graphics, tax stamp for 1899, 3 2/3" h. (ILLUS.) **$235**

New Martinsville Pink Satin Perfume Bottle

Perfume bottle & stopper, New Martinsville footed slender flaring lobed body
w/flaring neck, pink stain w/h.p. flowers,
6 3/4" h. (ILLUS.) **$75**

Perfume bottle & stopper, novelty-type,
"Naughty '90s" by Milart, molded glass
female torso w/a satin corset, w/dome,
full, ca. 1940s, 5 2/3" h............................... **$250**

Lady Figural Bottle for "Pois de Senteur"

Perfume bottle & stopper, "Pois de Senteur" by Joubert, figural clear & frosted
bottle, the base in the form of a large hoop
skirt, the stopper designed as the head &
arms of a lady holding a fan-shaped label,
cork stopper, in original colorful box, ca.
1925, 4 1/2" h. (ILLUS.) **$3,360**

Perfume bottle & stopper, pressed vaseline glass, waisted shape w/foot & pointed disc stopper w/broken dauber, Tiffin
Glass, ca. 1930s-40s, 7" h. **$90**

Figural Bottle for "Perfume No. 7"

Perfume bottle & stopper, "Perfume No. 7"
by Hattie Carnegie, wide narrow arched
clear glass bottle in the form of shoulders
fitted w/a frosted glass figural stylized
head of a woman, gilt wording around the
sides, labeled, in rare grass cloth box, ca.
1928, 2 1/2" h. (ILLUS.) **$450-900**

Fenton Lobed Ruby Perfume Bottle

Perfume bottle & stopper, ruby cased in
clear mold-blown glass in diamond optic
design, footed squatty spherical melon-
lobed form w/a short neck & applied clear
ruffled rim, clear ribbed & pointed stopper, Fenton Art Glass, ca. 1942, 4 1/2" h.
(ILLUS.)... **$75**

"Shari" by Langlois Czech-made Bottle

Perfume bottle & stopper, "Shari" by Langlois (United Drug), round widely flat base tapering sharply to the small neck w/fitted w/a bullet-form stopper, clear glass w/a decorative gold band around the base rim, original sticker label, sealed, base stenciled "Bottle Made in Czechoslovakia," ca. 1925, 4" h. (ILLUS.) **$900**

Squatty Glass & Brass Filigree Bottle

Perfume bottle & stopper, squatty bulbous clear glass bottle draped w/delicate brass filigree flowering leafy vines, the tall pierced brass stopper w/a keyhole form decorated w/a large blossom below a basket of flowers, long dauber, unsigned, probably American-made, ca. 1950s, 5" h. (ILLUS.) **$100-125**

Nan Duskin "Soirée" Rooster Bottle

Perfume bottle & stopper, "Soirée" by Nan Duskin, clear glass model of a rooster, head forms stopper, bottle made in France, ca. 1940s, 10" h. (ILLUS.)...... **$150-170**

Ornate Brass Filigree Perfume Bottle

Perfume bottle & stopper, tall upright brass filigree design w/a wide round scroll-cast foot supporting an upright flattened pierced disc w/a scroll border & a ring of amber cabochon stone around a large central flower blossom w/an amber stone center, the small brass bottle at the top supporting a tall fanned pierced stopper w/a bellflower design, ca. 1940s-50s, 7" h. (ILLUS.) **$100**

Extraordinary Lalique Presentation Set

Perfume bottle & stopper, "Trésor de la Mer" for Saks Fifth Avenue, a unique Lalique opalescent glass container, composed of a shell-shape box w/hinged cover opening to expose the pearl-shaped bottle, complete w/original red velvet presentation box lined in gold silk & blue velvet & corded label in the form of a booklet identifying this as No. 72 from a limited editon of 100, box also retains original Saks price tag affixed to the bottom indicating a price of fifty dollars, glass box retains partial label on inside of cover, box stenciled "R. Lalique - France," bottle engraved "R. Lalique - France," ca. 1936, box 5 x 7 1/2 x 8 1/4", glass box 5 3/4" w. (ILLUS.).................. **$216,000**

Perfume bottle & stopper, upright filigree brass design w/a round pierced leaf design foot supporting a large oval border w/brass beading framing two beveled glass panels enclosing a small cylindrical glass container enclosed in brass filigree & supported atop a small figural head, a large pierced & scroll-trimmed brass fleur-de-lis form stopper, ca. 1950, 9" h. (ILLUS.).. **$200-250**

Perfume bottle & stopper, "Violet Leaves" by Solon Palmer, clear cylinder bottle w/cylindrical neck fitted w/a cork stopper, good original label, ca. 1904, 3 1/4" h......... **$55**

Early "Viorenta" Boxed Perfume

Perfume bottle & stopper, "Viorenta" by Vantines, upright clear square bottle w/tall cylindrical neck & button stopper, w/original color-printed paper label, in handmade wooden box, base molded w/the Vantines flag logo, ca. 1908, 4 1/2" h. (ILLUS.) **$600-1,000**

"We Moderns" by Saks Fifth Avenue

Perfume bottle & stopper, "We Moderns" by Saks Fifth Avenue, flattened footed

Unusual Brass & Glass Tall Perfume

clear glass bottle w/stepped shoulders & enameled detail, clear flattened fan stopper, sealed, in original silver box, ca. 1928, 4 5/8" h. (ILLUS.) **$550-950**

Figural Globe Bottle with Original Box

"White Rose" Perfume Bottle by Allan

Perfume bottle & stopper, "White Rose" by Allan, upright gently swelled body enameled w/scattered flowers, facet-cut ball stopper, w/original label & silk-lined rectangular box, early 1900s, 5 3/4" h. (ILLUS.) **$550-800**

Perfume bottle w/cap, figural globe on metal stand, clear glass rotating globe on original stand w/original cap marked "Our Country," small label on side reads "Pat. Applied For," ground mouth, w/original box showing globe & labeled "The Earth - Filled with Choice Perfume - Wm. H. Brown & Co. - Perfumers - Baltimore, MD ...U.S.A.," ca. 1885-1910, 4 1/4" h. (ILLUS.)....................................... **$258**

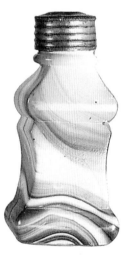

Sesquicentennial Liberty Bell Bottle

Perfume bottle w/cap, figural Liberty Bell, clear glass, embossed "E. Hoyt & Co. - Celebrated - Perfumers - Estb. 1868 - Sesqui Centennial - 1776-1926," tooled lip w/original neck foil, smooth base, 2 1/2" h. (ILLUS.) **$96**

Swirled Glass Perfume Bottle

Perfume bottle w/cap, blue & white swirled glass, four-sided slightly waisted form w/bulging shoulder tapering to rough sheared & ground lip w/original screw-on metal cap, marbled decoration in shades of blue on white, America, ca. 1860-90, two minor chips off edge of lip, possibly from time of manufacture, 2 1/8" h. (ILLUS.) **$364**

Mt. Washington Egg Perfume Bottle

Perfume bottle w/cap, Mt. Washington egg-shaped bottle, white opaque w/a pale beige ground h.p. w/irises in amethyst & blue, 4" h. (ILLUS., previous page) **$1,438**

Perfume bottle/powder box combination, pressed pink glass, stopper w/long dauber, Fostoria Glass, 6" h. **$50**

Clear Perfumes with Firebird Stoppers

Perfume bottles & stoppers, clear boule-shaped body w/molded ribs alternating w/diamond point panels, large oversized stoppers in the form of a firebirds, unsigned American, ca. 1940s, 6 1/4" h., pr. (ILLUS.) **$175**

Perfume bottles & stoppers, clear paperweight glass style, cranberry-trimmed ribs, stopper w/clear leaves & cranberry open flowers, unsigned Gunderson-Pairpoint, 6 1/2" h., pr. **$145**

Cornucopia-Shaped Perfume Bottles

Perfume bottles & stoppers, clear pressed glass, the bottle in the form of a cornucopia on a wave base, the tall pierced stopper designed as tall leaves w/a five-petal blossom, American-made, ca. 1940s-50s, 8 1/4" h., pr. (ILLUS.) **$175-225**

Evyan Boxed Three-Bottle Set

Perfume bottles & stoppers, "Great Lady," "Most Precious," & "White Shoulders," by Evyan, set composed of two flattened rectangular clear glass bottles & a smaller heart-shaped clear glass bottle, in a fitted satin-lined box, ca. 1950s, 2 3/8" 3 1/8" h., the set (ILLUS.) **$35-45**

Pair of Slender Lavender Heisey Perfumes

Perfume bottles & stoppers, mold-blown pale iridescent lavender glass, round foot & slender stem to the tall ovoid body tapering to a flared neck, paneled button-form stopper, marked by Heisey, ca. 1930-40, 7" h., pr. (ILLUS.) **$250**

Boxed Set of "Round The Clock" Scents in Original Box

Two Early Bottles in Basket Case

Perfume bottles & stoppers, "Pearls of Violets" & "Pearls of Lilies" by Wm. H. Brown of Baltimore, each simple flattened clear glass bottle w/a cork stopper, original labels, w/original woven basket case, ca. 1900, bottles 2 1/2" h., the set (ILLUS.).. **$150**

Perfume bottles & stoppers, plain clear glass cylindrical blown bottle w/glass screw-in stoppers, the "Round The Clock" set from Clock Perfumes of Chicago, held the scents "Morning," "Noon," & "Night," w/original plastic rack & clear plastic display box, bottles probably made in Czechoslovakia, the set (ILLUS., top of page) **$120**

Pair of Green & White Fenton Perfumes

Perfume bottles & stoppers, pressed green swirled w/white glass, footed ovoid body tapering to a flared & scalloped rim, clear frosted ribbed & pointed stopper, satin finish, Fenton Art Glass Co., ca. 1953, 5 3/4" h., pr. (ILLUS.) **$225**

Perfume bottles & stoppers, "White Roses" gift set by Yardley & Co., a pair of clear glass tapering squared bottles w/button stoppers, original paper labels & yellow neck ribbons, in original unusual Art Nouveau-style serpentine rectangular box, early 1900s, 4" h., the set (ILLUS., top next page) **$900**

"White Roses" Perfume Gift Set by Yardley & Co.

Perfume flask, mold-blown translucent pale blue cobalt blue glass, lightly dimpled tapered angular body w/a slender cylindrical neck, sheared flat base, possibly 9th to 11th century, some interior residue, 4" h. (ILLUS. far right with three other pungent bottles, top of next page) **$99**

Early American Sea Horse Pungent Bottle

Pungent bottle, clear blown glass in sea horse-form w/pale blue & applied trailing, probably late 18th - early 19th c., 3" l. (ILLUS.) **$300-400**

Pungent bottle, clear & white striped blown glass, dolphin- or mermaid-shaped, pungent-type, scrolled shaped applied w/cobalt blue rigaree, plain lip, possibly Boston & Sandwich Glass Co., first half 19th c., some losses & roughness to rigaree, 1 3/4" h. (ILLUS. far left with three other blown & pattern-molded pungent bottles, page 84) **$77**

Early Cobalt Cut Glass Pungent Bottle

Pungent bottle, cobalt blue cut glass flattened round form, probably American-made, ca. 1825-50, 2 1/4" w. (ILLUS.) **$200**

Pungent bottle, pattern molded bright peacock green glass, flattened tapering ovoid form w/16 ribs swirled to the right, plain rim, rough pontil, probably American, first half 19th c., 3 1/4" h. (ILLUS. far right with three other blown & pattern-molded pungent bottles, page 84) **$143**

Pungent bottle, teal blue pattern-molded glass, flattened tapering ovoid form w/24 vertical ribs, red swirl in the side, plain rim, rough pontil, American or English, first half 19th c., 2 7/8" h. (ILLUS. second from right with three other blown & pattern-molded pungent bottles, page 84) **$176**

Pungent bottle, yellowish amber pattern-molded glass, flattened tapering ovoid form w/26 vertical ribs, plain rim, rough pontil, American or English, tiny flake on lip, some wear, first half 19th c., 3" h. (ILLUS. second from right with three other blown & pattern-molded pungent bottles, top next page) **$165**

Group of Pungent & Perfume Bottles

Pungent bottle w/cap, mold-blown light fiery opalescent glass, paneled coffin form, pewter cap embossed w/roses, possibly Boston & Sandwich Glass Co., ca. 1850-70, 3 3/8" h. (ILLUS. far left with three other pungent bottles, top of page) **$121**

Pungent bottle w/cap, molded-blown opaque white glass, eight concave sides, tin cap, probably Boston & Sandwich Glass Co., ca. 1850-70, 2 3/8" h. (ILLUS. second from left with three other pungent bottles, top of page) **$22**

Scent bottle, cobalt blue glass, waisted form on flaring base, ringed neck w/inward rolled lip, the body decorated w/diamonds, scrolls & fans, medium color in center shading to light at sides, open pontil, America, ca. 1835-55, 5 5/8" h. (ILLUS.) **$2,128**

Early Blue Cut Glass Scent Bottle

Scent bottle, cut cobalt blue glass, flattened oblong form w/angled notches & panels w/almond-shaped cut waffle panels, sheared & polished lip, polished pontil, ca. 1850-80, 3 1/8" h. (ILLUS.) **$112**

Cobalt Blue Glass Scent Bottle

Very Early Blown Aqua Scent Bottle

Scent bottle, free-blown aqua glass, oval ring-form w/pinched-in center area, two bands of applied rigaree along the sides, pontil scar, sheared & tooled lip, Mid-Atlantic glasshouse, ca. 1800-30, 2 1/4" h. (ILLUS.)... **$464**

Blown Sea Horse Scent

Scent bottle, free-blown glass in sea horse form, small tapering & tightly scrolled shape in medium cobalt blue w/a white swirled stripe & applied clear rigaree, tooled mouth, pontil scarred base, ca. 1815-35, 2 3/4" h. (ILLUS.) **$532**

Scent bottle, free-blown glass in sea horse form, small tapering & tightly scrolled shape w/red, white, blue & clear swirled stripes & applied clear rigaree, tooled mouth, pontil scarred base, ca. 1815-35, 2 5/8" h. (ILLUS., top next column) **$1,008**

Scent bottle, free-blown sea horse-form, clear w/a tightly curled end, flattened sides copper-wheel engraved "T.S.N" above a bird on one side & "1792" above a flower on the other side, applied clear glass rigaree, pontil scar, tooled lip, very minor chip, rare, ca. 1792, 4 1/8" h. (ILLUS., middle next column) **$672**

Striped Sea Horse Scent

Dated Sea Horse Scent Bottle

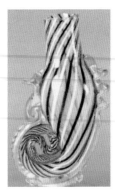

Sea Horse Scent

Scent bottle, free-blown sea horse-form, clear w/thin white & amethyst swirled bands ending in a tightly curled end, applied clear glass rigaree, pontil scar, tooled lip, slight lip edge roughness in the making, ca. 1815-35, 2 3/8" h. (ILLUS.)..... **$179**

Striped White & Cobalt Early Scent

Scent bottle, free-blown sea horse-form, clear w/thin white bands ending in a tightly curled end, applied cobalt blue glass rigaree, pontil scar, tooled lip, ca. 1815-35, 2" h. (ILLUS.) **$308**

Clear Thinly Striped Sea Horse Scent

Rare Large Early Sea Horse Scent Bottle

Scent bottle, free-blown sea horse-form, clear w/thin white bands ending in a tightly curled end, applied clear glass rigaree, pontil scar, tooled lip, slight lip edge roughness in the making, ca. 1815-35, rare large size, 4 3/4" h. (ILLUS.) **$672**

Scent bottle, free-blown sea horse-form, clear w/thin white, pink & blue bands ending in a tightly curled end, applied clear glass rigaree, pontil scar, tooled lip, ca. 1815-35, 3 3/16" h. (ILLUS., top next column) **$179**

Scent bottle, free-blown sea horse-form, clear w/wide white & amethyst bands ending in a tightly curled end, applied clear glass rigaree, pontil scar, tooled lip, tiny chip off rigaree end, ca. 1815-35, 3 1/4" h. (ILLUS., middle next column) **$235**

White & Amethyst-striped Sea Horse Scent

Cobalt Blue Blown Sea Horse Scent Bottle

Scent bottle, free-blown sea horse-form, cobalt blue w/a tightly curled base, applied clear glass rigaree, pontil scar, tooled lip, ca. 1815-35, 2 3/4" h. (ILLUS.) .. **$224**

Opalescent Milk Glass Monument Scent Bottle

Scent bottle, milk glass, monument form on rectangular base, w/short cylindrical neck & rolled lip, in fiery opalescent color, pontil, rare, America, 1835-55, 4 1/2" h. (ILLUS.) **$2,688**

Cobalt Blue Three-Lobed Scent Bottle

Scent bottle, mold-blown cobalt blue glass, triple-lobed form w/sheared & tooled lip, pontil scar, possibly Boston & Sandwich Glass Co., ca. 1840-60, 2 3/4" h. (ILLUS.) **$190**

Vertical-ribbed Cobalt Blue Scent Bottle

Scent bottle, mold-blown cobalt blue glass, flattened teardrop form w/26 vertical ribs, pontil scar, sheared & tooled lip, ca. 1840-60, 2 3/4" h. (ILLUS.) **$146**

Early Blue Concentric Ring Scent Bottle

Scent bottle, mold-blown glass, cobalt blue in a flattened concentric ring design w/notched edges, tooled lip, pontil scar on base, minor wear, rare, possibly from a New England glasshouse, ca. 1830-50, 2 1/4" h. (ILLUS.) **$224**

Early Teal Green Sunburst Scent Bottle

Scent bottle, mold-blown teal green glass, flattened round shaped w/molded sunburst design & notched edges, pontil scar, polished lip, pinhead size flake off side of lip, ca. 1830-50, 1 3/4" h. (ILLUS.)...................................... **$476**

Figural Lantern Scent Bottle

Scent bottle, teal glass & metal, figural lantern, center glass globe in metal cage w/stepped base, screw top & loop handle, original label on base reading "Use Tappan's Famous Sweet Bye & Bye Perfume, it is Fine Sold Everywhere," America, ca. 1890-1910, 3 3/8" h. (ILLUS.) **$90**

Rare Early American Scent Bottle

Scent bottle, teal green mold-blown glass, flattened ovoid shape w/a molded feathers & fern design, inward-rolled mouth, pontil scar, possibly early Pittsburgh district, 1820-40, 2 3/8" l. (ILLUS.).............. **$2,016**

Libbey-signed Alexandrite Scent Bottle

Scent bottle & stopper, Alexandrite art glass, the wide squatty bulbous optic-ribbed bottle centered by a small neck w/flared rim, tall amber stopper, bottom signed "Libbey," early 20th c., very slight interior staining, 4 1/2" h. (ILLUS.) **$460**

Flattened Round Ribbed Scent Bottle

Scent bottle & stopper mold-blown cobalt blue glass, flattened round form w/20 vertical ribs swirled to the right, polished pontil, sheared & tooled lip, original blown flattened tam stopper, ca. 1840-70, 2 3/4" h. (ILLUS.) **$448**

Scent bottle & stopper, paperweight-type, blown clear glass enclosing controlled bubbles & a paperweight base, oversized stopper w/three tiers of leaves, Gunderson-Pairpoint, ca. 1950, small chip, 6 1/2" h. **$125**

Joe St. Clair Paperweight Scent Bottles

Scent bottles & stoppers, paperweight-style, bulbous ovoid blown clear glass bottle w/controlled bubbles & encasing blue trumpet flowers, the tall ovoid stopper encasing blue flowers on pink stems, signed by Joe St. Clair, ca. 1945-90, 6 1/2" h., pr. (ILLUS.) **$750**

Tall Canary Yellow Toilet Water Bottle

Toilet water bottle, canary yellow glass, pattern-molded cylindrical body w/a tall slender neck w/molded mouth, eight vertical ribs swirled to the right on the neck, probably Pittsburgh district, ca. 1840-70, ring-ground pontil scar, 12 1/4" h. (ILLUS.) **$840**

Blue Mold-blown Toilet Water Bottle

Toilet water bottle w/original blown stopper, three-blown mold light cobalt blue glass, paneled 12-sided ovoid body tapering to a ringed cylindrical neck & tam stopper, smooth base, ca. 1850-80, 6" h. (ILLUS.) **$308**

Contemporary Makers

Modern Charles Lotton Blown Atomizer

Perfume atomizer w/fittings, blown art glass tapering bulb-shaped bottle w/green pulled leaves down over the pink ground, original pink cord & bulb covering, by Charles Lotton, ca. 2000, 7" h. (ILLUS.) **$550**

Contemporary Pink Glass Atomizer

Perfume atomizer w/fittings, ovoid pink glass bottle molded w/vertical leaves, brass fittings w/black tube & bulb w/tassel, unmarked, contemporary, 5" h. (ILLUS.)....... **$10**

Contemporary Atomizer & Perfume

Perfume atomizer w/fittings, spherical ribbed clear glass bottle w/a slightly iridescent finish, brass fittings & bulb, unmarked, contemporary, 3 3/4" h. (ILLUS. right with unmarked contemporary perfume bottle) **$5-10**

Perfume bottle & stopper, blown blue iridescent glass teardrop form bottle w/double twist at the bottom, w/a metal collar & stopper fitted w/a pointed purple glass jewel, suspended on a chain to be worn as a necklace, signed "John Gilvey," early 1990s, 3" l. (ILLUS., top next column) **$650**

Perfume bottle & stopper, blown clear glass teardrop shaped w/internal lily blossoms in green & white, signed & numbered by Orient & Flume, ca. 1970s-80s, 6 1/2" h. **$590**

Modern Blue Iridescent Necklace-Bottle

Modern Heart-shaped Perfume Bottle

Perfume bottle & stopper, blown flattened heart shape in clear enclosing a design of red heart-shaped leaves on green swirled stems, signed "Zellique 2001," 3" h. (ILLUS.) **$375**

Modern Flask-form Perfume Bottle

Perfume bottle & stopper, blown glass flattened flask shape in mottled shades of red, blue & tan, blown glass applied tapering horizontal stopper finial, signed "Baguere 1992," 3 3/4" h. (ILLUS.) **$175-225**

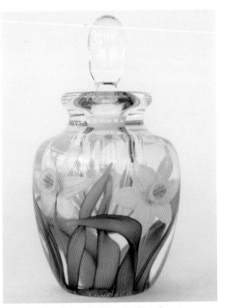

Lundberg Bottle with Narcissus

Perfume bottle & stopper, blown heavy clear glass encasing yellow & white narcissus & dark green leaves, clear blown ovoid stopper, signed "Steven Lundberg Studios 1980," 4" h. (ILLUS.) **$450-550**

Cased Glass Floral Lundberg Perfume

Perfume bottle & stopper, blown glass ovoid bottle in dark blue cased in clear & enclosing a band of stylized large white & yellow blossoms & green leaves, tall clear pointed stopper w/dauber, signed "Salazar" & "Steven Lundberg," Lundberg Studios, 1990, 7 1/3" h. (ILLUS.) **$165**

Modern Blown Black & White Perfume

Perfume bottle & stopper, blown ovoid black glass shape w/fused white glass

stylized flowers around the sides, knob stopper w/white swirls, signed "Pat Robison," ca. 1990s, 3 2/3" h. (ILLUS.)
.... **$175-225**

Two Modern Eloise Cotton Perfumes

Perfume bottle & stopper, blown tapering ovoid frosted clear glass bottle w/trailing stands encasing peach, frosted clear flame stopper, by Eloise Cotton, ca. 2000, 7 1/2" h. (ILLUS. left with matching perfume in blue) **$78**

Perfume bottle & stopper, blown tapering ovoid frosted clear glass bottle w/trailing stands encasing dark blue, frosted clear flame stopper, by Eloise Cotton, ca. 2000, 7 1/2" h. (ILLUS. right with matching perfume in peach) **$78**

Blown Clear Perfume with Colorful Canes

Perfume bottle & stopper, clear blown glass upright ovoid shape encasing a large cluster of colorful canes represent-

ing flower blossoms, by Shawn Messenger, ca. 2000, 5 1/2" h. (ILLUS.).... **$165**

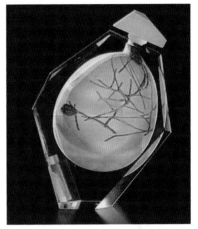

Steven Main Faceted Glass Perfume

Perfume bottle & stopper, clear upright angular glass enclosing a large bubble in peach shaded to light blue & trimmed w/a red bug on branches, angled faceted glass stopper, by Steven Main, ca. 2000, 6" h. (ILLUS.) **$500**

Perfume bottle & stopper, frosted & clear bottle w/fanned ribbing at the sides centered by a frosted stripe, frosted clear flower-molded stopper, unmarked, contemporary, 5" h. (ILLUS. left with contemporary atomizer, page 155)...................... **$5-10**

Contemporary Pyramidal Perfume Bottle

Perfume bottle & stopper, sharply tapering pyramidal body in mauve w/an iridescent finish, inverted pyramidal teal green stopper, unmarked, contemporary, 5" h. (ILLUS.) **$10**

Lundberg Bottle with Fuchsias

Perfume bottle & stopper, upright ovoid blown clear glass encasing pendent dusty rose fuchsia blossoms on green leafy stems, clear blown ovoid stopper, signed "Steven Lundberg 1987," 5 7/8" h. (ILLUS.).. **$300**

Dime Store Novelty-type,

Figural Dwarf Dopey Perfume Bottle

Perfume bottle & stopper, a clear glass figural bottle representing Dwarf Dopey from the Disney movie, Snow White and the Seven Dwarfs, maker unknown, 1960s, 4 1/4" h. (ILLUS.).............................. **$20**

"Apple Blossom" Bottles in Orange Holder

Perfume bottle & stopper, "Apple Blossom" by Laverne of New York, set of three small cylindrical clear bottles fitted in a model of a large metal orange on legs that opens in the middle, design used by other perfume makers, including Duvinne, ca. 1940s, each bottle 1 1/4" h., the set (ILLUS. open)............................. **$25-35**

Perfume bottle & stopper, "Bouquet" by Benjamin Ansehl, designed as a clear plastic typewriter, ca. 1930s........................ **$33**

Perfume bottle & stopper, "Gala Night" by Bouton, in a Bakelite ship's wheel w/an anchor holder, ca. 1928, 1 1/2" h. **$75**

"Harp d'Amour" Figural Harp Bottle

Perfume bottle & stopper, "Harp d'Amour" by Cleevelandt Corp., a slender clear glass vial w/a crown-form stopper mounted in a model of a upright floor harp, ca. 1940, 6 1/2" h. (ILLUS.) **$75**

Perfume bottle & stopper, "Heliotrope" by California Perfume Company, bottle w/an upright frosted stopper, good label, ca. 1916, 4 1/3" h. **$55**

Perfume bottle & stopper, "Imagination" by Loiret, clear glass in the shape of a dressmaker's dummy w/a pink enameled corset, ca. 1940s, 3 1/2" h. **$25**

Perfume bottle & stopper, "Milady's Strike" by Stuart Products, glass bottle in the form of a bowling pin, w/labels, ca. 1940s-50s, 3" h. **$35**

Novelty "Old Colonial" Perfume Bottle

Perfume bottle & stopper, "Old Colonial" by United Toilet Goods Co., designed as a hurricane lamp w/a wooden base & glass chimney enclosing the small bottle, good original label, ca. 1940s-60s, 2 1/4" h. (ILLUS.) **$25**

"PAR-fumes" Golf Clubs Novelty Set

Perfume bottle & stopper, "PAR-fumes" by Karoff, three small slender clear tubes w/metal caps shaped like golf clubs, fitted into a plaid cloth golf bag, w/label, ca. 1939, 5 1/2" h. (ILLUS.) **$125**

Novelty "Picanette" Figural Bottle

Perfume bottle & stopper, "Picanette" by Karoff, a clear glass bottle fitted w/a colorful skirt printed w/the faces of blacks, w/a wooden head stopper painted in black w/white & red accents, wearing a wide-brimmed felt hat, ca. 1938, 4 1/8"h. (ILLUS.) **$60-80**

Perfume bottle & stopper, "Queenly Moments" by Duchess of Paris, clear bottle in the form of a bust of Queen Victoria, on a wooden base, ca. 1938, 3 1/2" h. **$28**

Perfume bottle & stopper, "Springtime" by Bouton, designed as a piano formed by two miniature bottles, w/a worn box, ca. 1930s, 2" h. **$60**

Perfume bottle & stopper, "Sweet Pea" by Lander, bottle w/a red plastic tiara-form cap, 1940s, 3 1/2" h. **$20**

"The Duke" Figural Perfume Bottle

Perfume bottle & stopper, "The Duke" by Erte, clear glass in the shape of a standing man w/a mustache holding a cane & wearing a black hat stopper, trimmed in red & white enamel, under a glass dome w/a label, ca. 1930s, 3 7/8" h. (ILLUS.) **$60**

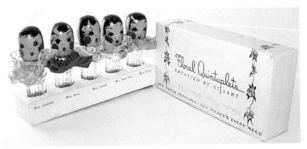

"Floral Quintuplets" Novelty Perfume Bottles Set

Perfume bottle & stopper, "The Winnah," a simple clear glass bottle in a trophy holder, by Artfield Creations, ca. 1940s **$60-75**

Perfume bottle & stopper, "Yesterday" by Babs Creations, glass designed in the shape of a lady holding a cloth bouquet, under a glass dome, ca. 1939, 4 1/4" h. **$35**

Novelty Bottles with Girl Head Stoppers

Perfume bottles & stoppers, "Apple Blossom" & "Gardenia" by Lander, a small ovoid clear glass bottle w/an overall knobby design, each w/a molded head of a girl w/hair forming the stopper, good labels on each, ca. 1940s, 5 1/2" h., each (ILLUS.)... **$35**

Perfume bottles & stoppers, "Castanettes" by Karoff, a set of three small glass bottles each wrapped in cloth & w/a painted wooden head stopper wearing a sombrero, w/original box, ca. 1937, each 2" h., the set (ILLUS., bottom of page) **$110-150**

Perfume bottles & stoppers, "Floral Quintuplets" by Karoff, a set of five small clear cylindrical bottles, each w/a painted wooden head stopper w/a cloth ruffle collar, fitted in original box, ca. 1940s, 2" h., the set (ILLUS., top of page) **$80-110**

"Castanettes" Figural Novelty Perfume Bottles Set

PERFUME, SCENT & COLOGNE BOTTLES

Perfume Atomizer Makers

United States

DeVilbiss

Fine DeVilbiss Four-Piece Dressing Table Set

Dressing table set: perfume bottle & stopper, atomizer, cov. powder box & tray; the perfume & atomizer w/a tall slender gilt-metal stem holding a short bulbous teal blue bottle w/gilt decoration, gilt-metal fitting or stopper, low round matching powder box, all on a round footed gilt-metal 11" d. tray, ca. 1930s, bottles 6 3/4" h., the set (ILLUS., top of page).... **$1,900**

Perfume atomizer & matching perfume bottle, each w/a thin round gold foot & slender swelled tall textured gold stem below an ovoid body in pink glass decorated w/a gilt lattice design trimmed w/stylized black blossoms, each w/gilt-metal fittings, the atomizer w/a gold fabric tube & bulb, the bottle w/a flat-topped stopper, signed "DeVilbiss," ca. 1926, 7" h., pr. (ILLUS.) **$1,560**

Fine DeVilbiss Atomizer & Perfume Set

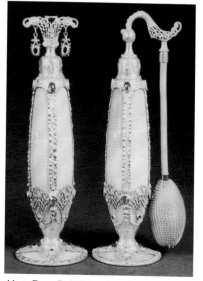

Very Rare DeVilbiss Atomizer-Bottle Set

Perfume atomizer & perfume bottle set, tall slender pale green glass Imperial bottles mounted in ornate gilt-metal filigree frames w/a round green glass foot, jeweled trim, domed top collar, the perfume w/a tall filigree two-armed stopper suspending filigree drops & w/a dauber, the atomizer w/matching top mount suspending original cord & gold mesh-covered bulb, signed, ca. 1920s, 7 7/8" h., pr. (ILLUS.)... **$13,500**

Fine Tall Black & Gold DeVilbiss Atomizer

Perfume atomizer w/fittings, thin round foot below the very tall slender tapering body w/original metal fitting w/a tall acorn-form finial, black background decorated w/thin gold stripes & stylized blossoms w/large orange leaves, marked "DeVilbiss," ca. 1926, 10" h. (ILLUS.) **$2,520**

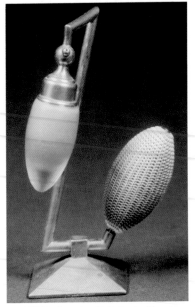

DeVilbiss Angular Debutante Atomizer

Perfume atomizer w/fittings, a rectangular pyramidal gilt-metal foot supporting a tall

angular metal tube suspending a tear-drop-shaped frosted bottle w/internal green paint, the bottom tip w/a gild mesh-covered bulb, unsigned, "Debutante Series," ca. 1928, 6" h. (ILLUS.) **$455**

Metal & Decorated Black Glass Atomizer

Perfume atomizer w/fittings, a round gilt-metal foot & tall slender stem supporting a gently swelled glass bottle enameled in black on the interior & trimmed w/a coral & gold ring & scroll design on the exterior, gilt metal fitting w/original gold tube & mesh-covered bulb, signed, 9 3/8" h. (ILLUS.)...................................... **$390**

DeVilbiss Debutante Perfume Atomizer

Perfume atomizer w/fittings, a round stepped gilt-metal foot supporting a tall slender S-scroll metal stem suspending a black glass bullet-shaped bottle & ending w/a back mesh-covered bulb, unsigned, part of "Debutante Series," ca. 1928, 6" h. (ILLUS., previous page) **$400**

Perfume atomizer w/fittings, blown light blue fading to yellow glass body trimmed w/an elegant jeweled DeVilbiss metal mount, glass made by Imperial, ca. 1920s, 6 7/8" h. (ILLUS.) **$1,700-2,000**

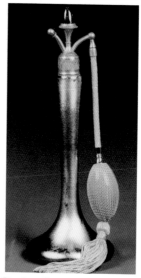

Gold DeVilbiss Atomizer with Label

Fine Steuben Aurene/DeVilbiss Atomizer

Perfume atomizer w/fittings a square glass foot on the upright ovoid body covered w/a textured gold finish, removable stopper w/original bulb, also w/a domed gilt cap, original DeVilbiss paper label, 1920s, 6 1/4" h. (ILLUS.) **$540**

Perfume atomizer w/fittings, blue Steuben Aurene glass container w/a flaring foot tapering to a tall very slender body, gilt-metal fittings w/a black faux jewel acorn finial & gold cord & mesh-covered bulb, signed, early 20th c., 10" h. (ILLUS.) **$900-1,100**

Quezal Gold Atomizer for DeVilbiss

Perfume atomizer w/fittings, deeply waisted cylindrical shape in gold iridescent Quezal glass w/blue highlights, signed by DeVilbiss, ca. 1920s, 6" h. (ILLUS.) **$650**

DeVilbiss Atomizer with Imperial Glass

DeVilbiss Atomizer of Cambridge Glass

Perfume atomizer w/fittings, footed slender tapering ovoid body in Azurite colored Cambridge glass w/an etched urn, scroll & swag decoration, gilt-metal fitting w/acorn-shaped finial, black fabric tube & bulb w/tassel, unsigned DeVilbiss, 1922, 8 5/8" h. (ILLUS.) **$660**

Lenox Penguin-form DeVilbiss Atomizer

Perfume atomizer w/fittings, Lenox porcelain figural bottle in the shape of a penguin topped w/a black felt cape concealing the bulb, signed by DeVilbiss & Lenox, 4 3/8" h. (ILLUS.).......................... **$260**

Steuben Gold Aurene DeVilbiss Atomizer

Perfume atomizer w/fittings, gold Steuben Aurene glass container w/a flat disk foot & a tall tapering cylindrical body, gilt metal fittings w/black tube & mesh-covered bulb, unsigned, early 20th c. 7 1/4" h. (ILLUS.)........................... **$475**

Perfume atomizer w/fittings, "Le Modern," a short domed clear glass container resting on a rectangular gilt-metal base & w/gilt-metal cap w/large round disk supporting the original black bulb, by DeVilbiss, w/original box, ca. 1928, 3" h.......... **$1,800**

DeVilbiss Atomizer with Silvered Metal Fittings

Perfume atomizer w/fittings, round silvered metal foot supporting a tall very slender stem topped by a flared cup supporting a squatty bulbous black glass container fitted w/a silvered cap & stem suspending the black fabric band & original oblong bulb, unsigned DeVilbiss, ca. 1928, 7 5/8" h. (ILLUS.) **$540**

Perfume atomizer w/fittings, small clear asymmetrical block-form glass bottle w/metal collar & fittings topped by a green Bakelite button, original green mesh-covered bulb, signed, w/original quarter-round green leatherette case, early 20th c., 2 1/2" h. (ILLUS., next page).. **$190**

Perfume atomizer w/fittings, tall slender blue opalescent Coin Dot glass patt., made for DeVilbiss by Fenton Art Glass, ca. 1930s-40s, 4" h. **$65**

Fine DeVilbiss Atomizer & Perfume Bottle Set with Original Box

Clear Blocky Glass DeVilbiss Atomizer

gilt-metal mounts, applied Delft blue foot & bottle stopper, probably made for DeVilbiss, 8 1/4" & 8 1/2" h., pr. **$450**

Perfume atomizers w/fittings & perfume bottle & stopper, tall slender gently swelled black glass bottle w/a gold-encrusted round foot & lower body & acid-etched gold leaves up from the base, gilt metal fittings, atomizer w/original black tube & mesh-covered bulb, the perfume bottle w/a disc-form stopper enameled in black on top, w/original textured gold box w/a tassel at the end, ca. 1930s, 7 1/2" h., pr. (ILLUS., top of page) **$1,500-1,750**

Small Green Glass DeVilbiss Perfume

DeVilbiss Purple Glass Atomizer

Perfume atomizer w/fittings, tapering cylindrical deep purple glass bottle w/metal mount fitted w/a purple jewel on top, original mesh-covered bulb, signed, ca. 1930s, 5" h. (ILLUS.) **$90**

Perfume atomizer w/fittings & bottle & stopper, Fry Foval glass body w/applied

Perfume bottle & stopper, squatty bulbous green glass bottle w/a gilt metal collar & disc-form stopper enameled in green, w/dauber, ca. 1940-60, 2 1/2" h. (ILLUS.)
.... **$45-50**

Perfume bottle & stopper, upright octagonal pink glass w/each panel trimmed in gold, metal collar & button stopper w/pink top, w/dauber, unsigned, 4 1/4" (ILLUS., next page) **$70**

DeVilbiss Octagonal Pink Perfume Bottle

DeVilbiss Black & Gold-etched Jar

Powder jar, cov., swelled cylindrical jar w/low domed cover, black enameled jar & cover each heavily decorated w/gold acid-etching & enameling, signed in white enamel, ca. 1920s-30s, 4 1/4" h. (ILLUS.).. **$300**

Volupté

Tall Decorative Volupté Atomizer

Perfume atomizer w/fittings, a clear glass round foot w/gold trim below the baluster- and spiral-twist clear stem supporting the ovoid bottle internally painted w/mauve & decorated on the exterior w/a black & gold geometric design, gilt metal fitting w/gold tube & mesh-covered bulb w/tassel, signed in gold, paper label on bottom reads "24 kt gold plated," 7" h. (ILLUS.) **$520**

Volupté Skyscraper-style Atomizer

Perfume atomizer w/fittings, Art Deco skyscraper design, a long narrow brass stepped base w/two stepped uprights supporting a flattened, ribbed & tiered clear glass skyscraper-form bottle w/brass fitting, mesh-covered bulb suspended in the interior, signed, ca. 1930, 6" h. (ILLUS.) **$750-900**

Art Deco-decorated Volupté Atomizer

Perfume atomizer w/fittings, round flat orange foot supporting a tall very slender bottle internally decorated in yellowish green & enameled on the exterior w/a detailed & colorful Jazz Age Art Deco design in red, green & black, gilt metal mount w/slender black tube & mesh-covered bulb, unsigned, ca. 1930s, 9 1/3" h. (ILLUS.)... **$1,250**

PERFUME, SCENT & COLOGNE BOTTLES

Perfume Bottle Designers

Austria - Czechoslovakia

Hoffman

Austrian Hoffman Black Perfume Bottle

Perfume bottle & stopper, black opaque & clear crystal, the flattened upright design w/a flat bottom & fanned octagonal sides decorated w/a metalwork spider & web design, designed by Hoffman, metal stamped "Austria," clear tall flattened arrow-form stopper, 7 1/4" h. (ILLUS.) **$4,500**

Fine Hoffman Black Crystal Perfume

Perfume bottle & stopper, black opaque crystal, upright flattened octagonal shape centered on each side w/a round malachite glass disk w/a jeweled spider design, matching stopper w/disks, de-

signed by Hoffman, ca. 1920s, 7 1/2" h. (ILLUS.) **$4,800**

Czechoslovakia

Rare Hoffman Bottle with Venus Stopper

Pefume bottle & stopper, cylindrical violet bottle molded w/a continuous band of dancing classical figures, a figural Venus de Milo stopper w/dauber, molded Hoffman butterfly logo & signed, ca. 1920s-30s, 7" h. (ILLUS.) **$3,750**

Blue Hoffman Bottle with Nudes

Pefume bottle & stopper, dark royal blue flattened domed bottle molded w/a female nude, the arched tiara-style stopper also molded w/nudes, signed by Hoffman, ca. 1920s-30s, 6 1/3" h. (ILLUS.) **$2,500-3,000**

Pefume bottle & stopper, footed squatty bulbous bottle in light blue molded around the sides w/blossoms on vines, the tall stopper molded w/two dancers, ca. 1920s-30s, 6 1/8" h. **$2,500-3,000**

Marked Hoffman Disc-form Bottle

Pefume bottle & stopper, light smokey-colored footed upright disc-shaped bottle w/a matching flat round stopper engraved w/a scene of a lady climbing a hill, w/dauber, butterfly logo of Hoffman, ca. 1930s, 6 1/3" h. (ILLUS.)........................... **$950**

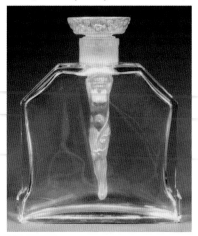

Rare Hoffman Bottle with Nude Dauber

Pefume bottle & stopper, upright flattened clear bottle w/beveled shoulders, small cylindrical neck & pale blue molded button-form stopper w/a long frosted figural nude dauber, Hoffman butterfly mark, 6 1/8" h. (ILLUS.) **$4,300**

Pink Hoffman Bottle w/Figures on Stopper

Pefume bottle & stopper, upright flattened pink square bottle w/beveled corners, the flat octagonal stopper etched w/a scene of a classical woman dancer w/a satyr & cupid, Hoffman butterfly logo, ca. 1930s, 5 3/8" h. (ILLUS.) **$800**

Extremely Rare Smoky Hoffman Bottle

Pefume bottle & stopper, upright flattened smoky square bottle w/beveled corners mounted on a base composed of turquoise panels, a bulbous ovoid stopper also mounted w/turquoise panels & ending in a figural nude female dauber, Hoffman butterfly logo, ca. 1930s, 6 3/8" h. (ILLUS.).. **$25,000**

Lapis Lazuli Flower-form Bottle

Pefume bottle & stopper, upright lapis lazuli crystal boldly molded flower-shaped bottle w/a matching flower stopper, designed by Hoffman, signed "Ingrid - Czechoslovakia," 5 2/3" h. (ILLUS.) **$1,200**

Hoffman Bottle with Nude on Stopper

Perfume bottle & stopper, pale blue crystal w/faceted tapering sides, metal-wrapped neck & tall oval stopper etched w/a dancing nude, on a gilt-metal four-footed jeweled & reeded base, marked in intaglio "Hoffman," 1930s, 6 1/2" h. (ILLUS.) **$3,000**

Green Hoffman Bottle with Filigree

Perfume bottle & stopper, green tapering bottle w/a short neck trimmed w/metal filigree, flat octagonal stopper etched w/a Cupid & Psyche scene & dauber, mounted in a high fancy metal filigree base trimmed w/enamel & a large oval green jewel, marked in intaglio "Hoffman," one jewel chip, 1920s, 3 1/4" h. (ILLUS.) **$1,300-1,600**

Scrolled Pale Purple Czech Bottle

Perfume bottle & stopper, pale purple crystal w/a flattened, arched & scroll-trimmed body, small neck w/gilt-metal band, tall oval flat stopper etched w/a scene of two putti complete w/dauber, fitted w/gilt-metal side panels & foot band enameled in green & trimmed w/jewels, attributed to Hoffman, w/original metal tag reading "Czechoslovakia", 1920s, 6 3/4" h. (ILLUS.) **$1,320**

Hoffman Pink Perfume with Pierced Stopper

Perfume bottle & stopper, pink crystal bottle in a long narrow shape w/angled shoulders, oval frosted pink stopper w/a pierced design of draped nudes, w/dauber, mounted on a four-footed gilt-metal base w/green enameling & a large green jewel, marked in intaglio "Hoffman," 1920s, 6" h. (ILLUS.)..................... **$1,600-2,000**

Rare Shoe-Shaped Czech Perfume Bottle

Perfume bottle & stopper, shoe-shaped black glass w/"jade" knot stopper & enameled & jeweled applied metalwork, Hoffman, stenciled "Made in Czechoslovkia," ca. 1920s, 4 1/2" l. (ILLUS.)........................... **$18,000**

Square Pink Crystal Czech Perfume Bottle

Perfume bottle & stopper, squared pink crystal w/angled shoulder & short neck w/a flat etched stopper w/a Cupid & Psyche scene & dauber, fitted in a filligree metal base decorated w/enameling & jewels, marked in intaglio "Hoffman," 1920s, 6 1/2" h. (ILLUS.).............. **$1,700-2,200**

Unusual Dralle "Tula" Perfume Bottle

Perfume bottle & stopper, "Tula" by Dralle of Germany, designed by Hoffman of Czechoslovakia, a low clear crystal bottle w/a heavily notched rockwork-like design, fitted w/a large upright blue disc stopper etched w/the figure of a kneeling nude male archer, w/paper label, ca. 1930, 5 1/2" h. (ILLUS.) **$1,440**

Perfume bottles & stoppers, clear & frosted crystal in a Modernist design, squatty bulbous oblong bottles w/short neck fitted w/tall rectangular stoppers etched w/female figures, designed by Hoffman, marked "Czechoslovakia," ca. 1930, 7" h., pr. **$2,000-3,000**

Two-bottle Czech Perfume Bottle Set

Perfume bottles & stoppers, green glass, two upright squared bottles w/angled shoulders w/gilt-metal neck band & flattened stoppers etched w/a Cupid & Psyche scene, in a fitted filigree gilt-metal stand, one w/dauber, marked in intaglio "Hoffman," 1920s, 6 1/2" h. (ILLUS.) **$1,500-3,000**

Green Glass Powder Jar on Base

Powder jar, cov., a cylindrical optic ribbed green glass box w/a flat cover etched in intaglio w/a scene of a dancing classical maiden & two cupids, gilt-metal filigree footed base set w/faux jewels, signed w/Hoffman butterfly logo, ca. 1930s, 1 2/3" h. (ILLUS.) **$700**

France

Sue et Mare

"Amour Amour" by Patou Perfume Bottle

Perfume bottle & stopper, "Amour Amour" by Jean Patou, clear glass domed glass bottle w/two labels, gold base & gold raspberry stopper, mint in box, ca. 1925, 3 1/2" h. (ILLUS.) **$350**

Perfume bottle & stopper, "Colony" by Jean Patou, clear glass bottle w/floriform stopper, ca. 1927, 5" h. **$390-425**

Perfume bottle & stopper, "Le Dandy" by D'Orsay, miniature upright flattened octagonal clear glass bottle w/square gold label, gold ball cap, ca. 1926, 1 2/3" h. **$25**

Perfume bottle & stopper, "Le Dandy" by D'Orsay, upright flattened octagonal black glass bottle w/square gold label, ca. 1926, 3" h. **$55**

Perfume bottle & stopper, "Le Dandy" by D'Orsay, upright flattened octagonal black glass bottle w/square gold label, ca. 1926, 3 1/2" h. **$375**

Patou "Normandie" Reissue Bottle

Perfume bottle & stopper, "Normandie" by Jean Patou, reissue of original Louis Sue designed bottle, mint in box, ca. 1980s, 3" h. (ILLUS., previous page) **$635-900**

"Toujours Fidele" Octagonal Bottle

Perfume bottle & stopper, "Toujours Fidele" by D'Orsay, upright flattened octagonal clear glass version of this bottle w/square gold label, mint in original box, ca. 1912, 2 1/2" h. (ILLUS.) **$25-50**

Perfume bottle & stopper, "Vacances" by Jean Patou, clear glass bottle w/upright Jean Patou stopper, mint in box, ca. 1934, 3 3/4" h. **$300**

Julien Viard

"Ambre de Carthage" Enameled Bottle

Perfume bottle & stopper, "Ambre de Carthage" by Isabey, clear flattened round bottle w/dripping orange enamel

on the stopper & down the shoulders, designed by Julien Viard & signed "J Viard," no label, ca. 1926, 2 1/3" h. **$650-700**

Perfume bottle & stopper, "Ambre de Carthage" by Isabey, clear & frosted glass bottle w/molded leaves w/grey stain, designed by Julien Viard & signed "JV," no label, ca. 1926, 3" h. **$355**

Perfume bottle & stopper, "Bleu de Chine" by Isabey, upright cylindrical body w/grey stained panels trimmed w/enameled flowers, designed by Julien Viard & signed "JV," no label, ca. 1926, 5 3/4" h. **$1,500**

Scarce Dubarry "Blue Lagoon" Bottle

Perfume bottle & stopper, "Blue Lagoon" by Dubarry, a J. Viard bottle in clear & frosted glass w/a multicolored patina, squatty four-lobed shape w/Egytian designs between each lobe, small molded hobs on the shoulder, short neck w/a figural stopper of a kneeling Egyptian woman, ca. 1919, 4" h. (ILLUS.) **$4,440**

A Circa 1900 "Bouquet Cavalieri" Bottle

Perfume bottle & stopper, "Bouquet Cavalieri" by Depinoix, a Monna Vanna J. Viard bottle in clear & frosted glass, tapering cylindrical shape w/molded panels trimmed w/enamel up the sides, metal pendant label, original box, ca. 1900, 5" h. (ILLUS., previous page) **$2,400**

Extremely Rare "Enigma" by Lubin Egyptian-style Bottle & Matching Box

Perfume bottle & stopper, "Enigma" by Lubin, a J. Viard bottle in clear glass, flattened triangle shape molded on the side w/an Egyptian sphinx & stylized vertical label in gold, triangular stopper, in original extremely rare decorative box w/a Nile tableau of flowering lotus blossoms inside & the name & an Egyptian scarab on the exterior, ca. 1921, 3 1/2" h. (ILLUS.).................................. **$27,600**

"Eva" Bottle with Figural Stopper

Perfume bottle & stopper, "Eva" by Lubin, bottle design by J. Viard, squatty bulbous clear blue-stained bottle trimmed w/leaf bands, stopper w/figure of Eve sitting

atop a coiled snake, unsigned, 3 3/4" h. (ILLUS.).. **$2,400-2,600**

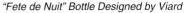

"Fete de Nuit" Bottle Designed by Viard

Perfume bottle & stopper, "Fete de Nuit" by Agnel, black glass paneled bell-shaped bottle w/upturned base, trimmed w/white bands & gold dots, full & sealed, designed by Julien Viard, ca. 1920, 3 1/8" h. (ILLUS.) **$1,250**

Perfume bottle & stopper, "Gotic" by Gueldy, glass decorated w/blue & black enamel, a gold label, designed by Julien Viard & signed, ca. 1922, 4 1/2" h............. **$550**

Rare "Le Prestige" by Gueldy Bottle

Perfume bottle & stopper, "Le Prestige" by Gueldy, J. Viard tall slender cylindrical clear glass bottle w/name in sepia patina around the top, fitted w/a figural sepia kneeling fairy stopper, based molded "J. Viard," w/original box w/hinge tear, ca. 1922, 6 1/8" h. (ILLUS.) **$4,800**

Perfume bottle & stopper, "Les Violettes," clear bottle w/embossed leaves w/a grey stain, designed by Julien Viard & signed "JV," ca. 1923, 5 1/8" h. **$1,859**

"Orchidee" by Depinoix J. Viard Bottle

Perfume bottle & stopper, "Orchidee" by Depinoix, a Renaud - J. Viard container in clear glass w/lavender patina, tapering ovoid shape w/molded stopper, w/label, cord sealed, in original box, ca. 1920s, 4 1/4" h. (ILLUS.) **$2,520**

Scarce "Promenade Matinale" Bottle

Perfume bottle & stopper, "Promenade Matinale" by Arys, J. Viard bottle made by Depinois, a footed flattened w/tapering ovoid shape in clear glass decorated w/frosted & sepia flower & leaf cluster, short neck w/a figural frosted & sepia kneeling nude stopper, w/original label & rectangular box, ca. 1920, 4 5/8" h. (ILLUS.) **$2,400**

"Sous la Charmille" Bottle for Brecher

Perfume bottle & stopper, "Sous la Charmille" by Brecher, a J. Viard bottle made by Depinoix, squatty bulbous clear glass tapering to a small neck & flattened blossom-form stopper, the sides enameled in shades of green & brown w/leaves, ca. 1924, 2 3/4" h. (ILLUS.)..... **$2,520**

Perfume bottle & stopper, "Vers la Joie" by Rigaud, squat frosted clear bottle w/gold trim, blue stopper & gold overcap, designed by Julien Viard, ca. 1927, 3 2/3" h. **$382**

Perfume Bottle Makers

England

Stevens & Williams

Fine Green & Clear Stevens & Williams Perfume

Perfume bottle & stopper, emerald green cut to clear upright bottle w/pinched-in sides (also called the "Kettroff" or "glug-glug"), sterling silver collar & emerald cut to clear ball stopper, cut leafy vine design, by Stevens & Williams, silver hallmarked 1897-98, 7 1/4" h. (ILLUS.) **$2,500-3,000**

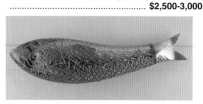

Stevens & Williams Fish-shaped Perfume

Perfume bottle & stopper, novelty fish shape composed of clear glass over mica chips & trimmed w/gold enamel details, unmarked silver tail forming the stopper, Stevens & Williams, ca. 1880, 5 1/2" l. (ILLUS., previous page) **$600-750**

Perfume bottle & stopper, satin glass, honey amber & bittersweet mother-of-pearl Swirl patt., spherical body w/a short flaring neck & matching ball stopper, creamy white interior, attributed to Stevens & Williams, England, late 19th c., 5 1/2" h. (ILLUS. left with other satin and Stevens & Williams perfume bottles, page 83).. **$748**

Perfume bottle w/cap, satin glass, turquoise blue mother-of-pearl Swirl patt., spherical body w/a sterling silver collar & bulbous leaf-cast cap dated Birmingham, England, 1887, bottle attributed to Stevens & Williams (ILLUS. center with other satin and Stevens & Williams perfumes, page 83)..... **$633**

Thomas Webb

Webb Shaded Red Netted Perfume Bottle

Perfume bottle & stopper, boule-shaped deep red shaded to pink cased glass bottle enclosed in gold netting, glossy finish, Thomas Webb & Sons, w/sterling silver collar & hinged cap w/hallmarks for London, 1885-86, 3 1/4" h. (ILLUS.) **$750-900**

Rare Four-Color Webb Cameo Perfume

Perfume bottle & stopper, cameo glass, boule-form four-color cameo bottle, opal cased in citron under red & white, cameo-carved around the body w/leafy blossoming branches, Thomas Webb butterfly emblem on the reverse, hinged sterling silver répoussé cap, ca. 1885, 4 1/2" h. (ILLUS.).. **$4,000-4,500**

Rare Webb Cameo Swan Head Perfume

Perfume bottle & stopper, cameo glass, figural swan's head cameo bottle in blue cased in white & cameo carved, sterling silver overcap on inner glass stopper, cap marked by Keller, Thomas Webb ca. 1885, 9 1/3" l. (ILLUS.)............... **$9,000-12,000**

Webb Green Cameo Teardrop Perfume

Perfume bottle & stopper, cameo glass flattened teardrop form, avocado green ground cased in white & cameo-cut w/trumpet-form blossoms on leafy vines, hinged sterling silver cap marked for Birmingham, 1887, Thomas Webb & Sons, 5" l. (ILLUS.).................................. **$2,400-2,750**

Webb Cameo Teardrop Perfume Bottle

Perfume bottle & stopper, cameo glass flattened teardrop form, teal blue ground cased in white & cameo-cut w/clusters of flowers on leafy vines, unmarked metal cap, Thomas Webb & Sons, some repair, ca. 1890, 3 1/3" l. (ILLUS.).............. **$900**

Webb Red Cameo Lay-down Perfume

Perfume bottle & stopper, cameo glass, flattened teardrop lay down-type, deep red cased in white & cameo-carved w/large blossoms on leafy stems, screw-off repoussé sterling silver cap, unsigned Thomas Webb, ca. 1890-1900, 4 1/2" l. (ILLUS.)... **$2,000**

Webb Novelty Egg with Chicken Head Perfume

Perfume bottle & stopper, novelty-type, a blown mottled egg yolk yellow egg-shaped bottle w/applied clear feet & fitted at the top w/a metal chicken head cap, Thomas Webb & Sons, ca. 1890, 4 1/4" h. (ILLUS.) **$400-500**

Two Fine English Perfume Bottles

Perfume bottle w/cap, cameo glass, lay-down type, flattened tapering form in dark green overlaid in white & cameo carved w/a butterly, sprigs & leaves, hallmarked sterling silver collar & ronded hinged cap, Thomas Webb & Sons, ca. 1890s, 4 1/2" l. (ILLUS. left with Thomas Webb perfume bottle).. **$1,434**

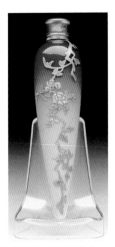

Fine Webb Shaded Pink Scent Bottle

Decorated Queen's Burmese Perfume

Perfume bottle w/cap, Queen's Burmese art glass, boule-shaped in salmon pink shaded to cream, enameled w/stylized leaves & berries trimmed in gold, silver cap w/English silver hallmarks for 1885, Thomas Webb, 3 1/4" h. (ILLUS.) **$1,500-2,000**

Scent bottle w/cap, art glass, lay-down type w/long pointed teardrop form in deep red shaded to pink & enameled in gold & white w/a long leafy stem w/blossoms & a gold butterfly, Thomas Webb, minor gold wear, 6 1/2" l. (ILLUS.) **$690**

Blue Cameo Thomas Webb Scent Bottle

Scent bottle & stopper, cameo glass, spherical body in light blue overlaid in white & cameo-carved w/a blue flower, leaves & branch, the reverse w/a different flower, three buds, leaves & branch, sterling collar & cap marked "Theodore B. Starr Sterling," bottle by Thomas Webb, 2 3/4" h. (ILLUS.) **$1,495**

Rare Webb Cameo Scent Bottle

Scent bottle w/cap, cameo glass, lay-down type w/a pointed teardrop shape, deep red overlaid in white & cameo-carved w/water lilies & a dragonfly, original gold-washed metal screw-on cap w/répoussé designs, 3 1/4" l. (ILLUS.) **$3,335**

France

Almeric Walter

Argy Rousseau Atomizer with Violets

Rare Walter Pate de Verre Atomizer

Perfume atomizer w/fittings, pate de verre, upright cylindrical form travel-type in shades of blue & a touch of orange molded w/stylized flowers, gilt-metal fittings, signed by Almeric Walter, ca. 1900-1910, 4 1/2" h. (ILLUS.) **$4,000-4,200**

Argy Rousseau
Perfume atomizer w/fittings, pate de verre, upright flat-bottomed tapering ovoid shaped w/a mottled pale green ground molded w/dark blue & green violets, gilt metal fittings, signed by Argy Rousseau, ca. 1920s 5 1/2" h. (ILLUS., top next column)........................... **$1,500-3,000**

Perfume atomizer w/fittings, pate de verre, upright pear-shaped body in mottled brown carved near the base w/a wide band of red poppies & amber foliage, original hardware & replacement black fabric-covered bulb, glass signed "G. Argy-Rousseau" in cameo, overall 6" h. (ILLUS., second from top next column)... **$3,600**

Fine Pate de Verre Perfume Atomizer

Baccarat
Dressing table set: five clear etched containers in an ornate gilt-bronze frame, includes two cylindrical bottles w/pointed stopper, two cylindrical atomizers & a central cylindrical covered box, Baccarat, ca. 1900, tallest 8" h., the set (ILLUS., bottom of page)............... **$6,000-7,000**

Rare Baccarat Five-Container Dressing Table Set in Frame

"Ideal" by Houbigant in Baccarat Bottle

Eau de toilette bottle & stopper, "Ideal" by Houbigant, upright square clear glass bottle w/faceted metal screw-on cap, unsigned by Baccarat, ca. 1900, 2 7/8" h. (ILLUS.).. **$25-30**

Perfume atomizer w/fittings, clear acid-etched glass decorated w/gilt swags, metal fittings, marked "Baccarat - MF (Marcel Franck)," ca. 1920s, 12" h... **$900-1,000**

Baccarat-attributed Panel Cut Atomizer

Perfume atomizer w/fittings, clear cylindrical crystal cut w/panels trimmed in gold, gilt-metal fitting & bulb, unmarked, attributed to Baccarat, ca. 1920s-30s, 6" h. (ILLUS.).. **$210**

Baccarat Atomizer with Flower Baskets

Perfume atomizer w/fittings, clear ovoid bottle enameled in dark blue w/oblong reserves enclosing baskets of flowers, banded trim & scattered tiny blossoms, metal fittings missing the bulb, signed "Baccarat - M Franck," ca. 1930s, 5 3/8" h. (ILLUS.) **$175-225**

Perfume bottle & stopper, "1000 Joies" by Myon, opaque green slag glass bottle w/dented brass overcap, no label, signed by Baccarat, ca. 1933, 3 7/8" h. **$710**

"12-34" by Premet Bottle by Baccarat

Perfume bottle & stopper, "12-34" by Premet, Baccarat upright rectangular clear glass bottle w/short neck w/facet-cut knob stopper, sealed, w/original label & silk-lined box, paper label w/"Baccarat," ca. 1910, 4 1/4" h. (ILLUS.) **$650-1,000**

"A Travers Champs" Bottle by Baccarat

Perfume bottle & stopper, "A Travers Champs" by Guerlain, a Baccarat container in clear glass, upright flattened ovoid shape w/frosted figural stopper, w/label, cord sealed, in original marbleized box, base marked "Baccarat," ca. 1924, 5" h. (ILLUS.) **$1,080**

Rare Baccarat Pink Bottle for "Astris" by Piver

Perfume bottle & stopper, "Astris" by Piver, a Baccarat upright hexagonal pink glass bottle w/button stopper, w/original large silver star-shaped label on the side, matching box, bottom stenciled "Baccarat," ca. 1927, 2 3/4" h. (ILLUS.) **$7,800**

Early Baccarat Bottle for "Astris"

Perfume bottle & stopper, "Astris" by L.T. Piver, clear upright square clear glass bottle w/beveled corners & a facet-cut stopper, trimmed w/gilt-metal bands & a medallion label on one side, signed by Baccarat, ca. 1908, 4 2/3" h. (ILLUS.).. **$300-400**

"Astris" by Piver Bottle by Baccarat

Perfume bottle & stopper, "Astris" by Piver, Baccarat upright clear glass bottle w/beveled corners, short neck w/face-cut knob stopper, in a decorative openwork gilt-metal holder, original fitted paper box w/some edge wear, ca. 1912 (ILLUS.) **$1,100-1,500**

Early Baccarat #1 Decorated Bottle

Perfume bottle & stopper, Baccarat #1 cylindrical clear bottle used for Violet & Oriza Legrand scents, decorated w/an overall design of black dots & black & yellow rings, flattened disc upright stopper, no brand label, signed by Baccarat, late 19th - early 20th c., 3 3/4" h. (ILLUS.)............ **$400**

"Caractère" & "Tendance" Baccarat Bottles

Perfume bottle & stopper, "Caractère" by Bruyere, clear square upright glass bottle w/beveled corners, short neck & faceted button stopper, original label, signed by Baccarat, ca. 1920s, 4 1/4" h. (ILLUS. right with Tendance bottle)........................ **$125**

"Bellodgia" by Caron Bottle by Baccarat

Perfume bottle & stopper, "Bellodgia" by Caron, short clear rectangular faceted bottle w/faceted knob stopper, good label, original box, unsigned by Baccarat, ca. 1927, 2 1/2" h. (ILLUS.) **$50-75**

Fine "Cascade" Bottle Made by Baccarat

Perfume bottle & stopper, "Cascade" by Gravier, Baccarat bottle in clear & frosted crystal w/pale green patina, the round upright three-tiered shape topped by a frosted figural dolphin stopper, bottom stenciled "Baccarat," 4 1/2" h. (ILLUS.) **$3,360**

Baccarat Turtle Bottle for Guerlain

Perfume bottle & stopper, "Champs Élysées" by Guerlain, a Baccarat bottle in clear glass, figural design of a turtle, a limited edition, w/orignal label, ca. 1904, original box not shown, 4 1/2" h. (ILLUS.) **$800-1,250**

Baccarat Etched Clear & Citron Bottle

Perfume bottle & stopper, clear cylindrical bottle w/narrow shoulder & short neck, flashed w/citron & acid-cut overall w/a design of leafy vines, by Baccarat, similar

bottles produced by Saint Lous & Val St. Lambert, ca. 1900, 6" h. (ILLUS.) **$350-400**

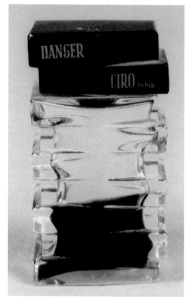

Baccarat Bottle for "Danger" by Ciro

Perfume bottle & stopper, "Danger" by Ciro, clear upright rectangular bottle in the form of staggered tiers, inner stopper & black crystal overcap, marked by Baccarat, ca. 1938, 3 1/8" h. (ILLUS.) **$100-150**

"Désir du Coeur" by Ybry Square Bottle

Perfume bottle & stopper, "Désir du Coeur" by Ybry, a Baccarat bottle in dark pink, an upright square w/a square red-enameled stopper at one corner, in box w/R. Lalique glass pendant & tassel, ca. 1926, 4" h. (ILLUS.) **$3,250**

"Devinez" by Ybry Bottle by Baccarat

Perfume bottle & stopper, "Devinez" by Ybry, flattened diamond-shaped bottle in opaque orange glass w/gilt metal round label on the side, orange metal overcap & inner stopper, w/original leather case, unsigned by Baccarat, ca. 1927, 2 1/8" h. (ILLUS.)... **$860-975**

Perfume bottle & stopper, "Diorissimo" by Christian Dior, a Baccarat clear glass bottle w/a tapering pedestal base below the ribbed ovoid body tapering to the gilded bronze rim & stopper topped by a gilded metal tall spray of roses & leaves, gilded label, in luxurious box w/interior satin, bottle base stenciled "Baccarat," ca. 1951, 8 1/2" h.. **$2,100**

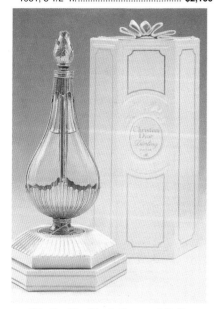

"Diorling" by Dior in Baccarat Bottle

Perfume bottle & stopper, "Diorling" by Dior, footed clear glass flask-shaped bottle w/heavy gilt-metal trim & a metal flower bud stopper, signed & numbered, w/box, 7 1/4" h. (ILLUS.) **$1,800-2,200**

Baccarat Opaline & Filigree Bottle

Perfume bottle & stopper, flattened ovoid white opaline bottle decorated at the shoulder w/ornate pierced scrolling gold filigree set w/tiny turquoise stones, hinged domed & scroll-engraved cap set w/tiny turquoise stones, by Baccarat, 3 3/4" h. (ILLUS.) **$3,000**

Baccarat Bottle for "Jasmin" by Mury

Perfume bottle & stopper, "Jasmin" by Mury, a Baccarat bottle in a conical form,

clear glass w/an enameled cobalt blue spiral down the sides, flared rim, clear ball stopper, ca. 1917, 4" h. (ILLUS.)
.... **$1,500-2,200**

Unusual Elephant-form "Kismet" Bottle

Perfume bottle & stopper, "Kismet" by Lubin, a Baccarat bottle in clear glass, figural design of an elephant w/black draping down the sides, the frosted stopper in the shape of its rider, base stenciled "Baccarat," ca. 1921, 4 1/8" h. (ILLUS.)
.... **$6,500-9,000**

Baccarat "L'Heure Romantique" Bottle

Perfume bottle & stopper, "L'Heure Romantique" by Corday, a Baccarat clear flattened arched bottle w/a deep fluted gold base band & gilt paneled gilt stopper, base stenciled "Baccarat," ca. 1928, 3" h. (ILLUS.) **$390**

Baccarat "L'Ocean Bleu" Dolphins Bottle

Perfume bottle & stopper, "L'Ocean Bleu" by Lubin, clear figural glass bottle designed as a pair of upright dolphins w/their tails touching, open center, small neck w/clear ball stopper, signed & numbered by Baccarat, designed for the Paris 1925 Exposition des Arts Decoratifs, ca. 1925, 6 1/8" h. (ILLUS.) **$375-400**

Baccarat "Le Parfum Ideal" Bottle

Perfume bottle & stopper, "Le Parfum Ideal" by Houbigant, upright square clear Baccarat glass bottle w/rounded shoulders, faceted button stopper, embossed gold label, w/original fabric-covered box, unsigned by Baccarat, ca. 1900, 4 1/8" (ILLUS.)... **$100-145**

Cut-Overlay Baccarat Bottle for Dior

1980s Limited Edition "Metal" Bottle

Perfume bottle & stopper, "Metal" by Paco Rabanne, a Baccarat clear flat upright rectangular bottle w/silvered metal mounts & rectangular block stopper, gilded label, in gold box & white outer box, base stenciled "Baccarat - Limited Edition - No. 437," ca. 1980, 5 3/4" h. (ILLUS.) **$2,100-2,800**

Perfume bottle & stopper, "Ming Toy" by Forest, designed as the figure of a seated Oriental lady, clear glass w/blue & gold enameling, signed & numbered by Baccarat, ca. 1923, 4 1/3" h. (ILLUS., top next column)................................. **$2,900-3,300**

Perfume bottle & stopper, "Miss Dior" by Dior, cut-overlay footed ovoid body in white cut to clear w/gold enameled details, matching cut ovoid stopper, mint in original satin-lined box, signed & numbered by Baccarat, 7" h. (ILLUS., top of page) **$1,500-2,000**

Perfume bottle & stopper, Molinard clear glass square bottle w/raised squares on each side, matching square stopper, used for several scents, no label, signed by Baccarat, ca. 1934, 4 1/2" h. (ILLUS., bottom next column).................................... **$125**

"Ming Toy" Figural Baccarat Perfume Bottle

Square Glass Baccarat Bottle for Molinard

Rare Baccarat Factice Bottle for Gabilla

Perfume bottle & stopper, "Mon Talisman" by Gabilla, a Baccarat factice footed ovoid opaque white glass bottle, the lower portion divided into panels below a scalloped band all trimmed in gold, the upper body molded in relief w/stylized flower blossoms, short cylindrical flared neck w/a gilt-trimmed cupped stopper centered by a gold ball, name printed in gold on the side, stenciled "Baccarat," minor gilt wear, ca. 1928, 10 3/4" h. (ILLUS.)....................... **$4,500**

Unusual Baccarat Bottle for "Muguet"

Perfume bottle & stopper, "Muguet" by Maudy, a Baccarat square crystal bottle w/the beveled corners decorated w/sil-

very grey stylized florals, the domed decorated cap w/four open arches ending at each rim corner, base stenciled "Baccarat," ca. 1928, 3 1/4" h. (ILLUS.) **$2,200-3,500**

"Black Glass Baccarat "Notturno" Bottle"

Perfume bottle & stopper, "Notturno" by Mury, a Baccarat upright black glass disk w/the name molded & trimmed in gold on the side, tiny gold neck & lobed ball stopper, base stenciled "Baccarat," ca. 1926, 3 3/8" h. (ILLUS.) **$400-650**

Houbigant "Premier Mai" Baccarat Bottle

Perfume bottle & stopper, "Premier Mai" by Houbigant, a Baccarat clear rectangular bottle w/rounded shoulder & short neck w/large button stopper, original label & silk-lined box, "Baccarat" paper label, ca. 1908, 4" h. (ILLUS.) **$650-1,000**

metal mounts, interior stopper present, in lavender suede box, molded "RL" on the metal, ca. 1912, 5 3/8" h. (ILLUS.) **$4,200**

"Rue Royale" by Molyneux Bottle

Perfume bottle & stopper, "Rue Royale" by Molyneux, clear cylindrical bottle w/tapering shoulder & short cylindrical neck w/flared rim, flat disc-form clear stopper, mint in original box, signed by Baccarat, ca. 1938, 4 1/3" (ILLUS.) **$200**

Rare Figural Pharoah Head Perfume

Perfume bottle & stopper, "Ramses IV" by Ramses, a J. Viard bottle in frosted clear glass w/a grey patina, figural design of an ancient Egyptian pharaoh's head w/a ball & feather stopper, ca. 1919, base stenciled "Baccarat," 4 3/4" h. (ILLUS.)
.... **$6,500-8,500**

Baccarat Bottle for "Ta Wao" by Madhva

Perfume bottle & stopper, "Ta Wao" by Madhva, a Baccarat container designed by J. Viard, wide thin disk-form base tapering sharply w/fluted sides enameled in gold below the black disk stopper w/original bead on stopper, base marked "Baccarat," ca. 1923, 2 1/2" h. (ILLUS.) .. **$6,000**

Perfume bottle & stopper, "Tendance" by Bruyere, clear square upright glass bottle w/beveled corners, short neck & faceted button stopper, original label, signed by Baccarat, ca. 1920s, 4 1/4" h. (ILLUS. left with Caractère bottle, page 181) **$125**

Scarce Baccarat-Lalique "Roses" Bottle

Perfume bottle & stopper, "Roses" by D'Orsay, a Baccarat bottle designed by Julien Viard, in frosted glass, slender cylindrial form w/an applied band of R. Lalique metalwork around the base, gilt-

Early Plassard Bottle Made by Baccarat

Perfume bottle & stopper, "Une Femme Passa" by Plassard, a Baccarat tapering ovoid clear crystal bottle w/an overall etched floral surface centered by a gold & white label, matching mushroom stopper, ca. 1911, 4 3/4" h. (ILLUS.) **$1,200-1,400**

Very Rare Baccarat Bottle for Delettrez

Perfume bottle & stopper, "XII" by Delettrez, a Baccarat container in molded pink opaque glass, a narrow upright rectangular form w/a molded oblong stopper, w/label, in original hand-painted box, first appearance of this bottle, base marked "Baccarat," ca. 1927, 4 1/2" h. (ILLUS.)................................. **$24,000**

Perfume bottles & stoppers, Baccarat Rose Tiente cylindrical bottles in the Swirl patt., two w/the Baccarat logo, 4 2/3" h., 6" h., 7" h., set of 3 .... **$550**

Guerlain "Vega" Bottle by Baccarat

Perfume bottle & stopper, "Vega" by Guerlain, Baccarat crystal bottle in a short slightly tapering ringed design w/a rounded shoulder to a small neck w/a knob stopper, resting on an octagonal base, sealed, in original octagonal box, bottled base stenciled "Baccarat," ca. 1926, 3" h. (ILLUS.).. **$1,200-2,100**

Houbigant Three Bottle Set in Holder

Perfume bottles & stoppers, Houbigant set of three square upright clear glass bottle w/faceted button stopper, in a fitted metal tantalus holder w/lock & key, unsigned by Baccarat, 2 3/4" h., the set (ILLUS.) **$125**

Rare Baccarat Boxed Set of Perfume Bottles & Atomizers for Ybry

Perfume bottles & stoppers & atomizers, Baccarat set for Ybry, three flattened diamond-shaped bottles in orange, green & deep rose glass & two small triangular atomizers in dark green & dark blue glass, complete in fitted suede case, signed by Baccarat, ca. 1920s, the set (ILLUS., top of page) **$7,000-8,000**

D'Argental

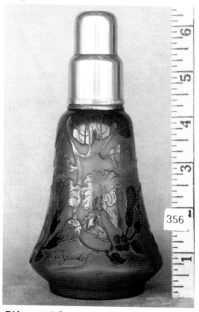

D'Argental Cameo Glass Perfume Burner

Perfume burner, cameo glass, footed tapering cylindrical bottle in dark yellow overlaid in dark red & cameo-carved w/leafy flowering vines, signed in cameo "d'Argental," ca. 1910-25, 7" h. (ILLUS.) **$1,500**

Daum - Nancy

Daum Nancy Cameo Glass Atomizer

Perfume atomizer w/fittings, cameo glass, bulbous tapering body in mottled amber carved & enameled in color w/leafy branches & red berries, original metal fittings but no cord or bulb, Daum - Nancy, ca. 1905-15, 6 1/2" h. (ILLUS.)
.... **$2,500-2,750**

Perfume atomizer w/fittings, cameo glass, cylindrical body in pink cased in white & carved & enameled w/trees, frosted glass ball stopper, signed by Daum - Nancy w/the Cross of Lorraine, 6" h......... **$1,900-2,200**

Fine Daum Nancy Cameo Perfume Bottle

Scent bottle & stopper, cameo glass, cylindrical body in rare raisin color cased in clear & cameo-carved w/a design of fleur de lis trimmed in gold, cylindrical chased silver cap set w/small turquoise stones, Daum - Nancy, ca. 1892, 3" h. (ILLUS.) **$3,000-4,000**

Fine Daum Cameo Scent Bottle

Scent bottle & stopper, Daum - Nancy cameo glass, spherical white body tapering to a short neck w/a clear stopper w/faceted edges trimmed in gold, the body cameo-cut & enameled w/a leafy vine of shaded red flowers & buds framing a black & white enameled scene of a road leading to a village, base signed w/etched signature, very small old chip inside lip, small flake on corner of stopper, 3 1/4" h. (ILLUS.) **$2,185**

DeVez

Daum Nancy Cameo Scent Bottle

Scent bottle & stopper, cameo glass, wide ovoid amethyst body w/a small cylindrical neck, cameo-carved w/floral blossoms & leaves trimmed in gold, frosted clear ball stopper, signed on bottom by Daum Nancy, late 19th - early 20th c., 6" h. (ILLUS.) **$1,035**

Fine DeVez Cameo Glass Atomizer

Perfume atomizer w/fittings, French cameo glass bottle w/a sharply tapering slender shape, light grey ground overlaid in dark green & cameo-carved w/leafy vines framing a lakeside landscape, signed "DeVez," ca. 1910-20, 11 1/2" h. (ILLUS.) **$1,500**

Franck (Marcel)

French Spatter Glass Perfume Atomizer

Perfume atomizer w/fittings, boule-shaped glass in a bold colorful spatter design in shades of orange, yellow, green, red & blue, metal collar & fittings w/black cord & mesh-covered bulb, metal mount marked "Marcel Franck - Brevete - SGDG," 5 1/2" h. (ILLUS.)..................... **$75-100**

Perfume atomizer w/fittings, cylindrical crystal cut in a hobstar, fan & zipper cut design, cylindrical silver plate mount w/plunger top, mount marked "Marcel Franck," ca. 1920s-30s, 4 1/4" h. (ILLUS. left with other cylindrical Franck atomizer).. **$100-125**

Two Cut Cylindrical Franck Atomizers

Perfume atomizer w/fittings, cylindrical crystal cut in an overall block design, cylindrical silver plate mount w/cord & bulb, mount marked "Marcel Franck," ca. 1920s-30s, 3 7/8" h. (ILLUS. right with other cylindrical Franck atomizer)....... **$100-125**

Two Marcel Franck Cut Atomizers

Perfume atomizer w/fittings, low rectangular clear cut crystal bottle w/metal mount marked "Marcel Franck Escale," ca. 1920-40, 3 1/2" h. (ILLUS. right with taller Franck atomizer)........... **$75-100**

Franck Goldtone Purse Atomizer

Perfume atomizer w/fittings, purse-sized, goldtone metal, flattened tapering pyramidal form w/a round dial device at the bottom front, pointed metal cap, ca. 1950s, 2 7/8" h. (ILLUS.)........................ **$35-40**

Perfume atomizer w/fittings, tall upright paneled circular clear cut crystal bottle w/metal mount marked "Marcel Franck Escale," ca. 1920-40, 5" h. (ILLUS. left with shorter Franck atomizer, previous page)... **$75-100**

Gallé

Gallé Cameo Perfume Atomizer

Perfume atomizer w/fittings, cameo glass, flat-bottomed ovoid shape tapering to the metal fittings missing the bulb, powder blue ground overlaid in purple & cameo carved w/boysenberries, vines & leaves, signed on the side by Gallé, late 19th - early 20th c., 5" h. (ILLUS.) **$690**

Gallé Cameo Glass Perfume Atomizer

Perfume atomizer w/fittings, slender slightly tapering cylindrical cameo glass form in light yellow ground overlaid in dark red & cameo-carved w/a design of

leafy branches w/berries, modern replacement metal fittings & yellow cord & silk-covered bulb, Gallé, signed in cameo, ca. 1920s, 9 3/4" h. (ILLUS.) **$550**

Perfume atomizer w/fittings, slender slightly tapering cylindrical cameo glass form w/a gold ground overlaid in brown & cameo-cut w/a design of flowering shrubs, Gallé, signed in cameo, ca. 1910-1920, 8" h. **$2,500**

Early Gallé Enameled Perfume Bottle

Perfume bottle & stopper, footed ovoid clear glass bottle w/a short neck & button stopper, enameled around the sides w/dark blue & purple blossoms w/slender green leaves & a butterfly to the side, signed by Gallé, ca. 1870-80, 3 3/4" h. (ILLUS.)... **$1,750-2,000**

Gallé Cameo Scent Bottle

Scent bottle w/cap, cameo glass, bulbous creamy white ground overlaid in orange & cameo-carved w/large flowers & leafy vines, a silver band on the small neck w/hinged cap opening to the original glass stopper, raised on a silver foot band, silver marked "C & M" & rearing lion & "G" in a shield, signed in cameo on the side, 5 1/2" h. (ILLUS., previous page) **$1,438**

Lalique

R. Lalique Atomizer Made for D'Heraud

Perfume atomizer w/fittings, for D'Heraud, a Lalique clear glass container, gently tapering squared form molded at each corner w/a vertical band of stylized leaves trimmed w/a black patina, original gilt-metal hardware, hose & hardened rubber bulb, molded "R. Lalique," ca. 1924, 6 1/2" h. (ILLUS.) **$1,140**

"L'Air du Temps" Atomizer by Lalique

Perfume atomizer w/fittings, "L'Air du Temps" by Nina Ricci, a Lalique clear & frosted glass container, short cylindrical shape decorated w/a soaring bird, w/atomizer fittings & bulb, in deluxe suede & fabric outer box, engraved "Lalique," 1950s, 3 1/2" h. (ILLUS.) **$1,020**

Lalique "Le Parisien" Perfume Atomizer

Perfume atomizer w/fittings, "Le Parisien" patt., frosted clear cylindrical shaped molded w/a repeated design of standing nude ladies & garlands, metal tapering collar & plunger top, glass signed "R. Lalique," metal stamped "SGDG," ca. 1920s, 7 1/3" h. (ILLUS.) **$650**

"Le Provencale" by Molinard Atomizer

Perfume atomizer w/fittings, "Le Provencale" by Molinard, a bulbous frosted clear bottle molded w/a continuous band of female nudes, metal fittings, etched signa-

ture "Molinard - Lalique - France," ca. 1940s, 5 1/3" h. (ILLUS.)............................ **$750**
Perfume bottle & stopper, "5 Fleurs" by Forvil, a Lalique perfume bottle in clear & frosted glass w/a grey patina, tall upright square shaped w/short neck & square stopper, cord sealed, molded "R. Lalique," ca. 1929, 4" h. **$3,600**

Rare Lalique "Amphitrite" Perfume

Perfume bottle & stopper, "Amphitrite," green glass in an upright snail shell design w/a small figural stopper, engraved "R. Lalique - France," a. 1920, 3 1/2" h. (ILLUS.).. **$5,100**

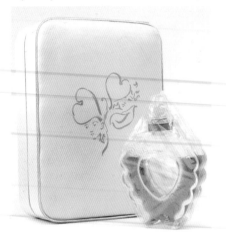

Lalique Bottle for "Coeur Joie" by Ricci

Perfume bottle & stopper, "Coeur Joie" by Nina Ricci, a Lalique frosted glass container, designed as an upright heart w/a scalloped border & large heart-shaped

center opening, sealed, in early silk box w/Christian Berard graphics, enameled "Lalique," 1940s, 4 3/4" h. (ILLUS.)..... **$550-800**
Perfume bottle & stopper, "Coeur Joie" by Nina Ricci, clear open heart-shaped bottle w/molded flowers, signed by Lalique, ca. 1946, 4" h. **$75-200**

Early "Cyclamen" by Coty Lalique Bottle

Perfume bottle & stopper, "Cyclamen" by Coty, a Lalique perfume bottle in clear & frosted glass w/a green patina, tall upright gently tapering shape w/short neck & disc stopper, w/original leather box, molded "R. Lalique," ca. 1909, 5 3/4" h. (ILLUS.).. **$3,900**

Round Lalique Perfume Bottle

Perfume bottle & stopper, "Dans La Nuit" by Worth, matte blue glass, round shape decorated w/randomly spaced & sized cameo stars on matte blue ground, matching stopper, bottle signed on bottom "R. Lalique," stopper held in place w/original metallic rope ties, each w/paper label reading "Worth, Paris" on one side & "Dans La Nuit" on other, in original box, wear to labels, box w/some wear & looseness to hinge, 3" h. (ILLUS.) **$403**

Rare "Elegance" Bottle by Lalique

Perfume bottle & stopper, "Elegance" by D'Orsay, a Lalique bottle in frosted glass w/a brown patina, upright flattened square shape w/an overall molded design of frolicking female figures, partial label, molded "R. Lalique," ca. 1914, 3 3/4" h. (ILLUS.) **$4,200**

Ricci "Farouche" Bottle by Lalique

Perfume bottle & stopper, "Farouche" by Nina Ricci, clear flattened round bottle w/an octagonal disc-form stopper, full & sealed, signed by Lalique in the mold, w/original red flocked box, ca. 1974, 3 3/8" h. (ILLUS.) **$110**

Smaller "Farouche" Lalique Bottle

Perfume bottle & stopper, "Farouche" by Nina Ricci, clear flattened round bottle w/an octagonal disc-form stopper, full & sealed, signed by Lalique in the mold, w/original red flocked box, 2 2/3" h. (ILLUS.)........................ **$88**

"Fille d'Eve" Apple-shaped Lalique Bottle

Perfume bottle & stopper, "Fille d'Eve" by Nina Ricci, frosted clear glass in the shape of an apple w/two clear leaves forming the stopper, signed by Lalique, ca. 1952 (ILLUS.) **$70-130**

Roger & Gallet "Flausa" Bottle by Lalique

Perfume bottle & stopper, "Flausa" by Roger & Gallet, clear & frosted Lalique bottle w/sepia patina, flattened ovoid body molded w/the seated figure of a half-nude classical maiden, molded "Lalique" on the button-form stopper, matching engraved control numbers, ca. 1914, 4 3/4" h. (ILLUS.) **$4,200**

Rare Lalique Frosted Glass Perfume

Perfume bottle & stopper, "Fleurs de Pommier" by Bouchon, Lalique frosted clear w/blue patina, the ovoid body molded w/bands of graduated arches, the high arched & pierced long stopper

molded w/a flowering tree, stopper engraved "R. Lalique - 939," matching number on the base, introduced in 1919, 5 1/2" h. (ILLUS.) **$10,755**

Lalique "Hélène" Bottle, Circa 1950

Perfume bottle & stopper, "Hélène," a Lalique frosted & clear container, squared shape w/four side panels molded w/a kneeling woman, large cylindrical ribbed cap enclosing the stopper, stenciled "Lalique - France," ca. 1950, 5 1/2" h. (ILLUS.) **$720**

R. Lalique "Imprudence" Bottle

Perfume bottle & stopper, "Imprudence" by Worth, a Lalique factice bottle in clear glass w/a tapering cylindrical boldly ringed design w/silver edge detail, small tapering stopper, base molded "R. Lalique," ca. 1938, 9 1/2" h. (ILLUS.) **$1,440**

Lalique Bottle for "Je Reviens" by Worth

Perfume bottle & stopper, "Je Reviens" by Worth, a Lalique blue & opaque blue glass container, upright cylindrical sky-scraper design w/ribbed sides & a stepped shoulder, blue domed stopper, in fitted silvered metal hexagonal case, ca. 1931, 5 1/2" h. (ILLUS.) **$1,800**

Perfume bottle & stopper, "L'Air du Temps" by Nina Ricci, clear round swirled glass bottle w/figural frosted peach stopper composed of a pair of flying birds, limited edition, mint in box, ca. 1990s, 3 1/2" h. **$165**

Perfume bottle & stopper, "L'Air du Temps" by Nina Ricci, clear round swirled glass bottle w/figural frosted stopper composed of flying birds, ca. 1948, signed by Lalique **$400**

Rare Early Lalique-Coty Perfume Bottle

Perfume bottle & stopper, "L'Effleur" by Coty, a Lalique bottle in clear & frosted glass w/a black patina, upright flattened rectangular shape w/a rectangular panel molded w/a mermaid among swirling waves, clear faceted ball stopper, applied "Lalique" glass label, first collaboration between Coty & René Lalique, ca. 1908, 4 1/2" h. (ILLUS.) **$3,600-4,500**

Rare Lalique Figural "La Phalène" Bottle

Perfume bottle & stopper, "La Phalène" by D'Heraud, a Lalique clear & frosted Amberina glass container, molded as a tiny nymph w/butterfly wings, flattened round stopper, molded "R. Lalique," ca. 1925, 3 1/2" h. (ILLUS.) **$7,200**

Burmann "La Sirene" Bottle by Lalique

Perfume bottle & stopper, "La Sirene" by Burmann, clear sharply tapering cylindrical clear glass bottle w/a small oblong concave panel w/a mermaid, disc-form stopper, ca. 1929, 4 1/3" h. (ILLUS.) **$2,750**

Lalique "Amelie" Pattern Perfume

Perfume bottle & stopper, Lalique "Amelie" patt., squatty bulbous clear frosted bottle w/a pale green patina, molded w/a design of graduated rows of overlapping leaves, molded & engraved "R. Lalique," ca. 1930s, 3" h. (ILLUS.) **$2,000**

Very Rare Lalique Clear & Red Perfume

Perfume bottle & stopper, Lalique "Bouchon Fleurs de Pommier" patt., gently swelled clear cylindrical bottle w/panels outlined in thin red stripes, very rare large arched & flower-molded stopper, signed "R. Lalique," ca. 1910-20, 5 2/3" h. (ILLUS. Too rare to price)

Perfume bottle & stopper, Lalique "Camilla" patt., squatty clear frosted bottle w/a blue patina, molded w/a design of deep ridges, signed "R. Lalique," ca. 1927, 2 1/2" h. **$550**

Nearly Unique "Orielles Lezards" Bottle

Perfume bottle & stopper, Lalique "Orielles Lezards" patt., heart-shaped clear bottle molded down each side w/lizards, flattened & arched molded stopper, only two known to exist, ca. 1912, 4 1/4" h. (ILLUS. Too rare to price)

Perfume bottle & stopper, Lalique "Panier des Roses" patt., clear frosted glass w/a blue patina, molded w/a band of roses around the shoulder & on the stopper, signed "R. Lalique," ca. 1930s, 4" h. **$3,300**

Perfume bottle & stopper, Lalique "Perles #3" patt., frosted clear bottle molded w/three rows of draped pearls, signed "R. Lalique," ca. 1926, 5 1/2" h. **$550**

Lalique "Telline" Pattern Perfume Bottle

Perfume bottle & stopper, Lalique "Telline" patt., frosted clear w/light blue patina upright clam shell form w/a flattened clam shell stopper, molded signature "R. Lalique," ca. 1930s, 3 7/8" h. (ILLUS.) **$2,500**

Perfume bottle & stopper, Lalique undocumented design in clear glass, plain flattened round bottle ribbed at the edges & w/a cylindrical neck & frosted bullet-shaped stopper w/gilt inclusion, molded

"Lalique," w/extended "L," ca. 1912, 6 1/2" h. **$2,000-3,000**

Early Undocumented Lalique Bottle

Perfume bottle & stopper, Lalique undocumented design in clear glass, the plain tall slightly tapering square bottle fitted w/a tall slender tapering pointed stopper molded w/stylized flora, molded "Lalique," w/extended "L," ca. 1912, 8 7/8" h. (ILLUS.)... **$780**

Lalique "Le Baiser du Faune" Bottle

Perfume bottle & stopper, "Le Baiser du Faune" by Molinard, clear & frosted Lalique bottle, an upright circle design enclosing an engraved plaque of a woman kissing a faun, small round stopper, molded "R. Lalique" & engraved "Moli-

nard - Paris, France," ca. 1928, 5 3/4" h. (ILLUS.).. **$4,800**

Very Rare "Le Baiser du Faune" Bottle

Perfume bottle & stopper, "Le Baiser du Faune" by Molinard, upright clear ring-form bottle w/a frosted inner panel etched w/a scene of a woman kissing a faun, sealed, signed "R. Lalique," ca. 1930, 5 2/3" h. (ILLUS.) **$5,000-6,000**

"Le Jade" Lalique Perfume Bottle

Perfume bottle & stopper, "Le Jade" by Roger & Gallet, jade green Lalique bottle w/grey patina, flattened ovoid body molded overall w/entwined vining, molded "R. L. - France," few flecks on inner rim, 3 3/4" h. (ILLUS.) **$2,400**

Lalique "Le Jade" Bottle for Roger et Gallet

Perfume bottle & stopper, "Le Jade" for Roger et Gallet, a Lalique jade green container w/a grey patina, flattened ovoid shape molded w/a spread-winged bird against a vining background, small domed stopper, meant to resemble a Chinese snuff bottle, molded "R. Lalique," first half 20th c., 3 1/4" h. (ILLUS.) **$1,800**

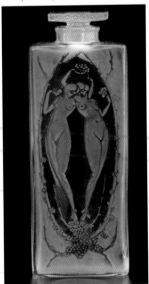

Rare Early Lalique Bottle for "Lepage"

Perfume bottle & stopper, "Lepage," a Lalique bottle in frosted & clear glass w/light

blue patina, tall slender upright square form w/a long almond-shaped reserve featuring stylized female nudes w/flowers, base molded "R. Lalique," ca. 1920, 4 1/2" h. (ILLUS.) **$5,100**

Lalique "Les Anemones" by Forvil Bottle

Perfume bottle & stopper, "Les Anemones" by Forvil, a Lalique perfume bottle in clear & frosted glass w/black enamel trim, clear spherical bottle w/a wide molded figural frosted stopper, w/label & original box, molded "R. Lalique," ca. 1929, 3 3/4" h. (ILLUS.) **$3,000**

Perfume bottle & stopper, "Les Yeux Bleus" by Canarina, blue glass bottle w/an overall pattern of eyes, signed "R. Lalique," ca. 1928, 2" h. **$1,600**

Perfume bottle & stopper, "Misti" by L.T. Piver, bottle w/impressed flowers, signed "R. Lalique," ca. 1923, 1 7/8" h. **$915**

Lalique "Misti" by Piver Bottle

Perfume bottle & stopper, "Misti" by Piver, a Lalique clear & frosted glass container w/a blue patina, squatty low round form molded overall w/butterflies, blossom-form button stopper, molded "R. Lalique," ca. 1913, 2" h. (ILLUS.)............ **$3,000**

Reissued Lalique Bottle for Molinard

Perfume bottle & stopper, "Molinard" by Molinard, flattened upright rectangular bottle, small on the lower half, a wide molded & frosted band of kneeling nudes on the upper half, w/original box, reissue of 1929 bottle for "Iles d'Or" by Molinard, bottle signed "Creation Lalique," sealed, ca. 1980s, 4 3/8" h. (ILLUS.) **$375**

Unusual "Muguet" Lalique Bottle

Perfume bottle & stopper, "Muguet," a Lalique perfume bottle in clear & frosted glass, a clear squatty bulbous bottle w/a high arched frosted floral stopper, stenciled "R. Lalique," ca. 1931, 4" h. (ILLUS.) **$4,000-5,000**

"Mystere" Black Bottle by Lalique

Perfume bottle & stopper, "Mystere" by D'Orsay, a Lalique black glass container w/whitish patina, an upright square w/a short neck, short square stopper centered by an upright stem, molded design around the rim & up the stem, w/original silk-lined leather presentation case, molded "R. Lalique," ca. 1912, 3 3/4" h. (ILLUS.) **$1,680**

Scarce "N" Skyscraper Bottle by Lalique

Perfume bottle & stopper, "N" by Lelong, a Lalique perfume bottle in clear & frosted enameled glass, upright square skyscraper-style bottle w/enameled swag bands around the sides, matching stopper, w/label & cord sealed, in rare green enameled metal box, molded "R. Lalique," ca. 1929, 4" h. (ILLUS.) **$8,400**

Lalique "Narkiss" Bottle for Chinese Market

Perfume bottle & stopper, "Narkiss" by Roger et Gallet, a Lalique bottle in clear glass w/light brown patina & enameled detail, flattened tapering ovoid shape molded on the sides as a large flower blossom w/a five-point star center, molded blossom button stopper, company label & Shanghai perfumer's label in Mandarin Chinese, intaglio molded "RL," ca. 1912, 4" h. (ILLUS.) **$1,920**

Very Early Lalique Bottle for "Niobe"

Perfume bottle & stopper, "Niobe" by Violet, a Lalique bottle in frosted & clear glass w/light blue patina, flattened ovoid shape w/a molded shoulder design of birds on branches, intaglio molded "RL," ca. 1912, 4 1/4" h. (ILLUS.)............ **$2,100**

Perfume bottle & stopper, "No. 7" for Morabito (luxury goods store in Paris), a Lalique opalescent butterscotch crystal container, footed bulbous ovoid shape tapering to a molded neck, the sides

molded w/large stylized leaves, four small molded turtles around the neck, bulbous scale patterned stopper, in silk box & outer box, stenciled "Lalique," ca. 1951, 4 3/8" h. **$6,500-8,500**

"Pan" Bottle by Rene Lalique

Perfume bottle & stopper, "Pan," clear & frosted Lalique bottle w/sepia patina, tall slender & slightly tapering frosted shape w/long swagged panels each topped by a relief-molded horned head, molded "R. Lalique" & engraved "Lalique," ca. 1920, 5" h. (ILLUS.) **$2,520**

Lalique Bottle for "Panier de Roses"

Perfume bottle & stopper, "Panier de Roses," a Lalique clear & frosted glass container w/a grey patina, designed as a slender upright ribbed cylinder molded around the shoulder w/a band of roses, stopper formed by a cluster of roses, engraved "Lalique," ca. 1912, 3 3/4" h. (ILLUS., previous page)......... **$2,040**

Late "Parfum Lalique" Factice Bottle

Perfume bottle & stopper, "Parfum Lalique," a Lalique factice perfume bottle in clear & frosted glass w/flat arched stopper, script signature "Lalique," ca. 1992, 10 1/2" h. (ILLUS.) **$660**

Very Rare Lalique "Quatre Soleils" Bottle

Perfume bottle & stopper, "Quatre Soleils," a Lalique clear & frosted glass container w/a sepia patina, wide flaring lower body below a sharply tapering upper body molded w/four panels enclosing stylized sunburst florettes backed w/reflecting foil, button-form stopper, engraved "R. Lalique," ca. 1912, 2 7/8" h. (ILLUS.)................................. **$10,200**
Perfume bottle & stopper, "Relief" by Forvil, a Lalique clear glass container, upright flattened disk shape molded overall

w/beaded spirals, w/round label, sealed, w/original box, molded "R. Lalique," ca. 1928, 6 1/2" h. **$1,700**

"Relief" by Forvil Bottle by Lalique

Perfume bottle & stopper, "Relief" by Forvil, a Lalique clear glass container, upright flattened disk shape molded overall w/beaded spirals, sealed w/round label, ca. 1920s, 8 1/2" h. (ILLUS.) **$2,200**
Perfume bottle & stopper, "Réplique" for Raphael, a Lalique frosted glass container, molded in the shape of an acorn w/gilded plastic top, ribbon label, in original box, enameled "Lalique" mark, ca. 1944, 1 7/8" l. **$175**

Lalique "Requete" by Worth Bottle

Perfume bottle & stopper, "Requete" by Worth, a Lalique clear glass container w/blue enamel trim, short pedestal base supporting an upright flattened disk form bottle w/a scalloped border all around, tapering cylindrical stopper w/blue enamel bands, labeled, sealed, w/seldom seen overall box, stenciled "Lalique," ca. 1944, 6 3/8" h. (ILLUS.) **$2,200-2,900**

Lalique "Roses" Bottle for D'Orsay

Perfume bottle & stopper, "Roses" by D'Orsay, clear & frosted Lalique bottle w/sepia patina, footed spherical bottle w/a short neck & tall figural stopper, molded "Lalique" w/extended "L," some interior residue, stopper frozen, ca. 1912, 4" h. (ILLUS.) **$3,360**

Perfume bottle & stopper, "Sans Adieu" by Worth, a Lalique green glass container, slender upright bottle w/a unique tall multi-tiered stopper, w/label, in original wooden box, molded "R. Lalique," ca. 1929, 4 1/4" h. **$1,080**

One-of-a-Kind Lalique "Sirene" Bottle

Perfume bottle & stopper, "Sirene" pattern by Lalique, the perfume bottle in clear & frosted glass w/a blue patina,

clear flattened upright disk shape molded w/the swirled figure of a siren trimmed in blue, matching mushroom stopper, first documented example w/conforming stopper, molded "R. Lalique," ca. 1927, 5" h. (ILLUS.) **$57,000**

Perfume bottle & stopper, "Tzigane" by Corday, a Lalique clear & frosted glass container, designed as an upright cluster of ropetwist bands, small disk stopper, enameled label, in violin-shaped easel-back silk display box w/edge wear, ca, 1937, 6 1/2" h. **$1,400-1,800**

Extraordinary Lalique Presentation Set

Perfume bottle & stopper, "Trésor de la Mer" for Saks Fifth Avenue, a unique Lalique opalescent glass container, composed of a shell-shape box w/hinged cover opening to expose the pearl-shaped bottle, complete w/original red velvet presentation box lined in gold silk & blue velvet & corded label in the form of a booklet identifying this as No. 72 from a limited editon of 100, box also retains original Saks price tag affixed to the bottom indicating a price of fifty dollars, glass box retains partial label on inside of cover, box stenciled "R. Lalique - France," bottle engraved "R. Lalique - France," ca. 1936, box 5 x 7 1/2 x 8 1/4", glass box 5 3/4" w. (ILLUS.) **$216,000**

Perfume bottle & stopper, "Tzigane" by Corday, an upright frosted notched cylindrical bottle w/disc stopper, molded Lalique signature, ca. 1949, 4 1/2" h. **$150-200**

Fine Lalique "Sirènes" Perfume Burner

Perfume burner, "Sirènes" patt., cylindrical base w/a dark amber stain molded in relief w/the figures of nude sirens, domed top, molded signature "R. Lalique," ca. 1930s, 6 3/4" h. (ILLUS.)........................ **$2,750**

Tall Lalique Scent Bottle Made for Arys

Scent bottle & stopper, Lalique bottle made for Arys, clear & frosted, tall slender upright cylindrical shape molded w/a design of vertical rows of stylized round flowerheads, button-shaped frosted stopper w/matching design around the rim, base marked in raised block letters "Arys - R. Lalique," some minor interior staining, small grind to lip, 7" h. (ILLUS.)........ **$1,035**

Le Verre Francais

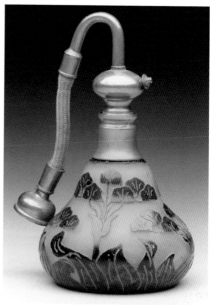

Le Verre Francais Cameo Atomizer

Cameo atomizer & fittings, squatty pear-shaped body in frosted yellow cased in mottled orange & brown & cameo-cut w/an Art Deco stylized flower & leaf design, original metal fittings, signed on the bottom, missing atomizer bulb, 6 1/2" h. (ILLUS.)... **$920**

Muller Freres

Muller Freres French Cameo Atomizer

Perfume atomizer w/fittings, French cameo tall slender swelled bottle in mottled orange cameo-carved & enameled in color w/tall trees in a lakeside landscape, signed "Muller Freres - Luneville - France," early 20th c., 8 1/2" h. (ILLUS., previous page) **$950**

Richard

French Cameo Richard Atomizer

Perfume atomizer w/fittings, French cameo glass bottle w/a bulbous base tapering to a slender cylindrical upper body, yellowish orange glass cased in dark red & cameo-carved w/a design of leafy hop vines, gilt-metal fitted w/long tube & mesh-covered bulb w/tassel, glass signed "Richard," mount unmarked, ca. 1930s, 8 3/4" h. (ILLUS.) **$475**

Richard Pink Cameo Perfume Atomizer

Perfume atomizer w/fittings, French cameo glass bottle w/a cushion foot below the gently tapering swelled body, light pink cased in dark maroon & cameo-carved a flowering stems up from the bottom, gilt metal fitting w/small mesh-covered bulb, glass signed "Richard," mount unmarked, ca. 1930s, 8" h. (ILLUS.) **$550**

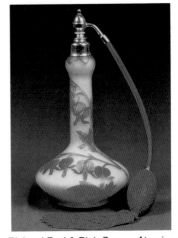

Richard Red & Pink Cameo Atomizer

Perfume atomizer w/fittings, French cameo glass bottle w/a footed squatty bulbous base tapering sharply to a tall slender cylindrical neck w/a bulbed top, pink cased in dark red & cameo-carved w/stems of bleeding heart, glass signed "Richard," mount apparently replaced, ca. 1930s, 8 3/8" h. (ILLUS.) **$1,400**

Saint Louis

St. Louis Green & Clear Etched Perfume

Perfume bottle & stopper, cylindrical clear bottle w/flattened shoulder & short neck, flashed w/peridot green & acid-etched overall w/a design of leafy vines against a leaf-etched ground, St. Louis, similar bottles made by Baccarat & Val St. Lambert, ca. 1900, 6" h. (ILLUS., previous page) **$350-400**

St. Louis White Latticino Perfume Bottle

Perfume bottle & stopper, footed bulbous ovoid glass bottle tapering to a slender neck, clear w/white swirled latticino threading up the sides, blue applied lip band, white latticino button stopper, St. Louis, ca. 1850-60, 4 1/4" h. (ILLUS.) **$375-425**

Rare "Ramses II" Obelisk Perfume Bottle

Perfume bottle & stopper, "Ramses II" by Bichara, a Saint Louis clear crystal Egyptian obelisk shape deeply etched overall w/hieroglyphics & labeling, silvery grey lustre patina, inner stopper present, ca. 1928, 8" h. (ILLUS.) **$7,000-10,500**

Fine French Latticino Perfume Bottle

Perfume bottle & stopper, squatty round tapering bottle in swirled blue & white latticino glass, matching blown bulbous stopper, probably by St. Louis, ca. 1870s, 5 1/2" h. (ILLUS.) **$450-600**

Germany

Meissen

Figural Meissen Perfume Atomizer

Pefume atomizer & fittings, figural porcelain, designed as a seated blackamoor boy in a colorful costume holding a pale blue ovoid bottle w/gilt metal collar, fittings & bulb w/gold mesh covering, blue Crossed swords Meissen mark, early 20th c., 5 1/2" h. (ILLUS.).................... **$250-300**

Unusual Figural Meissen Scent Bottle

Scent bottle w/stoppers, porcelain, figural, modeled as the figure of a standing bearded man in a long brown hooded robe holding the neck of a white goose in one hand & a basket of colored fruit over his other arm, a long basket holding a small child, the head of the child & the man form a stopper, Meissen blue crossed-swords mark & impressed "2472," late 19th c., 3" h. (ILLUS.) **$1,323**

Schuco
Perfume bottle & stopper, novelty-type, model of a blond mohair bear, 5" h. **$350**

Schuco Monkey Novelty Perfume Bottle

Perfume bottle & stopper, novelty-type, model of an auburn mohair monkey, removable head over interior glass tube insert, 5" h. (ILLUS.) **$300**

Perfume bottle & stopper, novelty-type, model of an auburn mohair monkey wearing a black suit & top hat, removable head over interior glass tube insert, 5" h.... **$450**

United States

Fry
Perfume bottle & stopper, tall slim milky Fry Foval glass body w/floral etching, Delft blue foot & stopper w/long dauber, 7 1/2" h.. **$325**

Quezal

Quezel Gold Perfume for Melba Company

Perfume bottle & stopper, slender tapering cylindrical shape w/four half ribs up from the base, small neck & button-form stopper, gold iridescent Quezal glass produced for the Melba Company, base marked "Q" & "Melba," ca. 1920, 6 1/2" h. (ILLUS.).. **$1,800-2,000**

Gold Iridescent Quezal Scent Bottle

Scent bottle w/disc stopper, blown art glass, tapering cylindrical form w/four ribs spaced around the sides, overall golden iridescence w/green highlights, hexagon stopper, Quezal, signed on the bottom, tiny fleabite on edge of stopper, early 20th c., 7 1/2" h. (ILLUS.)..... **$1,000-2,000**

Steuben

Steuben Blue Aurene Perfume Bottle

Perfume bottle & stopper, blue Aurene Steuben glass w/a wide bottom shape & squat pointed stopper, signed "Aurene 2833," 3 3/4" h. (ILLUS.) **$600**

Extremely Rare Steuben Perfume Bottle

Perfume bottle & stopper, deep purple Steuben glass w/a tapering ovoid shape w/molded columns down each corner forming side panels finely engraved w/draping flower & leaf swags, pointed disc stopper, variant of No. 6604, factory signature & original paper label, ca. 1920s, 8 1/4" h. (ILLUS. - Too rare to price)

Tall Steuben Blue Aurene Perfume Bottle

Perfume bottle & stopper, footed wide-waisted shape tapering to a tall slender neck w/flared rim & tall pointed stopper, Steuben blue Aurene glass, Shape No. 3175, signed "Aurene," ca. 1920s, 7" h. (ILLUS.)...................................... **$2,500-3,000**

Perfume bottle & stopper, mold-blown eight-lobed gourd shape w/ribbed & pointed stopper, Steuben gold Aurene glass, signed "Aurene 1455," 6 1/2" h. **$650-800**

Perfume bottle & stopper, squatty bulbous eight-lobed gourd shape in clear glass, a flame-shaped stopper w/silver overlay in a floral design, signed by Steuben, silver unsigned, 6 1/2" h. **$550**

Perfume bottle & stopper, squatty bulbous melon-lobed shape in clear engraved glass w/matching pointed stopper, Steuben Shape No. 1455, engraved & signed by J. Hoare, ca. 1910-20, 6" h. (ILLUS. center with two other similar Steuben perfume bottles, top next page) **$500-600**

Perfume bottle & stopper, squatty bulbous melon-lobed shape in clear glass decorated w/fancy silver overlay, matching pointed stopper, Steuben Shape No. 1455, unsigned, ca. 1910-20, 6" h. (ILLUS. right with two other similar Steuben perfume bottles, top next page) **$550-700**

Three Steuben Perfume Bottes in Shape No. 1455

Perfume bottle & stopper, squatty bulbous melon-lobed shape in Selenium Ruby w/matching pointed stopper, Steuben Shape No. 1455, ca. 1910-20, 6" h. (ILLUS. left with two other similar Steuben perfume bottles, top of page).............................. **$350-400**

Perfume bottle & stopper, squatty gold Aurene Steuben eight-lobed glass w/a ribbed & pointed matching stopper, signed "Aurene 1455," 5 3/4" h. **$525**

Steuben Verre de Soie & Celeste Blue Perfume

Steuben Verre de Soie & Jade Perfume

Perfume bottle & stopper, squatty translucent Verre de Soie Steuben eight-lobed glass w/a pointed Jade Green stopper w/dauber, unsigned, 4 1/2" h. (ILLUS.) **$600**

Perfume bottle & stopper, squatty Verre de Soie Steuben eight-lobed glass w/a ribbed & pointed Celeste Blue stopper, Shape No. 1455, ca. 1910-20, 4 3/4" h. (ILLUS., top next column) **$350-400**

Perfume bottle & stopper, tall slender green pilgrim bottle-shaped Steuben glass body raised on a swirled Cintra & mica-flecked ball stem & an amber foot, swirled Cintra & mica-flecked ball stopper w/long dauber, ca. 1920s, 11 3/4" h. (ILLUS., bottom next column) **$2,500-3,500**

Tall Green & Cintra Steuben Perfume

Three Steuben Shape 3294 Perfume Bottles

1920s, 7" h. (ILLUS. right with two similar perfume bottles, top of page) **$1,000-1,100**

Perfume bottle & stopper, tall slender tapering body w/a tall slender stopper, Green Jade, Steuben Shape No. 3294, ca. 1920s, 7" h. (ILLUS. center with two similar perfume bottles, top of page) **$700-1,000**

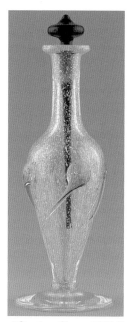

Unusual Steuben Shape 6309 Perfume

Perfume bottle & stopper, tall slender ovoid body w/a very tall slender neck & pointed button stopper, colorless glass layers enclosing mica flecks, the sides applied w/swirled Topaz drops, ruby stopper & dauber, Steuben Shape No. 6309, ca. 1920s, 6" h. (ILLUS.) **$2,500-3,000**

Perfume bottle & stopper, tall slender tapering body w/a tall slender stopper, deep Amethyst, Steuben Shape No. 3294, ca. 1920s, 7" h. (ILLUS. left with two similar perfume bottles, top of page) **$1,200-1,500**

Perfume bottle & stopper, tall slender tapering body w/a tall slender stopper, gold Aurene, Steuben Shape No. 3294, ca.

Tall Slender Blue Aurene Perfume Bottle

Perfume bottle & stopper, tall slightly tapering slender cylindrical footed body w/short flared neck, tall pointed stopper, Steuben blue Aurene, bottom signed "Aurene" & a paper label, 7 2/3" h. (ILLUS.) **$850**

Perfume bottle & stopper, tapering ovoid blue Aurene Steuben glass bottle w/a button-form stopper, Shape No. 2835, ca. 1915, 3 1/4" h. **$600-750**

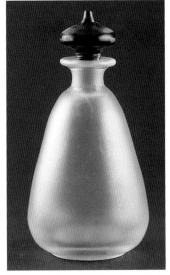

Steuben Shape 2835 Perfume Bottle

Perfume bottle & stopper, tapering ovoid Verre de Soie Steuben glass bottle w/a button-form Celeste Blue stopper, Shape No. 2835, ca. 1915, 3 1/4" h. (ILLUS.) **$275-300**

Blue Aurene "Atomic Cloud" Perfume

Perfume bottle & stopper, upright "Atomic Cloud" shaped Steuben blue Aurene

bottle w/ball stopper, four indents around the sides, unsigned, 1920s, 3 2/3" h. (ILLUS.)............................ **$2,800-3,300**

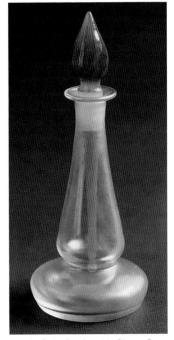

Verre de Soie Bottle with Cintra Stopper

Perfume bottle & stopper, Verre de Soie Steuben glass body w/pink Cintra stopper w/long dauber, Shape No. 6236, ca. 1920s, unsigned, 6" h. (ILLUS.) **$1,200-1,500**

Tiffany

Tiffany Favrile Perfume with Hearts & Vines

Perfume bottle & stopper, boule-shaped body w/short flared neck & ball-shaped stopper, gold iridescent Tiffany Favrile glass w/an overall green hearts & vines decoration, signed, ca. 1920s, 4 1/4" h. (ILLUS.)... **$750-900**

Cut Glass & Sterling Tiffany & Co. Scent Bottles

Fine Tiffany Double-Gourd Perfume

Perfume bottle & stopper, tapering double-gourd shape w/eight vertical ribs in Tiffany blue Favrile glass, signed, ca. 1909, 5 3/4" h. (ILLUS.) **$3,500-4,500**

Scent bottle w/cap, intaglio-carved paperweight glass, waisted cylindrical shape w/deep carved scrolls surrounding large deep rose pink blossoms & green leaves, ovoid leaf & flower cast sterling silver cap opening to a glass stopper, by Tiffany Studios & Tiffany & Company, glass engraved "L.C.T. o786," ca. 1905, 5" h. (ILLUS., top next column) **$19,120**

Extremely Rare Tiffany Scent Bottle

Scent bottles & stoppers, cut glass, spherical clear bodies cut w/a band of strawberry diamond & hobstars above a panel-cut bottom & shoulder w/a flaring neck, fitted w/an ornate pointed sterling-capped stopper, silver marked by Tiffany & Co., ca. 1900, 5 1/4" h., pr. (ILLUS., top of page) **$1,150**

Wheaton Glass Company,
After shave lotion, "Early American Old Spice" by Shulton, cylindrical w/an enameled girl on the front, upright glass stopper, unmarked by Wheaton, ca. 1937, 2" h. **$25-30**

Eau de cologne bottle & stopper, "Para Ti" by Tuya, clear glass bottle w/five bands & a tiered stopper, unsigned by Wheaton, ca. 1946, 5 3/4" h. **$25**

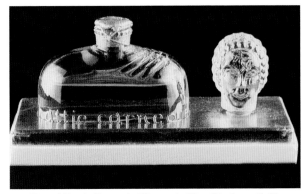

Figural Hattie Carnegie "Carnegie Blue "Perfume Bottle

Perfume bottle & stopper, "Carnegie Blue" by Hattie Carnegie, figural, in the shape of the shoulders of a woman trimmed in gold w/her clear head forming the stopper, ca. 1944, 4 1/4" h. (ILLUS., top of page) **$625-750**

Perfume bottle & stopper, "Sinner" by Adrian, columnar form bottle, unmarked by Wheaton, ca. 1944, 2 7/8" h. **$26**

Perfume Bottle Retailers

Irice

Filigree-mounted Irice - Czech Bottle

Perfume bottle & stopper, bulbous footed clear crystal bottle encased in delicate floral metal filigree set w/a large green jewel & smaller jewels, small cylindrical neck also mounted w/filigree & topped by a green jewel, Czechoslovakia mark, ca. 1930s, 2 1/2" h. (ILLUS.) **$125**

Perfume bottle & stopper, clear cut glass dram bottle w/a filigree metal cap w/a faux gem & dauber, dangling multicolored bead charms in the form of a boy & girl, ca. 1920s-30s, 2 2/3" h. **$153**

Perfume bottle & stopper, clear cut glass dram bottle w/a filigree metal cap w/faux

jewel & dauber, trimmed w/dangling dice charms, marked by Irice, ca. 1920s-30s, 2" h. **$128**

Perfume bottle & stopper, clear cut glass dram bottle w/a filigree metal cap w/faux jewel & dauber, trimmed w/a chain dangling a blue cat charm, ca. 1920s-30s, 2 2/3" h. **$450**

Irice Blue Bottle with Filigree Trim

Perfume bottle & stopper, flattened blue crystal bottle w/a stepped ovoid shape mounted w/a fancy metal filigree panel trimmed w/beads, flat blue asymmetrical stopper etched w/a cluster of lily-of-the-valley, no dauber, Irice paper label & signed, 4 7/8" h. (ILLUS.) **$300-400**

Perfume bottle & stopper, glass bottle w/a metal filigree-covered stopper w/faux jewel & glass dauber, a glass cherry & two leaves dangling from attached chain, signed w/an Irice Czech import mark, 2 3/4" h. **$175-225**

Miniature Crystal Irice Bottle with Charms

Perfume bottle & stopper, miniature clear tapering cylindrical cut crystal bottle w/a metal filigree-trimmed cap w/a domed red Bakelite top suspending two chains w/stylized boy & girl charms in black, white, blue & green beads, marked by Irice, ca. 1920s-30s, 2 2/3" h. (ILLUS.) **$135**

Miniature Filigree & Turquoise Jewel Bottle

Perfume bottle & stopper, miniature flattened upright clear bottle encased in delicate scrolling gilt metal filigree w/cross-form bands of delicate enameled flowers centered by a large turquoise-like jewel, cylindrical filigree neck w/turquoise jewel top, unsigned, ca. 1930s, 2 1/4" h. (ILLUS.) **$125-135**

Perfume Manufacturers

France

Bourjois
Eau de cologne bottle & stopper, "Ramage," clear glass bottle in original birds box, ca. 1951, 7 3/4" h. **$50**
Perfume atomizer w/fittings, "Evening in Paris," cobalt blue glass bottle w/silvertone metal fittings, ca. 1928, 2 1/4" h. **$25-50**
Perfume bottle & stopper, "Beau Belle," clear glass bottle shaped as the letter "B," good label, gold ball cap, ca. 1949, 5 3/4" h. **$170**
Perfume bottle & stopper, "Evening in Paris," cobalt blue glass bottle w/a silver V-shaped label & glass keyhole stopper, ca. 1928, 4 1/2" h. **$225**

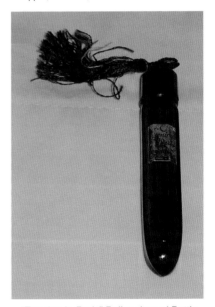

"Evening in Paris" Bullet-shaped Bottle

Perfume bottle & stopper, "Evening in Paris," cobalt blue miniature bullet-shaped lay-down style bottle w/gold label & silk tassel on the cap, ca. 1928, 3 1/2" l. (ILLUS.) **$16-20**

"Evening in Paris" Urn-shaped Bottle

Perfume bottle & stopper, "Evening in Paris," flattened, footed half-round urn-form cobalt blue glass bottle w/a short neck & high clear glass fan-shaped stopper, original silver label, w/original deluxe silver fabric box, empty, 4 1/4" h. (ILLUS.) **$300**

Bourjois "Evening in Paris" Bottle

Perfume bottle & stopper, "Evening in Paris," flattened upright cobalt blue bottle w/rounded shoulder, short neck & frosted glass upright stopper, original silver & black triangular label, in original blue & silver star-shaped box, ca. 1928, 2 3/4" h. (ILLUS.) **$75-100**

Perfume bottle & stopper, "Evening in Paris," miniature cobalt blue glass bottle w/original triangular silver label, in blue Bakelite shell-form case, ca. 1928, 2" h... **$70-125**

Perfume bottle & stopper, "Evening in Paris," miniature cobalt blue glass bottle w/original triangular silver label, in green Bakelite shell-form case, ca. 1928, 2" h. **$220-380**

Perfume bottle & stopper, "Evening in Paris," miniature cobalt blue glass bottle w/original triangular silver label, in figural

Eiffel Tower-shaped Bakelite case, ca. 1928, 2" h. **$220**

Perfume bottle & stopper, "Evening in Paris," miniature cobalt blue glass bottle w/original triangular silver label, in red Bakelite shell-form case, ca. 1928, 2" h. **$275**

"Evening in Paris" with Owl-form Case

Perfume bottle & stopper, "Evening in Paris," upright flattened rectangular cobalt blue glass bottle w/a black cap, original triangular silver label, w/original blue figural owl Bakelite case, ca. 1928, 2" h. (ILLUS.) **$100-225**

Bourjois "Kobako" Bottle & Case

Perfume bottle & stopper, "Kobako," clear frosted ovoid glass shaped like a Chinese snuff bottle & molded overall w/chrysanthemums, small metallic label, complete w/the red Bakelite inro-style case molded w/chrysanthemums, ca. 1953, 2 2/3" h. (ILLUS.) **$250-300**

Perfume bottle & stopper, "Mais Oui," cobalt blue bottle w/clear fan-shaped glass stopper, mint in box, ca. 1938, 4" h..... **$120-160**

"Mais Oui" Small Fan-shaped Bottle

Perfume bottle & stopper, "Mais Oui," small fan-shaped clear glass bottle w/blue cap fitted w/a silk tassel, ca. 1938, 1 3/4" h. (ILLUS.) **$30-45**

Miniature "On the Wind" Perfume Bottle

Perfume bottle & stopper, "On the Wind," miniature tapering ribbed clear bottle w/a yellow label & cap, ca. 1930, 1 3/4" h. (ILLUS.).. **$20-40**

Perfume bottle & stopper, "Premier Muguet," clear glass bottle w/white plastic flower-shaped stopper, mint in box, ca. 1955, 2 1/3" h... **$40**

Perfume bottle & stopper, "Soir de Paris," cobalt blue glass bottle w/a ribbed Bakelite stopper, ca. 1928, 3 1/3" h. **$40**

Unusual "Evening in Paris" Gift Set

Perfume gift set, "Evening in Paris," a shallow box in the form of a French sailor's hat holding cobalt blue glass perfume, eau de cologne & purse-sized bottles, a talcum container, face powder case & a lipstick, face powder & lipstick opened, ca. 1928, box 11" d. (ILLUS. of open & closed box) **$120-200**

Perfume set, "Evening in Paris," a small cobalt blue glass bottle sitting in the center of a flat rounded metal ashtray decorated w/scenes of Paris, ca. 1928, 2 1/4" h., the set **$355**

Caron

Miniature "Bellodgia" Bottle by Caron

Perfume bottle & stopper, "Bellodgia," miniature rectangular clear glass bottle w/a stepped shoulder & square black cap, w/original pink label, ca. 1927, 1" h. (ILLUS.) **$25**

Caron "Fete des Roses" Gold Bottle

Perfume bottle & stopper, "Fete des Roses," upright square glass bottle w/an overall molded small block design & covered w/gold enamel, matching tapering faceted stopper, label on bottom, sealed, ca. 1949, 4 1/4" h. (ILLUS.) **$325**

Caron "French Cancan" Bottle & Box

Perfume bottle & stopper, "French Cancan," clear glass ringed ovoid bottle w/a lace ruffle around the neck & a square white stopper, w/original drop-front box lined in white & decorated w/Cancan

dancers, bottle empty, ca. 1936, 3" h. (ILLUS.) **$100**

Caron "La Fete des Roses" Bottle & Box

Perfume bottle & stopper, "La Fete des Roses" by Caron, upright square glass bottle w/an overall checkered pattern covered in gold, pointed gold stopper, labeled, in a velvet drawer-slide box w/silk rose petals, ca. 1951, 4" h. (ILLUS.) **$1,900**

Caron "Nuit de Noel" Bottle & Box

Perfume bottle & stopper, "Nuit de Noel," flattened upright rectangular black glass Baccarat bottle w/gold label band & small knob stopper, w/original shagreen box w/tassel, unsigned by Baccarat, ca. 1922, 4 1/3" h. (ILLUS.) **$100**

Perfume bottle & stopper, "Poivre," laydown glass bottle in the shape of a pepper corn, w/leatherette case, ca. 1954, 3 1/2" l. **$25-45**

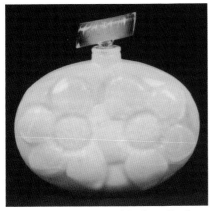

Caron "Voeu de Noel" Perfume Bottle

Perfume bottle & stopper, "Voeu de Noel," oblong opalescent white glass bottle molded w/large blossoms, bar-form glass stopper, name in gold enamel on the front, ca. 1939, 3 3/4" h. (ILLUS.) **$165-225**

Ciro

Perfume bottle & stopper, "Chevalier de la Nuit," flattened rounded upright black glass bottle molded to represent the torso of a knight, a figural plummed knight head stopper, ca. 1923, 4 1/2" h. **$200**

Perfume bottle & stopper, "Chevalier de la Nuit," flattened rounded upright clear glass bottle molded to represent the torso of a knight, a black glass figural plummed knight head stopper, ca. 1923, 2 1/3" h. **$800**

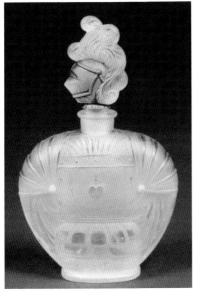

Ciro "Chevalier de la Nuit" Bottle

Perfume bottle & stopper, "Chevalier de la Nuit," flattened rounded upright frosted clear glass bottle molded to represent the torso of a knight, a figural plummed knight head stopper w/black patina, unsigned, ca. 1923, 7 1/2" h. (ILLUS.) **$175**

Perfume bottle & stopper, "New Horizons," clear glass curved bottle, mint in box, ca. 1941, 2 1/3" h. **$75**

Perfume bottle & stopper, "Oh La La," clear glass waisted cylindrical bottle w/a fan-shaped stopper, ca. 1959, 5 1/2" h. **$25-40**

Small Ciro "Oh La La" Bottle with Dress

Perfume bottle & stopper, "Oh La La," clear glass waisted cylindrical bottle wrapped in a black felt dress, white screw-on cap, ca. 1959, 2" h. (ILLUS.) **$60-75**

Perfume bottle & stopper, "Reflexions," miniature square clear glass bottle w/green & white label & screw-on white cap, full, ca. 1933, 1 1/4" h. **$25**

Corday

Perfume bottle & stopper, "Fame," clear glass bottle w/upright stopper, original damask box, ca. 1937, 2 1/2" h. **$65**

Perfume bottle & stopper, "Orchidée Bleue," clear glass Baccarat floriform bottle & stopper, signed by Baccarat, ca. 1925, 1 3/4" h. **$75**

Perfume bottle & stopper, "Quand?," black glass bottle w/black & gold stopper, original label, ca. 1925, 3 1/2" h. **$160-225**

Perfume bottle & stopper, "Toujours Moi," an upright clear glass flattened round bottle w/molded down the sides w/stylized flowers trimmed in gold, gold cap, original label, ca. 1950s, 2 1/2" h. **$40-58**

"Toujours Moi" Gold-trimmed Bottle

Perfume bottle & stopper, "Toujours Moi," an upright clear glass flattened round bottle w/molded down the sides w/stylized flowers trimmed in gold, original hang tab around the neck, flaring cylindrical cap, ca. 1924, 2 1/4" h. (ILLUS.) **$40**

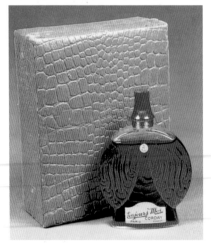

"Toujours Moi" Bottle & Box by Corday

Perfume bottle & stopper, "Toujours Moi," an upright clear glass flattened round bottle w/molded down the sides w/stylized flowers under a brown patina, orange Bakelite stopper, original label, w/original brown simulated alligator skin deluxe gift box, ca. 1935, 3" h. (ILLUS.) **$155**

Small "Toujours Moi" Bottle

Perfume bottle & stopper, "Toujours Moi," an upright clear glass flattened tapering ovoid body w/a molded shield on the front w/the original shield-shaped label, pink cap, ca. 1927, 1 2/3" h. (ILLUS.).................. **$30**

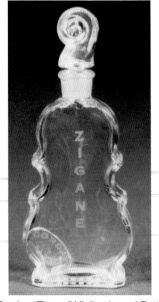

Corday "Zigane" Violin-shaped Bottle

Perfume bottle & stopper, "Zigane," an upright clear glass bottle in the shape of a violin, gold lettering on the front, empty, ca. 1949, 4 3/8" h. (ILLUS.)............ **$100**

Unusual Corday Lamppost Bottle Holder

Perfume bottles & stoppers, "Jet," "L'Ardente Nuit," & "Zigane," three miniature glass bottles w/original labels each fitted into a lantern atop a cast metal three-light lamppost mounted w/a signed reading "Rue del la Pax" & ending in a round ashtray base, Corday impressed mark on the bottom, ca. 1952, each bottle 1 1/3" h., the set (ILLUS.) **$180-510**

Coty

"L'Aimant" by Coty Eau de Toilette Set

Eau de toilette bottles & stoppers, "L'Aimant," a small & large upright squared clear glass bottle w/gold caps, original labels w/original gold box, ca. 1927, 1 2/3" & 3" h., the set (ILLUS.) **$35**
Perfume bottle & stopper, "A Suma," frosted boule-shaped glass bottle w/embossed flowers, in original Bakelite case

w/a black base & molded chrysanthemums, ca. 1934, 3 1/4" h.......... **$585**

Blue-Enameled Bottle Made for Coty

Perfume bottle & stopper, Coty bottle in upright oval crystal w/fancy enameled decoration, the blue banded shoulder above a narrow band of rings suspending overlapping stylized long blue leaves, domed blue-enameled stopper, attributed to Marcal Goupy, bottom molded "Coty - France," ca. 1925, 4 5/8" h. (ILLUS.) **$960**
Perfume bottle & stopper, "Emeraude," clear glass tall rectangular bottle w/a wave-molded stopper, set in a gold plastic high heeled shoe, w/outer box, mint in box, ca. 1936, 2 3/4" h **$98**

"Emeraude" by Coty Perfume Bottle

Perfume bottle & stopper, "Emeraude," upright flattened rectangular clear glass bottle w/incised bands around the body, flaring faceted stopper, original label, bottle originally used for "Le Vertige," ca. 1938, 4 1/8" h. (ILLUS., previous page)..... **$145**

Small "L'Aimant" Bottle Designed by Lalique

Perfume bottle & stopper, "L'Aimant," a small tapering rectangular clear glass Lalique bottle w/a rectangular waves stopper, original gold label, ca. 1927, 1 3/4" h. (ILLUS.) **$28**

Rare Coty "L'Effleur" Bottle by Lalique

Perfume bottle & stopper, "L'Effleur," upright rectangular clear & frosted Lalique glass bottle molded in the center panel w/an Art Nouveau female above waves, brown patina, probably first collaboration w/Lalique, ca. 1908, 4 1/3" h. (ILLUS.) **$4,500-4,750**

Coty "L'Or" Bottle by Baccarat

Perfume bottle & stopper, "L'Or," tall slender clear Baccarat teardrop-shaped glass bottle w/tall teardrop stopper, gold lettering near base, marked by Baccarat, ca. 1916, 6 1/4" h. (ILLUS.) **$225**

"L'Aimant" by Coty with Original Box

Perfume bottle & stopper, "L'Aimant" by Coty, an upright rectangular clear bottle w/frosted patterned domed stopper w/sepia patina, w/label, sealed, in upright square box, 1920s, 3 5/8" h. (ILLUS.) **$240**

Early "L'Origan" by Coty Perfume Bottle

Perfume bottle & stopper, "L'Origan," a small square clear bottle w/screw-off gold cap, original gold label, full, ca. 1903, 1 1/2" h. (ILLUS.) **$11**

Perfume bottle & stopper, "La Rose Jacqueminot," clear Baccarat glass bottle w/a floriform stopper, gold labels & original box, marked by Baccarat, ca. 1905, 4 2/3" h. **$305**

"Muguet" by Coty Perfume Bottle

Perfume bottle & stopper, "Muguet" by Coty, upright flattened rectangular clear glass bottle w/flat shoulders & flattened faceted diamond-shaped stopper, w/label, sealed, w/original box, 1930s, 5" h. (ILLUS.)... **$840**

Perfume bottle & stopper, "Muse," clear glass bottle w/a frosted overcap, ca. 1945, 3 1/8" h.. **$107**

Perfume bottle & stopper, "Styx," a clear glass unsigned Lalique bottle w/a briar stopper in the Serie Toilette, 1910, 2 1/3" h **$45-90**

Coty Three-Bottle Perfume Bottle Set

Perfume bottles & stoppers set, "La Rose," "Jasmin de Corse," & "L'Origan" by Coty, each a clear glass low square shape w/a squared & flattened stopper w/a molded design, sealed w/labels & in original black silk-lined leather case, bases stenciled "Cristal Coty," ca. 1923, 2 1/4" h., the set (ILLUS., above) **$1,800**

D'Orsay

"Ambre d'Orsay" Black Glass Bottle

Perfume bottle & stopper, "Ambre d'Orsay," a upright square black glass Lalique bottle w/a tall molded classical female figure at each corner, stopper w/stylized flowers, signed in the mold by Lalique, ca. 1913, 5 1/8" h. (ILLUS.) ... **$800-900**

D'Orsay "Belle de Jour" Reissue Bottle

Perfume bottle & stopper, "Belle de Jour," a clear tapering cylindrical Lalique bottle w/a high arched tiara stopper w/two nudes, an unusual reissue of a bottle designed for "Leur Ames" to celebrate the 25th anniversary of that scent, reissue bottle has a plastic stopper rather than a glass one, originally it sold for **$1**, missing the label, ca. 1938, 5 1/2" h. (ILLUS.) .. **$325-400**

Milk Glass "Belle de Jour" Bottle

Perfume bottle & stopper, "Belle de Jour," an upright oval asymmetrical milk glass bottle w/the stopper designed as a hand holding a bouquet of flowers, original label, ca. 1938, 3 1/2" h. (ILLUS.) **$225-300**

Very Rare "Grace d'Orsay" Perfume Bottle

Perfume bottle & stopper, "Grace d'Orsay," an upright square clear & frosted Lalique glass bottle w/reticulated upper corners & flaring reticulated stopper, brown patina, sealed, extremely rare, 1915-20, 5 1/8" h. (ILLUS.) **$20,000-30,000**

D'Orsay "Le Lys" Lalique Bottle

Perfume bottle & stopper, "Le Lys," an upright flattened ovoid clear & frosted Lalique glass bottle molded overall w/blossoms on stems, flat round flower-molded stopper, brown patina, unsigned by Lalique, 6 7/8" h. (ILLUS.)........................ **$325-400**

D'Orsay "Muguet" Baccarat Bottle

Perfume bottle & stopper, "Muguet," an upright flattened rectangular clear Baccarat glass bottle w/short neck & faceted knob stopper, gold label, etched Baccarat mark, ca. 1923, 4 1/2" h. (ILLUS.).......... **$600**

"Mystere d'Orsay" Black Lalique Bottle

Perfume bottle & stopper, "Mystere d'Orsay," upright rectangular flattened black glass Lalique bottle w/tall slender square stopper, engraved R. Lalique signature, ca. 1925, 3 7/8" h. (ILLUS.).................... **$900-1,000**

Perfume bottle & stopper, "Voulez Vous," a clear bottle w/black cap w/dauber, full, ca. 1965, 2 2/3" h. **$25-35**

Dior (Christian)

Mini "Miss Dior" Lay-down Bottle

Perfume bottle & stopper, "Miss Dior," miniature clear glass flattened oval lay-down bottle w/black lettering, screw-off cap, ca. 1953, 1 1/2" l. (ILLUS.)............. **$15-20**

Fine Baccarat "Diorling" Perfume Bottle

Perfume bottle & stopper, "Diorling," clear Baccarat glass footed & ribbed ovoid bottle w/a tall upright gilt-metal stopper composed of flowers on stems, signed & numbered by Baccarat, ca. 1956, 9" h. (ILLUS.).. **$1,000**

Fine "Miss Dior" Cut Baccarat Bottle

Perfume bottle & stopper, "Miss Dior," cobalt cut to clear Baccarat glass footed baluster-form bottle w/a tall cut teardrop stopper, gilt trim, name painted in gold, marked by Baccarat, ca. 1933, 7" h. (ILLUS.) **$525-700**

"Miss Dior" Clear Cut Baccarat Bottle

Perfume bottle & stopper, "Miss Dior," clear cut Baccarat glass footed baluster-form bottle w/a tall cut teardrop stopper, name painted in gold, marked by Baccarat, empty, ca. 1953, 7" h. (ILLUS.)...... **$140-175**

Two Dior Perfume Counter Testers

Perfume counter testers & fittings, "Diorling" & "Miss Dior," clear Baccarat glass footed & ribbed ovoid bottle w/a gilt-metal fittings & bases, ca. 1950s, 5" h., each (ILLUS.)... **$75**

Guerlain

"Vol de Nuit" Eau de Cologne Bottle

Eau de cologne bottle & stopper, "Vol de Nuit" by Guerlain, clear upright clear glass doughnut-shaped bottle w/label in the center, pointed stopper, "HP" mark of Pochet et de Courval, ca. 1937, 7 1/4" h. (ILLUS.) **$65**

Eau de toilette bottle & stopper, "Chamade," miniature clear glass teardrop-shaped bottle w/all-glass stopper, no box, ca. 1970, 2" h. **$39**

Eau de toilette bottle & stopper, "Chants d'Arome," miniature clear glass teardrop-shaped bottle w/all-glass stopper, w/box, ca. 1970, 2" h. **$51**

Black Glass "Chants d'Arome" Bottle

Eau de toilette bottle & stopper, "Chants d'Arome," upright flattened lyre-shaped black glass bottle w/gold

screw-off cap, worn label, full, ca. 1962, 2 7/8" h. (ILLUS.) **$55-70**

Eau de toilette bottle & stopper, "Jicky," miniature clear glass teardrop-shaped bottle w/all-glass stopper, no box, ca. 1970, 2" h. **$20**

"L'Heure Bleue" Eau de Toilette Bottle

Eau de toilette bottle & stopper, "L'Heure Bleue," upright flattened ovoid clear glass bottle w/frosted onion-dome stopper, good original label, ca. 1912, 6 1/2" h. (ILLUS.) **$55-70**

1970s "Parure" Eau de Toilette Bottle

Eau de toilette bottle & stopper, "Parure," clear flattened ovoid glass bottle w/frosted & bead-molded domed stopper, no box, ca. 1970, 2" h. (ILLUS.) **$25-35**

Eau de toilette bottle & stopper, "Shalimar," miniature clear glass teardrop-shaped bottle w/all-glass stopper, w/box, ca. 1970, 2" h. **$50**

Eau de toilette bottle & stopper, "Vol de Nuit," miniature clear glass teardrop-shaped bottle w/all-glass stopper, no box, ca. 1970, 2" h. **$57**

Scarce Guerlain "Champs Elysées" Bottle

Perfume bottle & stopper, "Champs Elysées," short rectangular flattened clear glass bottle w/rounded shoulder, short neck & rectangular faceted stopper, original silver & blue fountain design label, limited edition, ca. 1904, 2 1/8" h. (ILLUS.)... **$250-330**

Perfume bottle & stopper, "Coque d'Or," a short cobalt blue glass bow-shaped Baccarat bottle w/overall gold enamel, signed & numbered by Baccarat, same bottle used for the scent "Dawamesk" after 1946, this bottle ca. 1937, 3 1/2" h. (ILLUS. right with larger Coque d'Or bottle, bottom of page) **$900-1,000**

Perfume bottle & stopper, "Coque d'Or," a short cobalt blue glass bow-shaped Baccarat bottle w/overall gold enamel, signed & numbered by Baccarat, same bottle used for the scent "Dawamesk" after 1946, this bottle ca. 1937, 4 1/4" h. (ILLUS. left with smaller Coque d'Or bottle, bottom of page) **$750-800**

Lalique "Bouquet de Faunes" Bottle

Perfume bottle & stopper, "Bouquet de Faunes," footed rounded urn-form frosted Lalique glass bottle w/molded faun masks alternating w/masks of women around the shoulder, short neck w/molded button stopper, no label, unsigned by Lalique, ca. 1922, 4" h. (ILLUS.) **$450-750**

Perfume bottle & stopper, "Chamade," clear glass draped bottle w/a figural rosebud stopper, good label, "HP" mark of Pochet et de Courval, ca. 1969, 4 3/4" h. **$45**

A Large & Small "Coque d'Or" Perfume Bottle by Baccarat

Guerlain "Fleur de Feu" Bottle

Perfume bottle & stopper, "Fleur de Feu," clear slender tapering cylindrical ribbed body on a foot, flaring stopper, 4" h. (ILLUS.) **$85**

Early "Jicky" Bottle by Baccarat

Perfume bottle & stopper, "Jicky," a short clear paneled Baccarat bottle w/angled shoulder & quadrilobe stopper, mint & unopened in brown flocked box w/white satin interior, signed by Baccarat, scent introduced in 1889, bottle introduced ca. 1908, 3 3/4" h. (ILLUS.) **$120-190**

Perfume bottle & stopper, "L'Heure Bleue," miniature upright flattened square clear glass Baccarat bottle w/a scrolled shoulder, short neck & squatty openwork heart-shaped stopper, empty, no box, ca. 1932, 1 3/8" h. **$16**

Early Guerlain "Mitsouko" Bottle

Perfume bottle & stopper, "Mitsouko," a clear upright three-section glass bottle w/rectangular flattened stopper, early label w/horse design, sealed, ca. 1916, 4 1/8" h. (ILLUS.) **$250**

Guerlain "Mitsouko" Baccarat Bottle

Perfume bottle & stopper, "Mitsouko," upright flattened square clear glass Baccarat bottle w/a scrolled shoulder, short neck & squatty openwork heart-shaped stopper, original label, signed by Baccarat, ca. 1916, 4" h. (ILLUS.) **$50**

Guerlain "Nahéma" Bottle & Box

Perfume bottle & stopper, "Nahéma," clear flattened round glass bottle w/half-round foot & ball stopper, full & sealed, w/original box, discontinued scent, ca. 1979, 5 1/2" h. (ILLUS.) **$175**

Perfume bottle & stopper, "Pois de Senteur," a clear faceted glass bottle & stopper, large label, ca. 1940, 2 3/4" h. **$155**

Baluster-form "Shalimar" Bottle

Perfume bottle & stopper, "Shalimar," a clear & frosted baluster-form glass bottle w/a frosted drape wrapped around most of the body, tall upright molded rose bud stopper, original label, w/zebra design box, ca. 1921, 4 3/4" h. (ILLUS.) **$125-200**

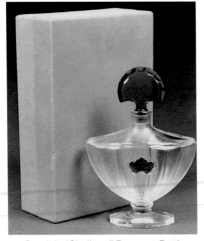

Guerlain "Shalimar" Baccarat Bottle

Perfume bottle & stopper, "Shalimar," a clear footed crystal fluted & fanned Baccarat bottle w/a small blue glass fanned stopper, original label & faded pink velour case, marked by Baccarat, ca. 1921, 6 1/3" h. (ILLUS.) **$100-165**

Modern Guerlain "Shalimar" Bottle

Perfume bottle & stopper, "Shalimar," a modern clear footed crystal fluted & fanned Baccarat bottle w/a small blue plastic fanned stopper, original label & purple velour case, marked "HP," ca. 1980s, 4" h. (ILLUS.) **$12-20**

Matching Bottles for Guerlain Scents

Perfume bottle & stopper, "Shalimar" or "Chamade," miniature upright flattened clear glass bottle w/a rounded shoulder, short neck & large black plastic button cap, used for several scents, 1 1/2" h., depending on the scent, each (ILLUS. of two) **$10-40**

Lancome "Magie" Teardrop Bottle

Perfume bottle & stopper, "Magie," clear glass teardrop-shaped pendant bottle w/metal collar & ring stopper, in original fitted box, ca. 1949, 3" h. (ILLUS.) **$75-90**

Early Guerlain "Sillage" Perfume Bottle

Perfume bottle & stopper, "Sillage" by Guerlain, wide clear octagonal form w/a gilt drapery around the edge of the shoulder, gilt-trimmed neck & button stopper, w/label, sealed, ca. 1910, 5 1/2" h. (ILLUS.) **$900**

Perfume bottle & stopper, "Tabac Fleuri," clear glass bottle w/fleur-de-lis shaped stopper, w/box, 3" h. **$96**

Perfume bottle & stopper, "Vol de Nuit" by Guerlain, small upright square grey glass bottle w/a molded sunburst design & circular gold ring label on the sides, short square clear stopper, sealed, in original zebra skin-patterned box, ca. 1933, 2 1/2" h. **$175**

Lancome

Perfume bottle & stopper, "Kypre," clear glass bottle w/upright engraved stopper, ca. 1935, 3 1/2" h. **$39**

Lancome "Magie" Twisted Baccarat Bottle

Perfume bottle & stopper, "Magie," clear upright square Baccarat glass bottle w/in-body twist, conforming block overcap & stopper, deluxe presentation box, unsigned by Baccarat, ca. 1949, 4 1/2" h. (ILLUS.)... **$150-250**

Perfume bottle & stopper, "Marrakech," clear glass bottle w/curved stopper, mint in box, ca. 1942, 3 2/3" h. **$210**

Lancome Trésor Bottle & Box

Perfume bottle & stopper, "Trésor," clear upright rectangular bottle w/a flattened engraved glass disk stopper, mint in original box, ca. 1953, 3" h. (ILLUS.) **$75**

Lancome Trésor Two-Bottle Set

Perfume bottles & stoppers, "Trésor," a clear glass tapering cylindrical ringed full bottle w/gold screw-on cap w/ribbon & a 1995 reissued clear glass flattened disk-form bottle w/a rayed design & faceted edges, gilt metal screw-on cap, the set (ILLUS.).. **$220**

Perfume bottles & stoppers set, "Tropiques" & "Magie" by Lancome, a pair of frosted glass tapering & fluted containers w/metal caps, original labels, in original box, Limited Edition "Jumelles" presentation set, ca. 1952, 3 1/2" h. **$1,600-2,100**

Lanvin

Lanvin "Arpege" Bath Oil Bottle

Bath oil bottle & stopper, "Arpege," upright flattened round clear glass bottle w/a flat base & relief-molded logo, screw-off gold cap, ca. 1927, 3 1/4" h. (ILLUS.)......... **$200-240**

Lanvin "Arpege" Round Black Glass Bottle

Perfume bottle & stopper, "Arpege," black boule-shaped glass bottle w/signature gold logo, older gilt raspberry-shaped stopper, mint in box, ca. 1927, 3 1/2" h. (ILLUS.).. **$220**

Tiny Rounded "Arpege" Bottle

Perfume bottle & stopper, "Arpege," tiny clear glass rounded bottle w/black screw-off cap, ca. 1927, 7/8" h. (ILLUS.) **$25**

Small Boule-shaped "Arpege" Bottle

Perfume bottle & stopper, "Arpege," clear boule-shaped glass bottle w/gold logo, gold ball-shaped ribbed stopper, full, ca. 1927, 1 3/4" h. (ILLUS.) **$8-10**

Rare Lanvin Miniature "Arpege" Bottle

Perfume bottle & stopper, "Arpege," rare miniature black boule-shaped glass bottle w/signature gold logo, gold screw-off cap, mint in box, ca. 1927, 1 1/3" h. (ILLUS.) **$1,000-1,300**

Unusual Miniature "Arpege" Bottle

Perfume bottle & stopper, "Arpege," unusual miniature rounded clear glass bottle w/banner label & black cap, ca. 1927, 1 1/2" h. (ILLUS.) **$25**

Perfume bottle & stopper, "Crescendo," miniature upright square clear glass bottle w/buff label & black screw-off cap, full, ca. 1939, 1 1/2" h. **$15**

"Scandal" by Lanvin Perfume Bottle

Perfume bottle & stopper, "Scandal" by Lanvin, clear spherical glass bottle printed in gold w/stylized figures of a woman & child, knobby gilded stopper, sealed w/label, in original box, ca. 1931, 2 1/4" h. (ILLUS.) **$250-350**

Scent bottles & stoppers, miniature glass bottles w/silver labels & black logo stoppers, in box, ca. 1920s, 1 7/8" h., set of 4 .... **$89**

LeLong (Lucien)

Eau de cologne bottle & stopper, "Impromptu," clear glass barber bottle-shaped bottle, mint in box, ca. 1935, 8" h. **$45**

5" Lelong "Indiscret" Ribbed Bottle

Perfume bottle & stopper, "Indiscret," frosted clear tall ribbed cylindrical glass bottle w/draped design around the flared base, upright metal bow-shaped stopper, labeled, ca. 1935, 5 1/8" h. (ILLUS.) **$28**

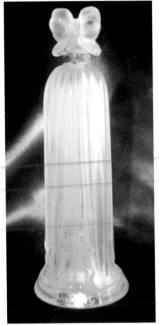

Lucien Lelong "Indiscret" Bottle

Perfume bottle & stopper, "Indiscret" by Lucien Lelong, slender tapering & reeded cylindrical frosted clear glass bottle w/a knob stopper, on a composition base, seated, w/original box, ca. 1935, 4 1/2" h. (ILLUS.) **$200-450**

Lelong Tall "Indiscret" Ribbed Bottle

Perfume bottle & stopper, "Indiscret," frosted clear tall ribbed cylindrical glass bottle w/draped design around the flared base, upright bow-shaped stopper, labeled, ca. 1935, 6 3/4" h. (ILLUS.) **$100**

Lucien LeLong "Jabot" Bottle & Box

Perfume bottle & stopper, "Jabot" by Lucien Lelong, clear glass bottle shaped like a skirt w/widely flaring hem, large frosted glass knot-shaped stopper, w/original label & round box, ca. 1939, 3" h. (ILLUS.) **$840**

Lelong "Jabot" Bow-topped Bottle

Perfume bottle & stopper, "Jabot," frosted clear wide domed & fluted bottle w/a large bow-shaped stopper, inner stopper & dauber, two labels, ca. 1939, 2 3/4" h. (ILLUS.) **$140-175**

Miniature Lelong "Mon Image" Bottle

Perfume bottle & stopper, "Mon Image," miniature upright tiered clear glass bottle w/flat rectangular stopper, original label, w/original mirrored case, ca. 1933, 1 2/3" h. (ILLUS.) **$130**

Lelong "Opening Night" Perfume Bottle

Perfume bottle & stopper, "Opening Night" by Lelong, a clear glass tiered pyramidal bottle enclosed in a rare amber & black Lucite box, cord sealed, w/labels, ca. 1939, 3" h. (ILLUS.) **$1,920**

Lelong "Opening Night" Bottle & Box

Perfume bottle & stopper, "Opening Night," clear squatty rounded & tapering bottle w/a wide flat shoulder & an overall incised block design, flat-topped half-round stopper w/matching design, in original stage-design box, ca. 1934, 2 1/8" h. (ILLUS.) **$225**

Lelong "Sirocco" Double-Twist Bottle

Perfume bottle & stopper, "Sirocco," upright clear glass double-twist design bottle, sealed, mint in box, ca. 1934, 3 3/8" h. (ILLUS.) **$100-125**

"Tailspin" Lucien LeLong Bottle-

Perfume bottle & stopper, "Tailspin" by Lucien Lelong, clear gently swelled cylindrical & paneled glass bottle w/faceted stopper, w/label, sealed, in unique armoire-shaped box, ca. 1940, 2 3/4" h. (ILLUS.) **$475**

Perfume bottle & stopper, "Tailspin," clear glass bottle shaped like a stack of poker chips, upright stopper, in original case, ca. 1947, 3 1/2" h. **$50**

Lelong Set of Small "Joli Petit" Bottles

Perfume bottles & stoppers, "Joli Petit," four miniature clear glass barber bottle-shaped bottles each tied w/a ribbon, mint in original red box, ca. 1940s, 2 1/2" h., the set (ILLUS.) **$75**

Lentheric

Miniature "À Bientot" Bottle & Box by Lentheric

Perfume bottle & stopper, "À Bientot," miniature upright square clear glass bottle w/gold ball cap, gold lettering, mint in fitted box, ca. 1930, 1 1/2" h. (ILLUS.) **$40-50**

Perfume bottle & stopper, "Confetti," miniature clear glass bottle w/gold cap & yellow banner label, original outer box, ca. 1939, 1 7/8" h. **$70**

Perfume bottle & stopper, "Dark Brilliance," clear glass bottle w/bow-shaped stopper, gold lettering, ca. 1946, 3 1/3" h. **$40-45**

Perfume bottle & stopper, "Miracle," frosted clear & polished columnar bottle w/hang tag, in original box, ca. 1924, 2 1/8" h. **$100**

Perfume bottle & stopper, "Repartée," clear glass knot-shaped bottle w/glass stopper, ca. 1949, 3 1/2" h. **$33**

Miniature "Shanghai" Bottle & Box

Perfume bottle & stopper, "Shanghai," miniature long low clear glass bottle w/stepped shoulder & gold ball cap, mint in box, ca. 1936, 1 1/3" h. (ILLUS.) **$45-50**

Perfume bottle & stopper, "Tweed," clear glass bottle w/wood cap, full, ca. 1935, 3 1/8" h. **$25**

Piver (L.T.)

L.T. Piver "Pompeia" Bottle & Box

Perfume bottle & stopper, "Pompeia" by L.T. Piver, upright square clear glass bottle w/rounded shoulder & cylindrical neck w/pointed faceted stopper, original labels, mint in original box, ca. 1922, 4 1/2" h. (ILLUS.) **$375**

Ricci (Nina)

"L'Air du Temps" Eau de Toilette Bottle

Eau de toilette bottle & stopper, "L'Air du Temps," tall ovoid twisted clear glass bottle w/a frosted stopper designed as two flying doves (Flacon aux Columbes), designed by Marc Lalique in 1947, often mistaken for a giant factice bottle, 12 7/8" h. (ILLUS.) **$1,250**

Small Capricci Glass Perfume Bottle

Perfume bottle & stopper, "Capricci" by Nina Ricci, small squatty bulbous clear glass bottle w/an overall diamond point design, screw-off gilt metal cap, ca. 1961, 1 1/8" h. (ILLUS.) **$25-30**

Lalique Bottle for "Capricci" by Ricci

Perfume bottle & stopper, "Capricci" by Nina Ricci, small squatty bulbous clear Lalique glass bottle w/an overall diamond point design, glass stopper, bottle signed by Lalique, 3" h. (ILLUS.) **$100**

"L'Air du Temps" Sunburst Bottle

Perfume bottle & stopper, "L'Air du Temps" by Nina Ricci, squatty flattened clear glass sunburst design w/a scalloped plastic case, gold metal cap, ca. 1948, 1 1/4" h. (ILLUS.) **$55-90**

Schiaparelli

Empty "Le Roi Soliel" Baccarat Bottle

Perfume bottle & stopper, "Le Roi Soliel," clear Baccarat glass round sharply tapering wave-molded bottle w/a large flattened upright stopper representing the sun w/the face composed of doves, designed to celebrate the liberation of France at the end of World War II, designed by Salvador Dali, missing gold metal shell-shaped case, bottle only, ca. 1945, 7" h. (ILLUS.) **$9,000-10,000**

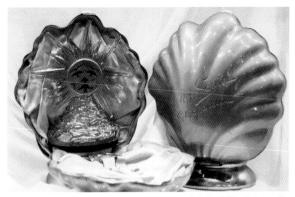

Rare Schiaparelli "Le Roi Soliel" Bottle in Original Shell-form Case

Perfume bottle & stopper, "Le Roi Soliel," clear Baccarat glass round sharply tapering wave-molded bottle w/a large flattened upright stopper representing the sun w/the face composed of doves, designed to celebrate the liberation of France at the end of World War II, designed by Salvador Dali, w/gold metal shell-shaped case, ca. 1945, empty in original case, 7" h. (ILLUS.) **$12,500**

Miniature Schiaparelli "S" Bottle

Perfume bottle & stopper, "S," miniature clear glass bottle in a flattened disc shape molded w/a script "S," gold ball stopper, sealed w/original hang tag, ca. 1965, 1 1/3" h. (ILLUS.) **$95-110**

Perfume bottle & stopper, "S," tiny clear glass bottle w/white cap, black script "S" label, small pink & transparent plastic box, ca. 1965, 1" h. (ILLUS., top next column) **$35**

Tiny Schiaparelli "S" Bottle & Box

Very Rare "Sans Souci" Presentation Set

Perfume bottle & stopper, "Sans Souci," clear glass bottle w/a tiny glass windmill inside, w/the original windmill-shaped presentation box w/movable blades, only known complete set, 1943, 3 1/2" h. (ILLUS.) **$8,000**

"Scent of Mystery" Bottle & Box

Perfume bottle & stopper, "Scent of Mystery," clear glass cylindrical bottle w/a black & gold label & black cap, created for Mike Todd's movie, "Scent of Mystery," meant to be sprayed in the theatres as "Smell-O-Vision," ca. 1969, w/original black & gold box, 2 1/2" h. (ILLUS.) **$500**

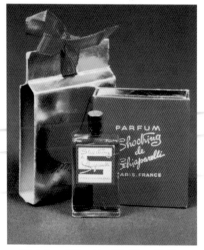

Miniature "Shocking" Bottle with Box

Perfume bottle & stopper, "Shocking," a miniature clear glass miniature upright rectangular bottle w/a gold cap, complete w/original pink & white label & in original pink box w/gold carrier, ca 1936, 2 1/8" h. (ILLUS.) **$65**

Schiaparelli "Shocking" Factice Bottle

Perfume bottle & stopper, "Shocking" by Schiaparelli, a factice clear glass bottle in the shape of a female mannequin, fitted w/a gold ball stopper, on original velvet display stand, ca. 1936, 18" h. (ILLUS.) **$3,500-4,000**

Schiaparelli "Shocking" Perfume Bottle

Perfume bottle & stopper, "Shocking," clear glass bottle molded in the shape of a dressmaker's dummy, glass flowers around the stopper, a tape measure around the neck w/the "S" label, all under a glass dome, ca. 1936, 6" h. (ILLUS.) **$350**

Schiaparelli Small "Shocking" Bottle & Box

Perfume bottle & stopper, "Shocking," figural, small clear glass bottle in the form of a female torso, gold nugget cap, w/original box, 2" h. (ILLUS.) **$110**

"Shocking Scamp" Bottle in Metal Body

Perfume bottle & stopper, "Shocking Scamp," a miniature clear glass bottle fitted inside a metal openwork stylized figure holding a sword above its painted stopper head, on metal stand, 5 1/2" h. (ILLUS.) **$2,335**

Miniature "Shocking" Perfume Bottle

Perfume bottle & stopper, "Shocking," miniature clear glass bottle in the shape of a female torso w/a dressmaker tape w/"S" label around the neck, gold cap, full, ca. 1936, 2" h. (ILLUS.) **$40-70**

"Si" by Schiaparelli Bottle & Box

Perfume bottle & stopper, "Si," clear glass bottle in the shape of a chianti bottle w/gold stripings, mint in cylindrical ribbed gold presentation box, ca. 1957, 4 3/4" h. (ILLUS.) **$800-900**

Miniature "Si" by Schiaparelli Bottle

Perfume bottle & stopper, "Si," miniature clear glass bottle in the shape of a chianti bottle, gold cap, label on bottom, ca. 1957, 1 1/3" h. (ILLUS.) **$145-290**

Schiaparelli "Sleeping" Candlestick Bottle

Perfume bottle & stopper, "Sleeping," clear glass candlestick-shaped bottle w/a red glass flame-shaped stopper, labeled, w/original snuffer-shaped bright pink box, ca. 1938, 8" h. (ILLUS.) **$650-750**

Perfume bottle & stopper, "Succes Fou," green opaque leaf-shaped glass bottle w/gold trim, in original bright pink heart-shaped pink box, ca. 1953, 4 1/4" h. (ILLUS., top next column).................. **$450-600**

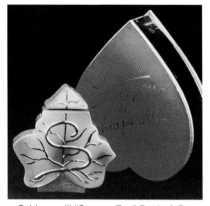

Schiaparelli "Succes Fou" Bottle & Box

Schiaparelli "Zut" Perfume Bottle & Box

Perfume bottle & stopper, "Zut" by Schiaparelli, clear & frosted glass, modeled as the lower torso of a lady wearing tights, her legs tapering down into round folds of fabric frosted & trimmed w/gold stars, gilded stopper, sealed, in original purple silk-lined box, ca. 1949, 5 1/2" h. (ILLUS.)........ **$900**

"Zut" by Schiaparelli Figural Bottle

Perfume bottle & stopper, "Zut," clear & frosted glass bottle in the shape of the lower body of a woman w/her slip puddled around her feet, gold designs around the waist & gold stars on the slip, gold metal cap & green neck ribbon, reportedly inspired by an accident that occurred to Elsa Schiaparelli when the waist elastic on her slip broke at a train station & the slip fell to her feet, ca. 1949, 4 3/4" h. (ILLUS.) **$345**

Perfume bottle & stopper, "Zut," miniature clear glass bottle in the shaped of the lower torso of a woman, metal stopper, empty, good label on bottom, ca. 1949, 2 1/8" h. **$500-600**

Miniature "Zut" by Schiaparelli Bottle

Perfume bottle & stopper, "Zut," miniature version of the clear glass bottle in the shape of the lower body of a woman w/her slip puddled around her feet, ca. 1949, 2 1/8" h. (ILLUS.) **$350**

Worth

Worth Blue Glass "Dans La Nuit" Bottle

Perfume bottle & stopper, "Dans La Nuit," small dark blue glass boule-shaped bottle w/upright blue disc stopper molded w/the name, w/original box, ca. 1920, 2 1/3" h. (ILLUS.) **$150**

"Je Reviens" Blue Lalique Glass Bottle

Perfume bottle & stopper, "Je Reviens," small blue Lalique glass cylindrical ribbed bottle w/a turquoise stopper, signed by Lalique, 3" h. (ILLUS.) **$100**

Scarce Worth "Requete" Lalique Bottle

Perfume bottle & stopper, "Requete," clear glass Lalique bottle w/a pedestal base supporting the upright round disc-form bottle w/a scalloped edge trimmed in blue enamel, clear tapering stopper, mint in box, marked by Lalique, ca. 1944, 6 1/8" h. (ILLUS., previous page) .. **$2,000-2,500**

Worth "Vers Toi" Lalique Bottle

Perfume bottle & stopper, "Vers Toi," clear frosted Lalique glass tapering cylindrical flowerpot-form bottle w/a flat shoulder, tiny neck & short cylindrical stopper, labeled, signed "R. Lalique," ca. 1933, 3" h. (ILLUS.) **$75**

Two Miniature "Je Reviens" Bottles

Perfume bottles & stoppers, "Je Reviens," a miniature upright reeded square blue Lalique glass bottle w/a match gold cap & a miniature flattened disc-form blue Lalique glass bottle w/a cylindrical cap, both empty & unsigned, ca. 1930s, 2" & 2 1/2" h., each (ILLUS.) **$20-25**

United States

Arden (Elizabeth)

Arden "Blue Grass" Figural Cologne

Cologne bottle, "Blue Grass," figural clear glass bottle in the form of the bust of a woman on plinth base, missing cork stopper, ca. 1934, 12 1/2" h. (ILLUS.)........ **$125**

Perfume bottle & stopper, "Blue Grass," clear upright rectangular glass bottle w/a blue horse overcap, full, w/two labels, ca. 1934, 3 1/4" h. **$66**

Miniature "Blue Grass" Arden Bottle

Perfume bottle & stopper, "Blue Grass," miniature clear upright rectangular glass bottle w/a gold overcap, empty, w/two labels, ca. 1934, 1 1/8" h. (ILLUS.).... **$110-125**

Fan-shaped "Cyclamen" Perfume Bottle

Perfume bottle & stopper, "Cyclamen" by Elizabeth Arden, a Baccarat figural bottle w/a white open fan resting on a clear faceted glass base, tall pointed square stopper, gilt trim, sealed w/metallic ribbon & jewel brooch, base stenciled "Baccarat," ca. 1938, 6 1/2" h. (ILLUS.)
.... **$2,400**

Baccarat "Cyclamen" Bottle for E. Arden

Perfume bottle & stopper, "Cyclamen," figural Baccarat glass bottle in the shape of an open white fan on clear feet & w/a tall pointed clear stopper, signed & numbered by Baccarat, ca. 1938, 6 3/8" h. (ILLUS.)... **$400-600**

Figural Baccarat Bottle for "It's You"

Perfume bottle & stopper, "It's You," clear figural Baccarat glass bottle in the form of an upright hand holding aloft a flaring bottle, a blue ring & blue flower stopper, sealed, w/hang tags, signed & numbered by Baccarat, lacking dome, ca. 1938, 6 1/2" h. (ILLUS.) **$1,200-1,500**
Perfume bottle & stopper, "It's You," figural Baccarat glass bottle in the form of an upright white hand holding aloft a gold flaring bottle, gold rose-shaped stopper, hang tag & original glass dome, mint in box, ca. 1935, 6 1/3" h. **$3,850**

Arden "Memoire Cherie" Figural Bottle

Perfume bottle & stopper, "Memoire Cherie," figural, a frosted clear glass model of a lady, label on the bottom, 3" h. (ILLUS.).. **$285**

"Mille Fleurs" by Elizabeth Arden Bottle & Presentation Box

Figural "On Dit" by Elizabeth Arden Bottle

Figural "Memoire Chérie" Perfume Bottle

Perfume bottle & stopper, "Memoire Chérie," frosted glass figural w/the bottle shaped like a woman's torso w/her gold-trimmed arms crossed at the front, head-shaped stopper w/gilt trim, deluxe holiday version, ca. 1953, 6 7/8" h. (ILLUS.)... **$750-1,200**

Perfume bottle & stopper, "Mille Fleurs," clear bulbous glass bottle w/an orange Bakelite cap, bottom label, mint in original presentation box, ca. 1942, 2 1/2" h. (ILLUS., top of page) **$175**

Perfume bottle & stopper, "My Love," clear glass bottle w/a feather-shaped stopper, good lettering, ca. 1949, 3 1/2" h. **$140**

Perfume bottle & stopper, "Night and Day," clear glass triangular bottle w/a flame-shaped stopper, good label, ca. 1935, 2" h. **$48**

Perfume bottle & stopper, "On Dit" by Elizabeth Arden, clear frosted container molded in the shape of two ladies' heads, one whispering to the other, curled topnot stopper, very rare box w/graphics by Rene Bouche, ca. 1948, 3 3/4" h. (ILLUS., top next column) **$6,600**

"On Dit" Figural Elizabeth Arden Bottle

Perfume bottle & stopper, "On Dit," figural clear & frosted glass bottle in the form of two stylized ladies' heads w/tightly curled hair whispering to each other, topknot forms stopper, ca. 1952, 4 1/4" h. (ILLUS., previous page) **$145-175**

Ayer (Harriet Hubbard)

"Muguet" Harriet Hubbard Ayer Bottle

Perfume bottle & stopper, "Muguet," J. Viard bottle in an upright flattened triangular shape, clear & frosted w/an overall blossom design w/a sepia patina, matching flattened arched stopper, w/original label, 1920s, 3 3/4" h. (ILLUS.) **$570**

Perfume bottle & stopper, "Yu," simple rectangular clear glass bottle w/a wide glass stopper, mint in box, ca. 1937, 2 2/3" h. **$55**

Chess (Mary)

Two Mary Chess Chessmen Bottles

Perfume bottle & stopper, chessman knight figural bottle, clear tapering & ringed bottle w/a gilt metal horse head stopper, ca. 1940s, 3" h. (ILLUS. left with tall Mary Chess knight bottle) **$20**

Perfume bottle & stopper, chessman knight figural bottle, clear tapering & ringed bottle w/a clear glass horse head stopper, ca. 1940s, 4 1/3" h. (ILLUS. right with short Mary Chess knight bottle) **$40**

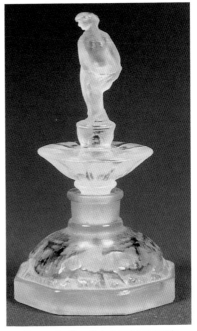

Souvenir d'un Soir Fountain Bottle

Perfume bottle & stopper, "Souvenir d'un Soir," a frosted & clear glass figural replica of the fountain in the Plaza Hotel in New York City, ca. 1956, 3 2/3" h. (ILLUS.)... **$310-590**

Set of Mary Chess Gold Chessmen Perfume Bottles

Perfumes bottle & stoppers, chessman figural bottles, gold-painted glass tapering & ringed bottle w/a chessman stopper, ca. 1940s, original gold box, 3" h., set of 4 (ILLUS.) **$89**

Colgate & Company

Early Colgate "Caprice" Perfume Bottle

Perfume bottle & stopper, "Caprice," simple slender slightly tapering clear bottle w/metal twist-off cap, good original label, ca. 1893, 3 1/8" h. (ILLUS.) **$20-30**

Perfume bottle & stopper, "Cha Ming," simple slender clear bottle w/glass stopper, original label w/floral graphics, in original box, ca. 1917, 3" h.......................... **$55**

Art Deco Lalique Bottle for "Orchis"

Perfume bottle & stopper, "Orchis," a Lalique bottle in clear & frosted glass w/a light rose patina, upright flattened rectangular shape w/an overall etched design of stylized flowers on the sides, w/label, molded "R. Lalique," ca. 1927, 3 5/8" h. (ILLUS.) **$2,520**

Colgate "The Unknown Flower" Bottle & Box

Perfume bottle & stopper, "The Unknown Flower," J. Viard frosted clear upright round bottle w/a sepia patina, the sides molded as a large four-petaled blossom, small blossom stopper, w/original disk-form box w/tassel, ca. 1921, stain to interior of box, 3 1/8" h. (ILLUS.) **$2,200-3,000**

Factor (Max)

Max Factor Novelty Perfume Set

Perfume bottle & stopper, "Hypnotique," novelty-type, a simple cylindrical glass bottle w/gold plastic cap packaged under a high plastic dome w/a seated stylized black cat, labeled around the base of the container "Sophisti-Cat," ca. 1958, bottle 2" h. (ILLUS.) **$18-22**

Max Factor Sophisti-Cat Novelty Set

Perfume bottle & stopper, "Primitif," novelty-type, a simple cylindrical glass bottle w/gold plastic cap packaged under a high plastic dome w/a seated stylized pink cat, labeled around the base of the container "Sophisti-Cat," ca. 1960, bottle 2" h. (ILLUS.) **$22-30**

Hudnut (Richard)

"Fadette" Bottle for Richard Hudnut

Perfume bottle & stopper, "Fadette," a J. Viard design in clear & frosted glass, cylindrical w/an overall molded floral swag design trimmed in sepia patina, figural stopper of nude lady, bottom molded "J. Viard," ca. 1924, 4" h. (ILLUS.).... **$1,600-2,300**

Perfume bottle & stopper, "Le Debut Blanc," a squatty octagonal white glass bottle w/a short neck & upright gold raspberry-shaped stopper, original label, empty, ca. 1927, 1 1/3" h. **$183**

Hudnut "Le Debut Noir" Black Bottle

Perfume bottle & stopper, "Le Debut Noir," footed squatty angular black glass bottle w/an upright frosted yellowish raspberry-shaped stopper, label on bottom, ca. 1927, 2 1/2" h. (ILLUS.) **$175-250**

Jade Green "Le Debut Vert" Bottle

Perfume bottle & stopper, "Le Debut Vert," a squatty octagonal jade green glass bottle w/a short neck & upright gold raspberry-shaped stopper, original label, empty, ca. 1927, 2 1/8" h. (ILLUS.) **$200**

Perfume bottle & stopper, "Mona Lisa," clear frosted bottle & stopper, gold label, ca. 1902, 3" h. **$21**

Hudnut "Three Flowers" Bottle

Perfume bottle & stopper, "Three Flowers," slightly tapering cylindrical frosted clear bottle w/clear & frosted arched stopper, original gold label, empty, ca. 1929, 6 2/3" h. (ILLUS.) **$45-50**

Hudnut "Violet Sec" 1940s Bottle & Box

Perfume bottle & stopper, "Violet Sec," clear upright tall slender square glass bottle w/a white plastic onion dome cap, original label & cylindrical presentation box, scent introduced in 1896, this bottle ca. 1940s, 3" h. (ILLUS.) **$25-55**

Hudnut Perfume & Compact Set

Perfume bottle & stopper & compact set, "Le Debut Noir," a squatty octagonal black glass bottle w/pointed gold stopper & original label in a fitted gold box beside an octagonal compact w/a black enameled lid, ca. 1927, bottle 2 1/8" h., the set (ILLUS.)....................................... **$1,200-2,000**

Prince Matchabelli

"Added Attraction" by Prince Matchabelli

Perfume bottle & stopper, "Added Attraction," clear glass crown-shaped bottle enameled in red & gold w/gold cross stopper, label on bottom, ca. 1956, 2 2/3" h. (ILLUS.) **$200-250**

Perfume bottle & stopper, "Added Attraction," miniature glass crown-shaped bottle w/red enamel trim & a screw-off cap, in velvet case, ca. 1956, 1 3/4" h. **$125-150**

Perfume bottle & stopper, "Ave Maria," clear & frosted crown-shaped bottle w/clear glass cross stopper, original label, ca. 1926, 2 1/4" h. **$25-40**

Perfume bottle & stopper, "Beloved," clear crown-shaped bottle enameled in blue & gold & w/a gold cross-form stopper, in original plastic case, ca. 1950, 3 1/4" h. **$113**

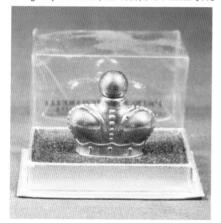

Gilt-Metal "Crown Jewel" Perfume Bottle

Perfume bottle & stopper, "Crown Jewel," miniature gilded metal crown-shaped bottle w/gold ball cap, in fitted box, ca. 1945, 1 1/2" h. (ILLUS.) **$100**

"Duchess of York" in Crown-form Bottle

Perfume bottle & stopper, "Duchess of York," clear glass crown-form bottle w/gold enamel trim & gold cross-form stopper, label & mark on the bottom, ca. 1934, 3 1/2" h. (ILLUS.) **$65-75**

Perfume bottle & stopper, "Empress of India," clear & frosted glass crown-shaped bottle w/cross stopper, original label, ca. 1930, 1 3/4" h. **$25-44**

Perfume bottle & stopper, "Infanta," all-clear glass crown-form bottle w/clear cross-form stopper, original box, ca. 1937, 1 1/2" h. **$128**

Perfume bottle & stopper, "Katherine the Great," all-black enameled crown-shaped bottle w/gold cross stopper, original label, ca. 1935, 2 1/3" h. **$550-580**

Perfume bottle & stopper, "Prophecy," white enameled crown-shaped bottle w/gold trim & gold cross stopper, original label, sealed, ca. 1974, 1 2/3" h. **$135**

"Royal Gardenia" with Special Box

Perfume bottle & stopper, "Royal Gardenia," clear glass crown-shaped bottle w/gold & black trim, gold cross stopper, full & sealed, w/original fitted heavy clear plastic cube box, ca. 1930, 2 2/3" h. (ILLUS., previous page) **$170**

"Wind Song" Crown Bottle in Box

Perfume bottle & stopper, "Wind Song," small bluish green & black enameled crown-shaped bottle w/a screw-off gold cap, fitted in velvet box, ca. 1953, 1 3/4" h. (ILLUS.) **$45-75**

Prince Matchabelli Miniature Bottles in Crown-shaped Presentation Box

Perfume bottles & stoppers, miniature set of three clear crown-shaped bottles w/gold caps, fitted in a presentation box w/a large gold & white crown-shaped cover w/gold cross finial, ca. 1950s, each 1 1/4" h., the set (ILLUS.).................... **$285-385**

Miscellaneous Specialty Perfume Bottles

Current Production Perfumes

"Matruska" Russian Doll-shaped Bottle

Air-Val International, "Matruska," Russian nesting doll figural bottle, mint in box, 4" h. (ILLUS.) **$20**

Clear Square "Amouage Gold" Bottle

Amouage, "Amouage Gold," square upright clear glass bottle w/a pointed domed metal stopper, also produced in a limited edition w/a genuine malachite & lapis bottles, ca. 1983, 5 1/8" h. (ILLUS.) **$175**

"Classique" Glass Torso Perfume Bottle

Gaultier (Jean Paul), "Classique," clear glass female torso spray bottle, ca. 1990s, 6" h. (ILLUS.)................................... **$30**

"Fragile" Snow Globe Gaultier Perfume

Gaultier (Jean Paul), "Fragile," designed as a snow globe enclosing the tiny figure of a lady wearing a long black dress & gloves, gilt metal base, mint in box, ca. 1999, 3" h. (ILLUS.) **$90**

Updated "Classique" Torso Bottle

Gaultier (Jean Paul), "Classique," updated clear glass female torso spray bottle w/black detailing, ca. 1990s, 6" h. (ILLUS.)..... **$55**

"Summer Fragrance" Glass Torso Bottle

Gaultier (Jean Paul), "Summer Fragrance," clear glass female torso atomizer bottle painted in bright pink & yellow in a South Seas motif, w/original metal can, 6" h. (ILLUS.)... **$60**

Sonja Rykiel One-Ounce Spray Bottle

Rykiel (Sonja), clear glass T-shaped one-ounce eau de perfum spray bottle w/orange cap, sealed, ca. 1990s, 3" h. (ILLUS.) **$6**

Factice Bottles

Chanel, "Chanel No. 5," giant all-glass design, 6 1/2" h. **$100-220**
Chanel, "Chanel No. 5," giant plastic design, 17" h. **$190-300**

Liz Claiborne "Realities" Factice

Claiborne (Liz), "Realities," frosted gold glass bottle designed as two stacked square blocks, frosted pale blue block stopper, good gold lettering, full, 9 1/2" h. (ILLUS.) **$100**

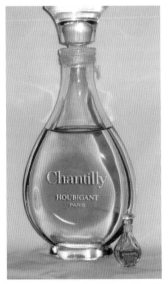

Houbigant "Chantilly" Glass Factice

Houbigant, "Chantilly," large footed tear-drop-shaped clear glass bottle w/gently flaring cylindrical clear glass stopper, ca. 1940s, 11 1/4" h. (ILLUS.).................. **$125-150**

1990s Calvin Klein "Eternity" Factice

Klein (Calvin), "Eternity," large upright rectangular clear glass bottle w/flattened rectangular metal stopper, ca. 1990s, 9 1/2" h. (ILLUS.) **$50**

Lagerfeld "Chloé" Factice

Lagerfeld (Karl), "Chloé," clear boule-shaped glass bottle w/large double blossom frosted glass stopper, marked "HP" on the bottom for glassmaker, Pochet et du Courval, 11" h. (ILLUS.) **$175-200**

Claude Montana "Montana" Acrylic Factice

Montana (Claude), "Montana," giant frosted acrylic stylized torso w/narrow banding, ca. 1990s, 16" h. (ILLUS.) **$175**
Prince Matchabelli, giant clear glass crown-shaped bottle enameled in light blue w/gold trim & a gold cross stopper, unlabeled, used to advertise a wide line of scents, ca. 1940s-60s, 8 1/2" h. **$2,717**

Prince Matchabelli Giant Crown Factice

Prince Matchabelli, giant clear glass crown-shaped bottle w/gold trim & a gold cross stopper, unlabeled, used to advertise a wide line of scents, ca. 1940s-60s, 8 1/2" h. (ILLUS.) **$650-725**

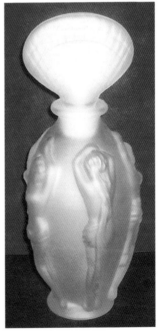

Vicky Tiel Green Glass Factice

Tiel (Vicky), large ovoid frosted green glass bottle molded w/standing female nudes & w/large shell-shaped stopper, used for several of her scents, 12 1/2" h. (ILLUS.) .. **$400**

Worth "Je Reviens" Factice by Lalique

Worth, "Je Reviens," tall cylindrical ribbed dark blue Lalique glass bottle w/stepped shoulder & cylindrical turquoise blue stopper, marked by Lalique on the bottom, ca. 1931, 11 1/3" h. (ILLUS.)......... **$250**

Miniature Perfume Bottles - General

"Muguet de Corday" Boxed Miniature

Corday, "Muguet de Corday," small clear glass ovoid bottle w/gilt metal cap, in original cellulose case, ca. 1931, 1 1/2" h. (ILLUS.) **$30-40**

"L'Origan" Mini Bottle with Head & Hat

Coty, "L'Origan," small clear glass cylindrical bottle w/gold lettering & gold cap topped by the painted head of a lady wearing a broad-brimmed black hat, ca. 1950s-60s, 1 1/2" h. (ILLUS.)...................... **$75**

Coty, "Paris," small cylindrical clear glass bottle tied to a plastic Christmas bell, ca. 1930, 1 1/2" h.. **$90**

Tiny "Paris" by Coty Miniature Bottle

Coty, "Paris," tiny square clear glass bottle w/original label & screw-off gold cap, ca. 1923, 1 1/8" h. (ILLUS.) **$25**

Miniature "Ecusson" Bottle in Box

d'Albret (Jean), "Ecusson," small flattened clear glass shield-shaped bottle w/gold label & gold screw-off cap, in original oblong plastic display box, ca. 1952, 1 1/2" h. (ILLUS.) **$20-50**

Desprez (Jean), "Sheherazade," small clear glass spire-shaped bottle, mint in box, ca. 1960s, 3" h. **$200**

Evyan, "White Shoulders," small clear glass lay-down type textured heart design, ca. 1943, 2 1/4" h. **$10**

Gabilla, "La Vierge," small clear glass bottle w/ tiered glass stopper, labeled, ca. 1913, 1 2/3" h. **$55-65**

Gourielli, "Five O'Clock," small clear glass model of a cocktail shaker, w/original box, ca. 1947, 1 1/2" h. **$25-30**

Miniature "Chantilly" Bottle with Chair

Houbigant, "Chantilly," small flattened ovoid clear glass bottle w/a white cap tied to the back of a miniature cafe chair w/red cushion seat, w/original box, ca. 1940, 2" h. (ILLUS.) **$50-125**

"Le Parfum Ideal" Miniature Bottle

Houbigant, "Le Parfum Ideal," small clear glass cylindrical ribbed Louis XV-style bottle w/a tall neck & gold cap, label on the bottom, ca. 1900, 2 1/2" h. (ILLUS.)....... **$42**

Isadora, "Isadora," small clear glass bottle w/plastic figural kneeling nude stopper, ca. 1970s, 1 1/2" h. **$12-18**

Miniature "Arpege" by Lanvin Bottle

Lanvin, "Arpege," small upright square clear glass bottle w/original label & black cap, w/original cylindrical black box, ca. 1927, 1 1/2" h. (ILLUS.) **$25**

Le Galion, "Sortilege," tiny clear glass bottle w/metal logo cap, mint in box, ca. 1937, 3/4" h. **$76**

Lelong (Lucien), "Passionment," small clear glass bottle w/a pearl-shaped top, ca. 1940, 1 1/8" h. **$18**

Myrurgia, "Joya," small clear glass faceted bottle w/gold cap, mint in box, ca. 1954, 1 1/2" h. **$25-50**

Paquin "9 x 9" Black Glass Miniature

Paquin, "9 x 9," small flattened upright black glass bottle w/original label, tapering fluted gold screw-on stopper set w/a blue stone, impressed mark on the bottom, ca. 1939, 2 1/8" h. (ILLUS.).......... **$140**

Park and Tilford, "No. 3," small clear glass bottle w/nude on the label, black cap, ca. 1931 .... **$16**

Patou "Moment Supreme" Miniature

Patou (Jean), "Moment Supreme," small clear glass bottle w/overall molded knobs, gold metal cap, gold label on bottom, w/original white box lined in blue silk, ca. 1929, 2 3/8" h. (ILLUS.) **$135**

Picasso (Paloma), "Paloma Picasso," flat round black glass bottle, full, ca. 1984, 2 1/8" h. **$5**

Picasso (Paloma), "Paloma Picasso," flat round white glass bottle, full, ca. 1984, 2 1/8" h. **$35**

Miniature "Lys Bleu" Bottle

Prince Henri d'Orleans, "Lys Bleu," small clear glass eau de toilette bottle w/rounded shoulders & short neck, upright plastic star-shaped stopper, black & gold label, full, ca. 1980, 3" h. (ILLUS.) **$27**

Redken Labs, "Pique," clear glass bottle w/plastic butterfly-shaped stopper, mint in box, ca. 1979, 2" h. **$29**

Renoir "Chi-Chi" Heart-shaped Mini

Renoir, "Chi-Chi," small clear & frosted glass bottle in the shape of a sideways heart raised on a foot, tan Bakelite screw-on cap, w/original box, ca. 1942, 2" h. (ILLUS.)... **$125-150**

"Detchema" by Revillon Miniature

Revillon, "Detchema," small flattened ovoid clear glass bottle w/original label & gold cap, ca. 1953, 1 1/8" h. (ILLUS.)................... **$15**

Rochas (Marcel) "Femme," small flattened round opaque white lay-down type glass bottle covered in floral design black lace, gilt-metal ball stopper w/long dauber, empty, w/black cloth pouch, 2 2/3" h. **$40-50**

"Heaven Sent" Miniature with Harlequin

Rubenstein (Helena) "Heaven Sent," a miniature upright flattened clear glass bottle w/a molded woodgrain design & a white cap being held by a small Harlequin doll, mint in box, ca. 1941, 2 1/2" h. (ILLUS.) **$50-75**

Rubenstein "Heaven Sent" Angel Bottle

Rubenstein (Helena), "Heaven Sent," small frosted clear glass bottle in the shape of a stylized baby angel, gold metal twist-off cap, empty, ca. 1941, 2 1/3" h. (ILLUS.)... **$40-60**

"Mischief" Miniature Bottle & Top Hat

Saville, "Mischief," small flattened upright black glass bottle w/a gold cap, labeled, w/miniature black plastic top hat holder & white oval hatbox box, ca. 1935, 1 3/4" h. (ILLUS.)... **$65-120**

Valois (Rose), "Marcotte," small glass bottle in plastic case designed as a woman wearing & white & red straw hat, ca. 1950, 2 1/3" h... **$371**

"A Concentrated Extract" Mini Bottle

Vanderbilt (Lucretia) "A Concentrated Extract," small flattened round blue glass bottle w/the silver butterfly logo, upright fanned blue glass stopper, tiny label on the bottom, 2 1/3" h. (ILLUS.) **$70-90**

Miniature Sets of Perfume Bottles

Chanel Four Miniature Bottle Set

Chanel, set of four small clear glass rectangular bottles w/plastic caps, fitted in original box, ca. 1990s, each 1 1/3" h., the set (ILLUS.) **$30-55**

Ciro Set of Five Miniature Bottles with Boxes & Case

Ciro, set of five bottles, "Danger," "New Horizons," "Reflexions," "Ricochet," "Replique," & "Surrender," each clear glass bottle in a different shape w/a gold cap, w/original individual boxes & presentation case, ca. 1940s, each 1 1/2" h., the set (ILLUS.) **$90-100**

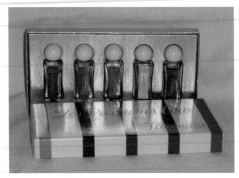

Ciro "Flaconettes" Set of Miniature Bottles

Ciro, set of five bottles, "Flaconettes," tiny upright square clear glass bottles each w/a different color label, white ball-shaped caps, in original fitted box, each 1 3/4" h., the set (ILLUS.) **$55-76**

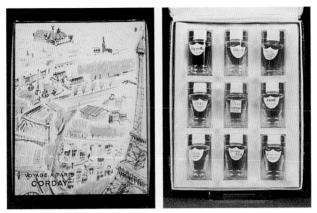

Corday "Voyage à Paris" Nine-Bottle Miniature Set

Corday, set of nine bottles, "Voyage à Paris" set, clear tapering cylindrical glass bottles w/shield-shaped paper labels, white caps, each in its individual cellulois case, ca. 1940s, mint in box, each 1 1/2" h., the set (ILLUS. of box cover & contents, top of page) **$175-225**

Coty, set of two bottles, "Emeraude," & "Paris," each clear simple rectangular glass bottle w/a finely ribbed gold cap, mint in original large white box, ca. 1940s, each 2" h., the set (ILLUS.) **$90-100**

Dior, set of three bottles, lay-down style, called pastilles or pebbles, w/paper labels, mint in box, ca. 1950s, each 1 1/2" h., the set **$188-355**

Marquay, set of four tiny faceted oval clear glass bottles w/pointed & faceted glass stopper, original labels, each w/individual velvet pouche in original box, ca. 1950s, each 1 1/2" h., the set (ILLUS., bottom of page) **$125**

Coty Set of Two Miniature Perfume Bottles

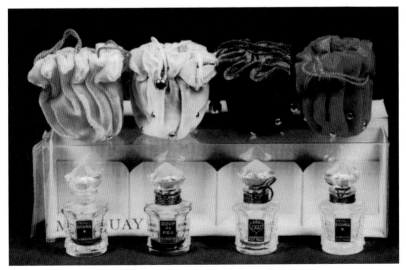

Marquay Four-Bottle Miniature Set

"Flor de Blason" Mini Perfume & Soap Set

Myrurgia, "Flor de Blason," a small clear glass square bottle w/gold metal stopper, labeled, w/matching wrapped bar of soap, mint in box, ca. 1927, bottle 2 7/8" h., the set (ILLUS.)............................ **$85**

Prince Matchabelli, set of four bottles, "Perfume Honors," each clear glass bottle mint in original 11 1/3" l. box, each 1 1/4" h., the set..................................... **$29-49**

Prince Matchabelli, set of four bottles, "Perfume Honors," each clear glass bottle mint in original square pink box, each 1 1/4" h., the set... **$76**

Three Miniature Raphael Bottles

Raphael, set of three bottles, "Demon," "Plaisir" & "Replique," each clear squared glass w/a flattened clear glass blossom-form stopper w/an engraved "R," labeled, full & sealed, in green cloth carrying case, ca. 1940s, each 2" h., the set (ILLUS.)... **$300**

Ricci (Nina), set of five bottles, "L'Air du Temps," each clear glass bottle w/a colored plastic double-dove stopper in a cage presentation box, mint, ca. 1990s, each 1 3/4" h., the set **$95-130**

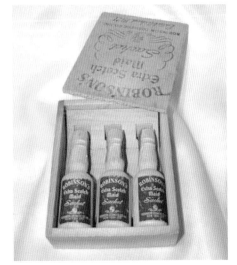

Set of "Extra Scotch Maid Sachet" Sachet Bottles

Robinson, set of three bottles, "Extra Scotch Maid Sachet," each a wooden model of a whiskey bottle w/a blue & white label, in a fitted rectangular wooden case, ca. 1940s-50s, each 2 1/2" h., the set (ILLUS.)... **$125**

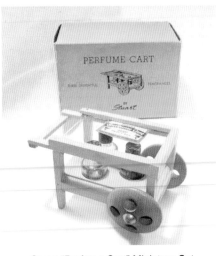

Stuart "Perfume Cart" Miniature Set

Stuart, set of three bottles, "Perfume Cart," a pink wood cart w/movable wheels holds three tiny cylindrical clear glass bottle w/caps, w/original box, 1940s, each 1 1/4" h., the set (ILLUS.).................... **$125-160**

Set of Six Rose Valois Miniature Bottles

Valois (Rose), set of six small tapering cylindrical ribbed bottles w/plastic head-shaped stoppers each wearing a different fancy hat, mint in original display box, Rose Valois was a haute couture hat designer, ca. 1950, 2 3/8" h., the set (ILLUS., top of page) **$1,000-1,100**

Perfume Tester Bottles

Arden (Elizabeth), "Cupid's Breath," clear glass bottle w/glass ball stopper w/dauber, labeled, original wooden case, ca. 1928, 2 2/3" h. **$24-46**

Balmain (Pierre), "Jolie Madame," clear glass bottle w/glass stopper w/dauber, full, ca. 1952, 2 1/3" h. **$29**

Caron, "Le Muguet de Bonheur," clear glass bottle w/white label & metal cap w/dauber, ca. 1952, 2 1/2" h. **$20-42**

Caron, set of 8 small bottles, clear glass w/white labels & screw-off caps w/daubers, mint in box, ca. 1950s, each 2 1/2" h., the set **$315**

Two Dana Tester Bottles

Old Chanel No. 5 Tester Bottle

Chanel, "No. 5," upright square clear glass bottle w/label, upright flat oval glass stopper w/dauber, original label, ca. 1921, 2 1/2" h. (ILLUS.) **$25**

Dana, "Ambush," upright square clear glass bottle w/label, glass ball stopper w/dauber, ca. 1950s, 2 1/4" h. (ILLUS. right with Dana Platine tester bottle, top next column) **$30**

"Bolero" by Dana Square Tester Bottle

Dana, "Bolero," upright square clear glass bottle w/squared clear glass stopper w/long dauber, good original label, ca. 1932, 2 3/4" h. (ILLUS.) **$35-50**

Dana, "Platine," upright square clear glass bottle w/label, glass ball stopper w/dauber, ca. 1950s, 2 1/4" h. (ILLUS. left with Dana Ambush tester bottle, previous page)..................................... **$30**

Desses (Jean), "Celui," clear glass bottle w/glass stopper w/dauber, ca. 1938, 2 3/4" h. **$23**

Dralle "Illusion Rose" Tester Bottle &Case

Dralle, "Illusion Rose," clear cylindrical bottle w/flat oval glass stopper impressed w/a flying bird, red diamond-shaped label, plain wood upright lighthouse-form case w/red & black paper label, Germany, ca. 1918, 2 3/8" h. (ILLUS.).. **$90-100**

Dralle "Veilchen" Tester Bottle & Case

Dralle, "Veilchen (Violet)," upright paneled clear bottle w/flat oval stopper impressed w/a flying bird, original label, w/upright cylindrical red wood case in the form of a lighthouse, Germany, ca. 1920-30s, 2 3/8" h. (ILLUS.) **$80-120**

Houbigant, "Quelques Fleurs," clear glass bottle w/glass stopper w/dauber, ca. 1912, 2 1/4" h... **$20**

Purse Bottles

Perfume bottle & stopper, cased glass w/pink over white cut to clear, brass overcap & finger ring & inner stopper, Europe, late 19th c., 3 3/4" l. **$600**

English Cranberry Glass Purse Perfume

Perfume bottle & stopper, cylindrical cranberry glass bottle w/a floral-stamped cylindrical sterling silver screw-on cap, hallmarked 1876, England, 2 1/2" h. (ILLUS.)... **$250**

Bird Claw-shaped Purse Perfume Bottle

Long Sterling Chased Perfume Bottle

Perfume bottle & stopper, figural, silver plated model of a bird's foot w/claws, American or European, ca. 1890, 2 1/2" l. (ILLUS., previous page) **$400**

Czech Lapis Purse Perfume Bottle

Perfume bottle & stopper, flattened footed round lapis lazuli glass molded in high-relief w/a large blossom & leaves, metal filigree screw-on cap w/a blue faux jewel, metal tag marked "Czecho-Slovakia," ca. 1920, 2 1/2" h. (ILLUS.) **$200**

Fine Blue Cut-Overlay Purse Perfume

Perfume bottle & stopper, flattened oblong cut-overlay glass in clear cased in blue over white & cut w/a long rectangular panel trimmed in gold & enclosing colorful flowers on a white ground, cut round windows down one edge, gilt-silver collar & decorated cap, Bohemia or France, ca. 1875-1900, 3 1/2" h. (ILLUS.) **$400-500**

Perfume bottle & stopper, long slender cylindrical sterling silver case chased overall w/flower & leaves, hinged domed cap, England, ca. 1900, 8" l. (ILLUS., top of page) **$400**

Rare Rutilated Quartz Perfume Bottle

Perfume bottle & stopper, long square rutilated quartz hardstone bottle w/a leaf-stamped silver-gilt collar & hinged cap marked by Krementz, American, dated 1898, 2 3/4" h. (ILLUS.) **$1,000**

Czech Malachite Glass Purse Perfume

Perfume bottle & stopper, molded footed round malachite glass decorated w/flowers & ropetwist bands, red Bakelite screw-on cap, signed "Ingrid - Czecho-Slovakia," ca. 1920, 2 1/4" h. (ILLUS., previous page) **$300**

Souvenir-Type

Blown Glass & Silver "Duluth" Souvenir

Perfume bottle & stopper, blown bulbous dark green bottle tapering to a short flaring neck, decorated w/overall silver overlay w/loops spelling out the name "Duluth" (Minnesota), unknown maker, probably late 19th - early 20th c., 3 1/2" h. (ILLUS.) **$85**

Blue Glass Souvenir Perfume for Venice

Perfume bottle & stopper, blown cobalt blue glass in a boule shape enameled overall in gilt leafy flower sprigs surround-ing the gold inscription "Venise" (Venice in French), metal collar, overcap & chain w/large ring, late 19th - early 20th c., 2" h. (ILLUS.)... **$250**

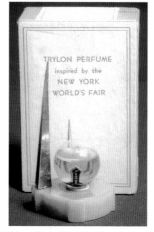

1939 New York World's Fair Perfume Set

Perfume bottle & stopper, figural design of the Trylon & Perisphere of the 1939 New York World's Fair, a squared yellowish green Bakelite platform supports a clear glass Perisphere w/Rubicon sticker beside a tall slender metal model of the Trylon, complete w/original box, 3 1/4" h. (ILLUS.).. **$305-480**

Porcelain Exposition Souvenir Perfume

Perfume bottle & stopper, flattened oval gilt-brass mounted porcelain w/a printed color scene of a large unknown exposition building, gilt-brass collar, cap & long chain w/finger ring, probably late 19th c., 4" h. (ILLUS.) **$450**

Red Perfume with Notre Dame Scene

Perfume bottle & stopper, short cylindrical red glass shape w/a rounded shoulder to the metal collar & overcap decorated at the top w/a color scene of Notre Dame Cathedral, Paris, late 19th c., 2 7/8" h. (ILLUS.) **$150**

Perfume Related Collectibles

Men's Scents

Dana "Canoe" Figural Cologne Bottle

Dana, "Canoe," figural cologne bottle, a ceramic decanter in the shape of a French sailor standing on a dock, realistic painting, full, brand name on cap, ca. 1946, 15" h. (ILLUS.) **$75-100**

"HIS Northwoods After Shave Lotion"

House for Men, "HIS Northwoods After Shave Lotion," glass bottle molded in the shape & a man's torso & enameled in dark red, square stylized head white plastic cap, small round label, ca. 1940, 6 1/3" h. (ILLUS.) **$60-90**

Patou "Voyageur" Eau de Toilette Bottle

Patou (Jean), "Voyageur" eau de toilette, a small cylindrical cobalt blue glass bottle w/a silver cap resting in a miniature model of an ocean liner, w/original dark blue & silver presentation box, ca. 1990s, bottle 1 1/2" h.(ILLUS.)................................ **$15-30**

Rabanne "Eau de Calandre" Bottle

Rabanne (Paco), "Eau de Calandre," small upright square clear glass bottle w/black cap, ca. 1990s, 2" h. (ILLUS.) **$1**

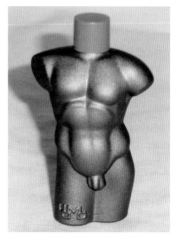

Uomo Male Torso "Hero" Bottle

Uomo, "Hero," figural grey nude male torso bottle w/grey plastic cap, full, ca. 1992, 2 1/3" h. (ILLUS.) **$12**

Perfume Lamps

DeVilbiss Perfume Lamp with White Shade

Brass & glass, round brass base & support ring holding a cylindrical white glass shade decorated around the base w/small black dancing figures & w/orange & black swags around the top, metal domed cap w/pierced holes, unsigned DeVilbiss, United States, 1930s, 7 1/2" h. (ILLUS.) **$600**

Elizabeth Taylor "Passion for Men" Factice

Taylor (Elizabeth), "Passion for Men," upright rectangular deep purple large factice bottle w/fanned ribs at sides, large rectangular wood cap, 11 1/2" h. (ILLUS.) **$50-70**

Fulper Figural Dancer Perfume Lamp

Ceramic, figural, model of a curtseying dancer holding out her ruffled skirt, atop a low cylindrical dark pink base, rewired, Fulper Pottery, United States, signed, ca. 1920s, 6" h. (ILLUS.)................................. **$600**

DeVilbiss Perfume Lamp with Nymph

Metal & glass, gilt-metal footed base supporting a cylindrical white shade decorated in black w/a sea nymph raised on waves & blowing a long horn, pierced metal cap, unsigned DeVilbiss, United States, ca. 1930s, 7 3/4" h. (ILLUS.).......... **$550**

DeVilbiss Orange-shaded Perfume Lamp

Metal & glass, footed metal base supporting a tall slender cylindrical shade in dark orange glass internally decorated in black w/nude fairies & foliage, pierced metal cap, DeVilbiss, United States, ca. 1930s, 8 1/2" h. (ILLUS.)............................ **$500**

Etling Figural Indian Perfume Lamp

Porcelain, figural, a seated Native American holding a golden bowl where scent emerges, in shades of cream & red, rewired, by Etling, signed "Chuparus," France, ca. 1920s, 7" h. (ILLUS.)............... **$800**

Figural Bambi Goebel Perfume Lamp

Porcelain, figural, in the shape of Bambi standing above green foliage, licensed by Disney, signed by Goebel, Germany, rewired, ca. 1940s, 6 1/2" h. (ILLUS.) **$600**

Goebel Porcelain Owl Perfume Lamp

Porcelain, figural, a stylized owl in brown, tan & yellow w/large amber glass eyes, marked w/the Goebel trademark, Germany, ca. 1930s, 5" h. (ILLUS.) **$350**

German Porcelain Kitten Perfume Lamp

Porcelain, figural, modeled as a brown & white kitten seated on a white pillow, unmarked, unwired, German, 6 1/2" h. (ILLUS.) **$55-90**

Pottery, molded in two pieces as a ballerina, blue & violet w/painted face, air vents on the side of dancer's head, rewired, bottom signed very faintly "Fulper" in an impressed oval, 6" h **$440**

Art Deco Figural Porcelain Perfume Lamp

Porcelain, figural, all-white, a standing figure of an Art Deco lady holding a cup on an oval base w/a ringed urn in front of her fitted w/a yellow glass ball shade etched w/roses, Germany or perhaps Czechoslovakia, ca. 1930s, 7" h. (ILLUS.).... **$350**

Carved DeVilbiss Perfume Lamp

Wooden, cylindrical shade on a wooden base, black carved to white w/a design of a sailing ship & sea gulls on stormy seas, perfume well missing, DeVilbiss, United States, ca. 1930s, 6 1/3" h. (ILLUS.).......... **$350**

Solid Perfumes

Mary Chess "Emerald Clover" Perfume

Chess (Mary), "Emerald Clover," gilt metal four-leaved clover set w/four green heart-shaped stones, pendant attachment, original labeled box, ca. 1970s, 1 3/8" h. (ILLUS.)... **$50**

Corday "Tourjours Moi" Carousel

Corday, "Tourjours Moi," Le Carousel design box, round gilt-metal base mounted w/a movable carousal unicorn below a parasol w/banner, labeled, full, 2 1/2" h. (ILLUS.)... **$145-175**

Corday "Tourjours Moi" in Horse Box

Corday, "Tourjours Moi," Le Cheval style box w/the gilt metal case topped by the model of a reclining horse in tan plastic imitating hard stone, labeled, full, 1 2/3" h. (ILLUS.)... **$115-145**
Dana, "Tabu," designed as a pendant decorated w/a raised lady head, mint in box, ca. 1970s, 2 1/8" h. **$22**
Factor (Max), "Aquarius," gilt metal miniature circus seal pendant w/chain, full, no box, ca. 1970s, 1 1/2" h. **$27**
Factor (Max), "Hypnotique," gilt metal miniature flower cart w/movable wheels, mint in box, ca. 1970s, 1 1/2" h...................... **$55-75**

Max Factor "Hypnotique" Rocking Horse

Factor (Max), "Hypnotique," gilt metal miniature rocking horse container, full, no label, ca. 1958, 2" h. (ILLUS.) **$45**

Fragonard, "Banjo," designed as a Bakelite penguin figure, labeled, ca. 1930s, 1 2/3" h. **$155**

Houbigant, "Chantilly," designed as a white plastic compact w/a crystal in the center top, mint in box, ca. 1970s, 2" l. **$23**

Lancome, "Trésor," designed as a stepped compact w/a pink bow, mint in box, ca. 1980s, 2" l. **$15-35**

Lauder (Estée), "Aliage Christmas Camellia," in a faux carved jade camellia-shaped box, empty, original label & box, 1981, 1 1/4" l. **$433**

Lauder (Estée), "Beautiful," a model of a jeweled cowboy boot, "Beautiful to Boot," mint in box, ca. 1998, 2" h. **$158**

Lauder (Estée), "Beautiful," designed as a replica of King Tut's gold burial mask, mint in box, ca. 2001, 2" h. **$61**

Lauder (Estée), "Cinnabar," a composition model of Chinese foo dog seated atop a square box, from the Imperial Series, empty, no label, ca. 1979, 1 7/8" h. (ILLUS., top next column) **$350**

Lauder (Estée), "Cinnabar," a model of a seated Chinese Imperial foo dog in faux ivory seated on a compact, used, labeled, ca. 1984, 1 3/4" h. **$200**

Estée Lauder "Cinnabar" Solid Perfume

Lauder "Cinnabar" in Box with Cat

Lauder (Estée), "Cinnabar," an oval gilt metal box compact with the top mounted by a faux ivory model of a cat scratching its neck, from the Ivory Series, labeled, used, ca. 1982, 1 3/8" h. (ILLUS.).............. **$150**

Lauder "Dazzling" Statue of Liberty

Lauder (Estée), "Dazzling," a model of the Statue of Liberty in gold, statues holds lipstick, mint in box, ca. 2000, 3 2/3" h. (ILLUS.) **$79**

Lauder (Estée), "Knowing," a model of a jeweled bee on a honeycomb, labeled, full, ca. 1994, 1 7/8" l. **$108**

Lauder (Estée), "Pleasures," a model of a cactus decorated w/green crystals, mint in box, ca. 2001, 2 3/4" h. **$75-120**

Lauder (Estée), "Pleasures," a model of a crab representing the zodiac symbol, from the Zodiac Series, full, labeled & w/pouch, 1 1/2" l. **$58**

Lauder "Pleasures" Champagne Bottle

Lauder (Estée), "Pleasures," a model of an ice-filled bucket holding the perfume in the shape of a bottle of champagne, full, no box, ca. 2000, 2" h. (ILLUS.) **$55**

Lauder "Pleasures" Gold Kitten, No Box

Lauder (Estée), "Pleasures," designed as a gilt metal model of a kitten w/a pink ball, full, no box, ca. 2000, 1 3/4" h. (ILLUS.) **$40**

Lauder "Pleasures" in Gold Kitten

Lauder (Estée), "Pleasures," designed as a gilt metal model of a kitten w/a pink ball, complete in original fitted box, ca. 2000, 1 3/4" h. (ILLUS.) **$68**

"Pleasures Perfect Peach" Solid Perfume

Lauder (Estée), "Pleasures Perfect Peach," a model of a realistic peach w/gold stem & leaf set w/rhinestones, tiny label on the bottom, ca. 2000, 1 3/4" h. (ILLUS.) **$55-80**

Lauder (Estée), "White Linen," a model of a beige plastic snail, mint in box, ca. 1994, 2" l. **$49-85**

Lauder (Estée), "White Linen," a model of a metal lady bug enameled in red & black, empty, no label, 1998, 2 1/4" l. **$35**

Lauder (Estée), "White Linen," a model of an open-winged butterfly compact in purple & green, mint in box, ca. 1993, 1 3/4" l. **$116**

Lauder (Estée), "Youth Dew," an oval box with the top set w/a faux cameo w/an amber background w/raised white figures of dancing ladies, label on the back, original box w/price tag, ca. 1982, 1 3/4" l. (ILLUS., next page) **$130**

Lauder "Youth Dew" in Faux Cameo Box

Lauder (Estée), "Youth Dew," an oval gilt metal compact box w/a faux cameo top w/the white relief head of a lady, ca. 1984, 1 1/2" l. **$289**

Lauder (Estée), "Youth Dew," in a blue enameled box w/an orange enameled flower in the top center, labeled, used, ca. 1979, 1 3/4" l. **$45**

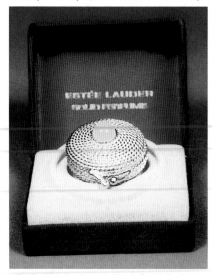

Estée Lauder "Youth Dew" Solid Perfume

Lauder (Estée), "Youth Dew," in a gilt-metal round coiled rope box w/a turquoise colored stone centered on top, mint in box, ca. 1968, 1 1/2" d. (ILLUS.) **$20**

Lauder "Youth Dew" in Jeweled Box

Lauder (Estée), "Youth Dew," in a low rectangular compact box w/gilt metal border, the top set w/beige plastic imitating agate & set w/a blue jewel, full, no box, ca. 1974, 2" l. (ILLUS.) **$90**

Lauder "Youth Dew" in Compact

Lauder (Estée), "Youth Dew," Parma Paisley round gilt metal compact box decorated w/dark blue enamel, no label, empty, ca. 1974, 1 3/4" d. (ILLUS.) **$35**

Millot, "Crepe de Chine," designed as a gilt metal fortune cookie, mint in box, ca. 1970s, 1 3/4" h. **$38**

Two Molinard "Concretas" with Girls

Molinard, a pink & a yellow "concreta," each h.p. w/a scene of a girl smoking, labeled, full, 3/4" d., each (ILLUS. of two).. **$20-35**

Molinard, "Baiser du Faune," a yellow cylindrical Bakelite "concreta" h.p. on the pot w/a faun, labeled, full, ca. 1930s, 1 1/8" h. **$65-75**

Molinard, "Habinita," a "concreta" decorated w/a girl smoking, in a plastic ring box, ca. 1930s, 7/8" d. **$60**

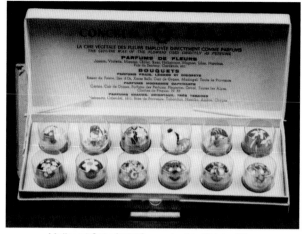

Molinard Set of 12 "Concretas" in Original Box

Molinard, set of 12 round "concretas" in Bakelite, each decorated w/a different flower, mint in box, ca. 1930s, each 7/8" d., the set (ILLUS., top of page) **$150-225**

Set of 5 Molinard Die-shaped "Concreta"

Molinard, set of 5 square "concretas" in Bakelite shaped like dice, each a different color, scents are "Carino," "Fleurettes," "Naniko," "Tabatchin" & "Xmas Bells," in original leatherette case, ca. 1930s, each 3/4" w., the set (ILLUS.) **$150**

Molinard Set with Decorated Boxes

Molinard, set of three cylindrical small pots, each a different color & h.p. on top w/flowers or a girl smoking, ca. 1930s, 1 1/8" h., the set (ILLUS.) **$75-120**

Molinard, set of three, each in the form of a French sailor's hat, mint in box, ca. 1930s, each 1" w., the set **$185-342**

Patou (Jean), "Joy," container w/crystal logo top, mint in box, ca. 1990s, 2" h. **$50**

Prince Matchabelli, "Aviance," designed as a rectangular gilt metal rectangular pendant w/woven top & chain, labeled, ca. 1970s, 1 1/2" h. **$15-23**

Prince Matchabelli, "Wind Song," designed as a gilt metal cat w/green jewel eyes, full, no box, 1 1/4" h. **$25**

Revlon "Moon Drops" in Elephant

Revlon, "Moon Drops," designed as "The Rajah's Elephant," a gilt metal elephant-shaped container w/enameled howdah & green stone eye, full, in original box, 2 3/8" h. (ILLUS.) **$40-50**

Revlon "Ultima" Compact with Portrait

Revlon, "Ultima," octagonal gilt-metal compact w/center oval miniature portrait of a lady under glass, labeled on the back, full, ca. 1970s, 2" l. (ILLUS.) **$20-30**

Rubenstein (Helena) "Emotion," designed as a jeweled purse, mint in box, ca. 1970s, 1 3/4" l. **$30**

Rubenstein (Helena) "Heaven Sent," designed as a gilt metal bracelet, labeled, full, ca. 1941, 2" l. **$122**

"Heaven Sent" Toad Solid Perfume

Rubenstein (Helena) "Heaven Sent," gilt metal model of a toad w/a bumpy back & red jewel eyes, nearly empty, w/original box, ca. 1941, 1 2/3" l. (ILLUS.) **$30**

Rubenstein "Heaven Sent" Solid Perfume

Rubenstein (Helena) "Heaven Sent," round disc-form gilt-metal compact design w/a large yellow stone set into the top, label on the bottom, w/original box, ca. 1941, 1 2/3" d. (ILLUS.) **$25**

Schiaparelli "Shocking" Solid Perfume

Schiaparelli, "Shocking," designed as a gilt metal heart-shaped locket w/a latticework center set w/pink rhinestones & S-scrolls around the border, labeled on the bottom, w/original box, ca. 1936, 1 1/3" h. (ILLUS.) **$140**

Unknown maker, unknown scene, Bakelite designed as "Le Jazz" black man wearing a top hat, no label, ca. 1920s-30s, 1 3/8" h. **$83**

Vanda "Limoge" in Owl Pin

Vanda, "Limoge," gilt metal pin in the form of an owl w/green stone eyes, in original box, ca. 1960s-70s, 1 7/8" h. (ILLUS.) **$20-30**

Miscellaneous

Guerlain Advertising Booklet

Advertising booklet, published by Guerlain, color photos of various Guerlain perfume products, ca. 1970s (ILLUS.) **$35**

Lelong "Indiscret" Body Powder Box

Body powder, "Indiscret" by Lucien LeLong, large round cream box w/a molded sunbrust design on the top, ca. 1935, 3 1/8" h. (ILLUS.) **$35-45**

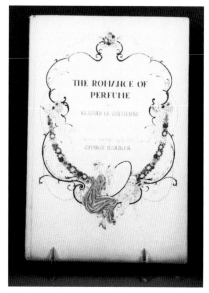

"The Romance of Perfume" Book

Book, "The Romance of Perfume" by Richard le Galliene, drawings by George Barbier, w/enclosed pamphlet about Richard Hudnut (ILLUS.) **$175**

Dior Bracelet-form Perfume Holder

Bracelet, bangle-type, wearable painted glass & metal snake-form holding "Poison" by Christian Dior, mint in box, ca. 1990s, 4" d. (ILLUS.).......................... **$125-175**

Baccarat Store Dealer Sign

Dealer sign, "Baccarat," long rectangular clear glass sheet on a black wooden stand, 3 1/8" h. (ILLUS.)...................... **$175-200**

Dealer sign, "Guerlain," long rectangular green glass w/black lettering, 6" l........... **$25-35**

"Lanvin" Black Dealer Sign

Dealer sign, "Lanvin," long rectangular black glass w/gold lettering, 6" l. (ILLUS.) **$25-35**

Lalique "Fleurs d'Amour" Face Powder Tin

Face powder, "Fleurs d'Amour" by Roger et Gallet, a low round metal tin w/an impressed design of exotic birds on the lid, reddish-orange stain, signed by Lalique, 3" d. (ILLUS.) **$100-125**

Early "Shalimar" by Guerlain Face Powder

Face powder, "Shalimar" by Guerlain, low disc-form box in black w/ornate gilt leafy scrolls & loops on the top, opened, ca. 1912, 1 1/2" d. (ILLUS.) **$30**

Lamp, display lamps w/printed shades & glass bases in the shape of candle-form bottles used for "Sleeping" perfume, 9 1/2" h., pr.. **$1,850**

Italian Micromosaic Lavaliere

Lavaliere, silver-gilt flattened ovoid jug-form pendant decorated overall w/micromosaic designs in various colors, suspended on chains for a fancy micromosaic bar pin, Italy, ca. 1900, 2 3/4" l. (ILLUS.)... **$450-500**

1947 Magazine Ad for D'Orsay "Divine"

Magazine advertisement, "Divine" by D'Orsay, from a 1947 French magazine, 9 1/2 x 12" (ILLUS.).. $5

Early Glass Golliwogg Perfume Pin

Pin, "Le Golliwogg" by Vigny, black glass face of a smiling Golliwogg w/gold, red & white trim, ca. 1919, 1" w. (ILLUS.)..... **$250-350**

Estée Lauder "Cinnabar" Pendant

Pendant, "Cinnabar" by Estée Lauder, flattened oval faux cinnabar lacquer bottle carved overall w/leaves & blossoms, gilt metal shoulder, cap & chain, ca. 1978, 2" l. (ILLUS.).. $36

Paneled Green Jar with Lady on Cover

Powder jar, cov., green glass w/a cylindrical paneled jar w/a stepped paneled rim, matching flattened domed cover centered by the frosted green figure of a kneeling lady, unmarked, Europe, ca. 1930s, 6" h. (ILLUS.)................................ $300

Figural Lady Porcelain Powder Jar

Powder jar, cov., porcelain, figural, model of a lady in 18th c. court costume, gown in yellow & pink, high hairdo w/feathers, unmarked, Germany, ca. 1920s-30s, 4 1/2" h. (ILLUS.) **$95-110**

Porcelain Spanish Lady Powder Jar

Powder jar, cov., porcelain, figural, model of a Spanish lady wearing a deep pink gown & white shawl trimmed in green,

yellow & black, unmarked, Germany, ca. 1920s-30s, 11 1/2" h. (ILLUS.)............ **$100-110**

Jeannette Powder Jar with Donkey

Powder jar, cov., short cylindrical clear box w/the matching cover molded w/model of a walking donkey, Jeannette Glass Co., 1930s-50s, 5 3/8" h. (ILLUS.)...................... **$25**

Pink Powder Jar with Scottie Dog

Powder jar, cov., short cylindrical pale pink box w/the matching cover molded w/model of a seated Scottie dog, Jeannette Glass Co., 1930s-50s, 5 3/8" h. (ILLUS.) **$45**

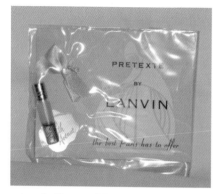

Lanvin "Pretexte" Sample Card for Saks

Sample card, "Pretexte" by Lanvin, a tiny cylindrical glass tube on the original advertising card from Saks Fifth Avenue, ca. 1929, tube 1" l. (ILLUS.)........... **$40**

"Sculptura" Figural Soap Bar Holder

Soap holder, round black plastic dish molded w/a female nude, made to hold a figural nude soap bar in "Sculptura" by Jovan (ILLUS.)... **$25**

Trade card, Escada, white w/black sketch of an elegant lady, gold wording along the bottom, unsprayed, ca. 2006, 5" l. **$1-2**

APPENDIX I

SCENT NAMES

A.

A Bientot (Lentheric)
Added Attraction (Prince Matchabelli)
A Go Go (Hattie Carnegie)
Aladin (Rosine)
Aliage "Christmas Camellia (Estee Lauder)
Ambre de Carthage (Isabey)
Ambre de Delhi (Babani)
Ambre d'Orsay (D'Orsay)
Amouage Gold (Amouage)
Amour Amour (Jean Patou)
Apogee (Veolay)
Apple Blossom (Lander)
April Violets (Yardley)
Aquarius (Max Factor)
Arpege (Lanvin)
Astris (L. T. Piver)
A'Suma (Coty)
Au Soliel (Lubin)
Ave Maria (Prince Matchabelli)
Aviance (Prince Matchabelli)
A Vos Ordres (Forvil)

B.

Baiser du Faune (Molinard)
Banjo (Fragonard)
Beau Belle (Bourjois)
Beautiful "Beautiful to Boot" (Estee Lauder)
Beautiful "Sphinx" (Estee Lauder)
Belle de Jour (D'Orsay)
Bellodgia (Caron)
Beloved (Prince Matchabelli)
Ben Hur (Andrew Jergens)
Bermuda Angel Fish (Peniston-Brown)
Bleu de Chine (Isabey)
Blue Grass (Elizabeth Arden)
Bolero (Dana)
Bouquet (Benjamin Ansehl)
Bouquet des Faunes (Guerlain)

C.

Calandre (Paco Rabanne)
Can Can (Mary Sherman)
Canoe (Dana)
Capricci (Nina Ricci)

Caprice (Colgate)
Carnegie Blue (Hattie Carnegie)
Carnegie, Hattie (Hattie Carnegie)
Carnet de Bal (Revillon)
Casque (Jean d'Albert)
Cassandra (Weil)
Castanettes (Karoff)
Celui (Jean Desses)
Chamade (Guerlain)
Cha Ming (Colgate)
Champs Elysses (Guerlain)
Chanel #5 (Chanel)
Chanel #22 (Chanel)
Chantilly (Houbigant)
Chants d'Arome (Guerlain)
Chevalier de la Nuit (Ciro)
Chi Chi (Renoir)
Chloe (Karl Lagerfeld)
Cinnabar "Contented Cat" (Estee Lauder)
Cinnabar "Imperial Foo Dog" (Estee Lauder)
Cinnabar "Imperial Dog" (Estee Lauder)
Circe (Moiret)
Classique (Jean Paul Gaultier)
Coeur Joie (Nina Ricci)
Colony (Jean Patou)
Confetti (Lentheric)
Coque d'Or (Guerlain)
Coup de Chapeau (Gilbert Orcel)
Crepe de Chine (Millot)
Crescendo (Lanvin)
Crown Jewel (Prince Matchabelli)
Cuir de Russie (Bienaime)
Cuir de Russie (L. T. Piver)
Cupid's Breath (Elizabeth Arden)
Cyclamen (Elizabeth Arden

D.

Danger (Ciro)
Dans la Nuit (Worth)
Dark Brilliance (Lentheric)
Dawamesk (Guerlain)
Dazzling Gold "Statue of Liberty" (Estee Lauder)
Debutante International (Jean Desprez)
Detchma (Revillon)
Devinez (Ybry)
Diorling (Christian Dior)
Djer Kiss (Kerkoff)

Duchess of York (Prince Matchabelli)
Duke, The (Erte)
Duska (Langlois)

E.

Early American Old Spice (Shulton)
Ecusson (Jean d'Albert)
847A (Eisenberg Brothers)
Emerald Clover (Mary Chess)
Emeraude (Coty)
Emotion (Helena Rubenstein)
Empress of India (Prince Matchabelli)
Escarlate de Suzy (Suzy)
Essence Rare (Houbigant)
Eternity (Calvin Klein)
Eva (Lubin)
Evening in Paris (Bourjois)
Extra Scotch Maid (Robinson)

F.

Fame (Corday)
Fan Toi (Fannie J. London)
Farouche (Nina Ricci)
Femme (Marcel Rochas)
Fete de Nuit (Agnel)
Fete des Roses (Caron)
Fille d'Eve (Nina Ricci)
Five O'clock (Gourelli)
Fleurs d'Amour (Roget et Gallet)
Fleurs du Monde (Faberge)
Floral Quintuplets (Karoff)
Flor de Blason (Myrurgia)
Fragile (Jean Paul Gaultier)
French Cancan (Caron)

G.

Gala Night (Bouton)
Gala Performance (Helena Rubenstein)
Gardenia (Valois)
Gardenia (Lander)
Golden Laughter (Suzy)
Golliwogg (Vigny)
Gotic (Gueldy)
Grace d'Orsay (D'Orsay)
Guy Six (Jeannette Renaud)

H.

Habanita (Molinard)
Harp d'Amour (Cleevelandt)

Heart's Delight (Dubarry)
Heaven Sent (Helena Rubenstein)
Heliotrope (California Perfume Co)
Hero (Uomo)
HIS Northwoods (House For Men)
HRH (Chevalier Garde)
Hypnotique (Max Factor)

I.

Ideal (Houbigant)
Illusion Rose (Dralle)
Imagination (Lioret)
Impromptu (Lucien Lelong)
Indiscret (Lucien Lelong)
Infanta (Prince Matchabelli)
Isadora (Isadora)
It's You (Elizabeth Arden)

J.

Jabot (Lucien Lelong)
Jasmin (Lander)
Jasmine (Giraud Fils)
Jasmine of Southern France (United Drug Co)
Je Reviens (Worth)
Jicky (Guerlain)
Jolie Madame (Pierre Balmain)
Jolie Petit (Lucien Lelong)
Joy (Jean Patou)
Joya (Myrurgia)

K.

Katherine the Great (Prince Matchabelli)
Knowing "Honeycomb" (Estee Lauder)
Kobako (Bourjois)
Kypre (Lancome)

L.

La Boheme (Arly)
L'Aimant (Coty)
L' Air du Temps (Nina Ricci)
La Rose Jacqueminot (Coty)
La Sirene (Burmann)
La Vierge Folle (Gabilla)
Le Baiser du Faune (Molinard)
Le Chic Chic (Vigny)
Le Dandy (D'Orsay)
Le Debut Blanc (Richard Hudnut)
Le Debut Noir (Richard Hudnut)
Le Debut Vert (Richard Hudnut)

L'Effleur (Coty)
Le Jade (Roger et Gallet)
Le Jazz (unknown maker)
Le Golliwogg (Vigny)
Le Lys (D'Orsay)
Le Muguet de Bonheur (Caron)
Le Parfum Ideal (Houbigant)
Le Prestige (Moiret)
Le Provencale (Molinard)
Le Roi Soliel (Schiaparelli)
Les Violettes (Molinard)
Les Yeux Bleus (Canarina)
L'Heure Bleu (Guerlain)
L'Heure est Venue (de Marcy)
Limoge (Vanda)
L'Ocean Bleu (Lubin)
L'Or (Coty)
L'Origan (Coty)
Lov' Me (Melba)
Lys Bleu (Prince Henri d'Orleans)

M.

Mademoiselle Chanel No. 1 (Chanel)
Maderas de Orient (Myrurgia)
Magie (Lancome)
Maharajah (Rosine)
Mais Oui (Bourjois)
Marotte (Rose Valois)
Marrakech (Lancome)
Matruska (Air-Val)
May Bloom (Solon Palmer)
Milady's Strike (Stuart Products)
Mille Fleurs (Elizabeth Arden)
Ming Toy (Forest)
Miracle (Lentheric)
Mischief (Saville)
Miss Dior (Christian Dior)
Misti (L. T. Piver)
Mitsouko (Guerlain)
Molinard de Molinard (Molinard)
Moment Supreme (Jean Patou)
Mona Lisa (Richard Hudnut)
Mon Image (Lucien Lelong)
Montana (Claude Montana)
Moon Drops "The Rajah's Elephant" (Revlon)
Muguet (Corday)
Muguet (D'Orsay)
Muse (Coty)
My Love (Elizabeth Arden)
Mystere d'Orsay (D'Orsay)

N.

Nahema (Guerlain)
Narcisse Bleu (Caron)
Narcisse Bleu (Mury)

Narcisse Noir (Caron)
Naughty 90s (Milart)
New Horizons (Ciro)
Night and Day (Elizabeth Arden)
Niki First Edition (Niki de St. Phalle)
9 x 9 (Paquin)
No. 3 (Park & Tilford)
Normandie (Jean Patou)
Nuit de Noel (Caron)

O.

Oh La La (Ciro)
Old Colonial (United Toilet Goods)
Ondine (Suzanne Thierry)
On Dit (Elizabeth Arden)
1000 Joies (Myon)
On The Wind (Bourjois)
Opening Night (Lucien Lelong)
Orchidee Blue (Corday)
Ouvrez Moi (Lubin)

P.

Para Ti (Tuya)
PAR-fumes (Karoff)
Parfum Pour les Blondes (Lionceau)
Parfum Pour les Brunes (Lionceau)
Paris (Coty)
Parure (Guerlain)
Passion For Men (Elizabeth Taylor)
Passionment (Lucien Lelong)
Picanette (Karoff)
Picasso, Paloma (Paloma Picasso)
Pearls of Lilies (Wm. H. Brown)
Pearls of Violets (Wm. H. Brown)
Penthouse (Lancome)
Pique (Redken Labs)
Platine (Dana)
Pleasures "Bubbly" (Estee Lauder)
Pleasures "Cactus" (Estee Lauder)
Pleasures "Cancer" (Estee Lauder)
Pleasures "Delightful Kitten" (Estee Lauder)
Pleasures "Perfect Peach" (Estee Lauder)
Pois de Senteur (Guerlain)
Poison (Christian Dior)
Poivre (Caron)
Pompeia (L. T. Piver)
Premier Muguet (Bourjois)
Pretexte (Lanvin)
Primitif (Max Factor)
Prince Douka (Marquay)
Prophecy (Prince Matchabelli)

Q.

Quand? (Corday)
Queenly Moments (Duchess of Paris)
Quelques Fleurs (Houbigant)

R.

Ramage (Bourjois)
Realities (Liz Claiborne)
Reflexions (Ciro)
Relief (Forvil)
Repartee (Lentheric)
Replique (Raphael)
Requete (Worth)
Royal Gardenia (Prince Matchabelli)
Rue de la Paix (Corday)
Rue Royal (Molyneux)
Rykiel, Sonia (Sonia Rykiel)

S.

S (Schiaparelli)
Sans Souci (Schiaparelli)
Savoire Faire (Dorothy Gray)
Scent of Mystery (Schiaparelli)
Sheherazade (Jean Desprez)
Sculptura (Jovan)
Shalimar (Guerlain)
Shanghai (Lentheric)
Shari (Langlois)
Shocking (Schiaparelli)
Shocking Scamp (Schiaparelli)
Si (Schiaparelli)
Side Glance (Anjou)
Sinner (Adrian)
Sirocco (Lucien Lelong)
Sleeping (Schiaparelli)
Slumber Song (Helena Rubenstein)
Soir de Paris (Bourjois)
Soiree (Nan Duskin)
Sortilege (Le Galion)
Souvenir d'un Soir (Mary Chess)
Springtime (Bouton)
Styx (Coty)
Succes Fou (Schiaparelli)
Suivez Moi (Tre Jur)
Summer Fragrance (Jean Paul Gaultier)
Sweet Pea (Lander)
Sweet Pea (Renaud)

T.

Tabac Doux (Edhia)
Tabac Fleuri (Marcel Guerlain)
Tabu (Dana)
Tailspin (Lucien Lelong)
Three Flowers (Richard Hudnut)
Tiel, Vicky (Vicky Tiel)
Tigress (Faberge)

Toujours Fidele (D'Orsay)
Toujours Moi (Corday)
Toujours Moi "Le Carousel" (Corday
Toujours Moi "Le Cheval" (Corday)
Toujours Toi (Corday)
Tresor (Lancome)
Triomphe (Leon Laraine)
Tryst (Villon)
Tweed (Lentheric)
Tzigane (Corday)

U.

Ultima (Revlon)

V.

Vacances (Jean Patou)
Vanderbilt, Lucretia (Lucretia Vanderbilt)
Veilchen (Dralle)
Vers la Joie (Rigaud)
Vers Toi (Worth)
Violet Leaves (Solon Palmer)
Violet Sec (Richard Hudnut)
Voeu de Noel (Caron)
Vol de Nuit (Guerlain)
Votre Main (Jean Desprez)
Voulez Vous (D'Orsay)
Voyageur (Jean Patou)

W.

White Linen "Butterfly" (Estee Lauder)
White Linen "Lady Bug" (Estee Lauder)
White Linen "Snail" (Estee Lauder)
White Shoulders (Evyan)
Wind Song (Prince Matchabelli)
Winnah, The (Artfield Creations)

X.

Xmas Bells (Molinard)

Y.

Yesteryear (Babs Creations)
Youth Dew (Estee Lauder)
Youth Dew "Cameo Dancers" (Estee Lauder)
Youth Dew "Fragrant Flower (Estee Lauder)
Youth Dew "Golden Cameo" (Estee Lauder)
Youth Dew "Jeweler's Treasure" (Estee Lauder)
Youth Dew "Parma Paisley" (Estee Lauder)
YU (Harriet Hubbard Ayer)

Z.

Ze Zan (Tuvache)
Zibeline (Weil)
Zigane (Corday)
Zut (Schiaparelli)

APPENDIX II
Perfume Bottle & Container Manufacturers

Belgium
Val St. Lambert

Bohemia
Harrach
Ingrid Company
Ludwig Moser & Son
Joseph Riedel

England
Stevens & Williams
Thomas Webb & Sons

France
Porcelain:
William Guerin & Company, Limoges
Haviland & Company, Limoges
J. Pouyat, Limoges
Glass:
Argy-Rousseau (Gabriel)
Baccarat
Brosse (Verreries Brosse)
Cristallerie de St. Louis
Daum, Nancy
Franck (Marcel) - Atomizers
Galle (Emile)
Lalique (Rene)
Le Verre Francais (Schneider/Charder)
Manon Freres
Pochet et du Courval
Richard
Romesnil
Sabino
Saint Gobain-Desjonqueres
Sue et Mare
Viard (Julien)
Walter (Almeric)

Germany
Schuco

Italy
Barbini
Barovier and Toso
Cenedese
Venini

Sweden
Kosta Boda
Orrefors

United States
Boston & Sandwich Glass Company - (Sandwich, Masschusetts)
Cambridge Glass Company – (Cambridge, Ohio)
Clark (T.B.) – (Honesdale, Pennsylvania)
Consolidated Lamp & Glass Company – (Coraopolis, Pennsylvania)
DeVilbiss – (Toledo, Ohio) – Atomizers
Dorflinger (Christian) & Sons – (White Mills, Pennsylvania)
Duncan & Miller Glass Company – (Washington, Pennsylvania)
Fenton Art Glass Company – (Williamsport, West Virginia)
Fostoria Glass Company – (Moundsville, West Virginia)
Fry (H.C.) Glass Company – (Rochester, Pennsylvania)
Gunderson-Pairpoint Glass – (Sagamore, Massachusetts)
Hawkes (T.J.) Glass Company – (Corning, New York)
Heisey Glass Company – (Newark, Ohio)
Imperial Glass Company – (Bellaire, Ohio)
Libbey Glass Company – (Toledo, Ohio)
Littleton (Harvey)
Lotton (Charles) – (Chicago, Illinois)
Lundberg Studio – (Davenport, California)
Morgantown Glass Works – (Morgantown, West Virginia)
Mt. Washington Glass Company – (New Bedford, Massachusetts)
Orient and Flume – (Chico, California)
Pyramid - Atomizers
St. Clair Glass Company – (Elwood, Indiana)
Smith (L.E.) Glass Company – (Mount Pleasant, Pennsylvania)
Steuben Glass Works – (Corning, New York)
Stiegel (William Henry) – (Manheim, Pennsylvania)
Tiffany Glass and Decorating Company – (Corona, New York)
Tiffin Glass Company – (Tiffin, Ohio)
Volupte – Atomizers
Wheaton Glassworks, Millville, New Jersey

APPENDIX III
Perfume Bottle Designers, Retailers & French and American Couturiers

Bottle Designers

Georges Chevalier (France)
Salvidor Dali (France)
George Delhomme (France
Heinrich Hoffman (Bohemia)
Julien Viard (France)

French Couturiers with Perfume Lines

Cristobal Balenciaga
Pierre Balmain
Marie-Louise Bruyere
Callot Soeurs
Pierre Cardin
Cartier
Carven
Coco Chanel
Jean Desses
Christian Dior
Jacques Fath
Jean Paul Gaultier
Givenchy
Gres – Madame Gres
Jacques Griffe
Jacques Heim
Hermes
Karl Lagerfeld
Lanvin
Germaine Lecomte
Lucien LeLong
Lentheric
Edward Molyneux
Claude Montana
Jeanne Paquin
Jean Patou
Paul Poiret
Paco Rabanne
Revillon (furs)
Nina Ricci
Marcel Rochas

Sonia Rykiel
Yves St. Laurent
Elsa Schiaparelli
Suzy (hats)
Madeleine Vionnet
Weil
Worth

American Couturiers with Perfume Lines

Adrian
Hattie Carnegie
Ceil Chapman
Liz Claiborne
Lilly Dache
Eisenberg Brothers
Barbara Gould
Peggy Hoyt
Calvin Klein
Jay Thorpe
Gilbert Orcel (hats)
Nettie Rosenstein
Adele Simpson
Gloria Vanderbilt

Perfume Retailers Marketing Their Own Brands

Bernard Altman (U.S.A.)
Henri Bendel (France)
Bergdorf Goodman (U.S.A.)
Bonwit Teller (U.S.A.)
Cartier (France)
Etling (France)
Nan Duskin (United States)
Irice (U.S.A.)
Lord & Taylor (U.S.A.)
Marshall Field (U.S.A.)
Peniston-Brown Company (Bermuda)
Robj (France – porcelain dealer)
John Wanamaker (U.S.A.)

APPENDIX IV

Perfume Manufacturers Worldwide

Agnel (France)
Air-Val International (Spain)
Alys (France)
Amboise (France)
Amouage (Oman)
Anjou (U.S.A.)
Benjamin Anseht (U.S.A.)
Antoine de Paris (France)
Elizabeth Arden (U.S.A.)
Arly (France)
Arys (France)
Atkinson (England)
Avenel (France)
Avon (U.S.A.)
Harriet Hubbard Ayer (U.S.A.)
Babani (France)
Babs Creations (U.S.A.)
Henri Bendel (U.S.A.)
Benoit (France)
Bichara (France)
Bienaime (France)
Biro (U.S.A.)
John Blocki (U.S.A.)
Boissard (France)
Borsari (Italy)
Bourjois (France)
Brajan (France)
Bryenne (France)
Burmann (France)
California Perfume Company (U.S.A.)
Canarina (France)
Caron (France)
Charbert (U.S.A.)
Charles of the Ritz (U.S.A.)
Cheramy (France)
Mary Chess (U.S.A.)
Ciro (France)
Clammy (France)
Jacqueline Cochran (France)
Colgate (U.S.A.)
Consolidated Cosmetics (U.S.A.)

Corday (France)
Coryse Salome (France)
Coty (France)
Crown Perfumery (England)
Jean d'Albert (France)
Dana (France)
De Heriot (U.S.A.)
Delettrez (France)
de Marcy (France)
Jean de Parys (France)
De Raymond (France)
De Seghers (France)
Jean Desprez (France)
D'Orsay (France)
Georg Dralle (Germany)
Dubarry (England)
Pierre Dune (France)
Mary Dunhill (England)
Gi Vi Emme (Italy)
Erasmic (France)
Esme (France)
Evyan (U.S.A.)
Faberge (U.S.A.)
Max Factor (U.S.A.)
Charles Fay (France)
Fioret (France)
Forest (France)
Forvil (France)
Fragonard (France)
Fuller Brush (U.S.A.)
Gabilla (France)
Gelle Freres (France)
Giraud Fils (France)
Godet (France)
Gourelli (U.S.A.)
A. Gravier (France)
Dorothy Gray (U.S.A.)
Grenoville (France)
Gres (France)
Jacques Griffe (France)
Grossmith & Son (England)
Gueldy (France)
Guerlain (France)
Marcel Guerlain (France – Not related to Guerlain)

Guermantes (France)
Gui (France)
Ann Haviland (U.S.A.)
Heraud (France)
Houbigant (France)
House For Men (U.S.A.)
Richard Hudnut (U.S.A.)
Isabey (France)
Isadora (France)
Andrew Jergens (U.S.A.)
Jeurelle (U.S.A.)
Thomas Jones (France)
Joubert (U.S.A.)
Jovoy (France)
Jussy (France)
Karoff (U.S.A.)
Kathryn (U.S.A.)
Kerkoff (France)
Lalique (France)
Lanchere (U.S.A.)
Lancome (France)
Lander (U.S.A.)
Langlois (France)
Lanselle (France)
Lanvin (France)
Estee Lauder (U.S.A.)
Lazell (U.S.A.)
Le Galion (France)
Legrain (France)
Legrand (France)
Leigh – aka Shulton (U.S.A.)
Lengyel (U.S.A.)
Lever Brothers (U.S.A.)
Lionceau (France)
Lioret (France)
Fannie London (U.S.A.)
L'Oreal (France)
L'Orle (U.S.A.)
Lubin (France)
Lundborg (England)
Marceau (France)
Massenet (France)
Marquay (France)
Maudy (France)

Melba (U.S.A.)
Mellier (U.S.A.)
Milart (U.S.A.)
F. Millot (France)
Miro Dena (France)
Moiret (France)
Molinard (France)
Molinelle (England)
Morny (England)
Mullens & Kropff (Germany)
Mury (France)
Myon (France)
Myrurgia (Spain)
Nesly (France)
Nipola (U.S.A.)
Merle Norman (U.S.A.)
Odeon (France)
Odlys (France)
Gilbert Orcel (France)
Oriza Legrand (France)
Orloff (U.S.A.)
Ota (France)
Solon Palmer (U.S.A.)
Park & Tilford (U.S.A.)
Paloma Picasso (France)
Piguet (France)
Edward Pinaud (France)
L.T. Piver (France)
Plassard (France)
Pleville (France)
Prince Henri d'Orleans
  (France)
Prince Matchabelli (U.S.A.)
Raffy (France)

Rallet (France)
Ramses (France)
Raphael (France)
Raquel (U.S.A.)
Redken Labs (U.S.A.)
Jean Claude Renard (India)
Jeannette Renard (France)
Renaud (France)
Renoir (France)
Revlon (U.S.A.)
Rigaud (France)
Rimmel (France)
Robertet (France)
Robinson Cosmetics
  Company (U.S.A.)
Rochambeau (U.S.A.)
Rodin (France)
Roger et Gallet (France)
Rosine – Paul Poiret
  (France)
Rouff (France
Helena Rubenstein (U.S.A.)
Rubicon (U.S.A.)
St. Denis (France)
Salome (France)
Sauze Freres (France)
Saville (England)
Scherk (Germany)
Sheisedo (Japan)'
Shulton (U.S.A.)
Silka (France)
Societe Hygenique (France)
Ahmed Soliman (Egypt)
Stuart (U.S.A.)

Suzanne Thierry (France)
Jay Thorpe (U.S.A.)
Vicky Tiel (U.S.A.)
Elizabeth Taylor (U.S.A.)
Tokalon (France)
Tre-Jur (U.S.A.)
Tussy (U.S.A.)
Tuvache (U.S.A.)
United Drug Company
  (U.S.A.)
Uomo (Italy)
Valois (U.S.A.)
Rose Valois (France)
Vanda (Canada)
Monna Vanna (France)
Lucretia Vanderbilt (U.S.A.)
Vantine (U.S.A.)
Varva (U.S.A.)
Vega (France)
Verlayne (France)
Vigny or deVigny (France)
Vinolia (England)
Violet or Veolay (France)
Vivaudou (France)
Volnay (France)
Ganna Walska (France)
J.R. Watkins (U.S.A.)
Wolff & Sohn (Germany)
Woodworth (U.S.A.)
Wisley (U.S.A.)
Yardley (England)
Ybry (France)
Zofaly (France)

**For additional listings of Perfume Manufacturers see the reference book,
"Commerical Perfume Bottles" by Jacquelyne Y. Jones-North
(Schiffer Publishing, Ltd., 1987).**

More Glorious Glass Guides

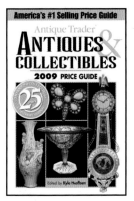

25th Anniversary Edition

by Kyle Husfloen

This twenty-fifth anniversary edition of the most sought-after price guide contains more than 5,500 color photos, and covers key antiques and collectibles categories including glass, ceramics, toys, furniture and more. With nearly 10,000 listings, and the most extensive descriptions of any price guide, this book delivers the most information of any collectibles reference available today.

Softcover • 6 x 9 • 1,008 pages • 5,500 color photos
Item# Z2045 • $19.99

6th Edition

by Michael Polak

Loaded with listings, up-to-date market values and trademark data for 19th and 20th century bottles, this new edition of the ultimate bottle book allows you to accurately identify and assess more than 50 categories of bottles. With 650 auction-quality color photos and concise descriptions which contain maker information, year of production and identifying details and pricing, this book is built to make sense of today's bottle market.

Softcover • 6 x 9 • 552 pages • 650+ color photos
Item# Z2815 • $21.99

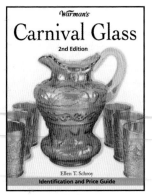

2nd Edition

by Ellen T. Schroy

Everything you need to assess carnival glass is in this new edition. A revamped listings format includes dimensions, color and price range, while 250 patterns help you identify pieces. From color and cut to design and identifying details, the world of Depression Glass is at your fingertips.

Softcover • 8-1/4 x 10-7/8 • 256 pages
1,000+ color photos
Item# Z1048 • $24.99

2nd Edition

by Mark Moran

Identifying and assessing the value of your Fenton pieces has never been so easy, or so accurate. In addition to identifying and pricing details, this book also provides a helpful and insightful history of the Fenton Glass Co.

Softcover • 8-1/4 x 10-7/8 • 256 pages
1,000+ color photos
Item# Z1050 • $24.99